A Biblical Kingdom Theology
A Biblical Study of the Kingdom of God in the Context of His *Missio Dei*

Dr. Ian A. Fair

HCU Media LLC

Accra, Ghana ◆ Frisco, TX

A Biblical Kingdom Theology

HCU Media LLC

Published and Copyright © 2020
By Dr. Ian A. Fair & HCU Media LLC

ISBN-13: 978-1-939468-17-8 (Paperback Edition)

Also available in Kindle Format

ALL RIGHTS RESERVED

No part of this publication may be reproduced, sored in a retrieval system, or transmitted in any form by any means – electronic, mechanical, photocopying, recording or otherwise – without prior consent from publishers.

Scripture quotations, unless otherwise noted, are from The Holy Bible, Revised Standard Version, copyright 1971, Zondervan Bible Publishers.

(Cataloguing Data:
Christianity. Theology. Kingdom Theology.)

Cover Design by Dale Henry – www.dalehenrydesign.com

First Edition December 2020
10 9 8 7 6 5 4 3 2 1

CONTENTS

WHAT IS THIS BOOK ALL ABOUT? II

BIBLIOGRAPHY IV

THE KINGDOM OF HEAVEN IN A PARABLE 1

CHAPTER 1 INTRODUCTION – SOME PERSONAL REFLECTIONS 5

CHAPTER 2 A NECESSARY INTRODUCTION TO KINGDOM THEOLOGY 23

CHAPTER 3 JESUS AND THE KINGDOM 49

CHAPTER 4 SEVERAL BIBLICAL TERMS USED TO DESCRIBE KINGDOM PEOPLE 77

CHAPTER 5 KINGDOM THEOLOGY AND UNITY 85

CHAPTER 6 THE CHURCH AS THE AGENT OF THE *MISSIO DEI* 93

CHAPTER 7 KINGDOM THEOLOGY, THE *MISSIO DEI*, KINGDOM LIVING, THE CHURCH, AND CHURCH MINISTRIES 111

CHAPTER 8 THE GREAT COMMISSION AND THE KINGDOM 171

CHAPTER 9 THE APOSTOLIC PRACTICE AND THE MISSION AND EXPANSION OF THE NEW TESTAMENT CHURCH AND KINGDOM *MISSIO DEI* 179

CHAPTER 10 WHAT DOES A MISSIONAL KINGDOM CHURCH LOOK LIKE? 189

What Is This Book All About?

Obviously, it is all about Kingdom Theology!
But it is not simply about kingdom *living*!
Kingdom *living* is important, but this book is not about kingdom *living*!
Neither is this book about a theology of the kingdom!
It is about Kingdom *theology*, and there is a difference!

Kingdom Theology

The Kingdom is the major theological narrative of Biblical theology! Theologies flowing from kingdom theology like kingdom living and a theology of social concern are necessary, yet are "subcategory" theological themes. They function within the major Kingdom theology narrative! Both are related and important topics within the major Kingdom theology!

The Church and Kingdom Living

If kingdom living is not grounded and experienced within Church life, then it is not Kingdom theology!
The failure of the Church to meet some kingdom living standards does not negate the true value and role of the Church in Kingdom theology.
Unfortunately, a negative attitude toward the Church is adopted by some who stress kingdom living without the primacy of a theology of the Church.
So, if kingdom living is divorced from the Church it is not Kingdom theology!
Unfortunately, the concept of Church is maligned and marginalized in some quasi-theological post-modern groups.
It has been expressed by some within our post-modern culture that a Christian can be in a relationship with Jesus, but not necessarily be a member of a Church congregation!
That is not Kingdom theology!

Kingdom theology and the *Missio Dei*:
Missio Dei refers to the mission in which God is involved in restoring his fallen creation to its former glory.
It is God working his redemptive purpose through his church and chosen people.
Kingdom theology is the theological expression of what God is doing to redeem his creation.
Hence kingdom *theology* and the *Missio Dei* are evangelistic and missional.

If this does not make sense, then be patient with me, and read on!

Bibliography

Bibles

The Holy Bible: The Revised Standard Version, Zondervan, 1971. Unless otherwise stated all quotations or references to scripture are based on *The Revised Standard Version*.

The Holy Bible: New International Version, Zondervan, 1996.

The Greek New Testament, United Bible Society, 4th revised edition of the 26th edition of the *Novum Testamentum Graece*, 2001, Barbara Aland, et al., United Bible Society.

On occasion I have italicized certain words in the cited text for emphasis.

General Bibliography:

Allen, C. Leonard, *Distant Voices*, Abilene: ACU Press, 1993.

Allen, Roland, *Missionary Methods: St. Paul's and Ours*, 1912, Kindle Ed., 2011.

Allen, Roland, *Missionary Principles and Practices*, Lutterworth Press, 1913, Kindle Ed., 2006.

Allen, Roland, *The Spontaneous Expansion of the Church: And the Causes That Hinder It*, Oregon: Wipf & Stock Publishers 1927, 1997.

Ash, Tony, *Directions for Disciples*, Hillcrest Publishers, 2002.

Ashford, Bruce Edward, Ed., *Theology and Practice of Mission*, Nashville: B & H Publishers, 2001.

Aune, David, *Revelation*, 3 Vols, Word Biblical Commentary, 1997.

Barth, Karl, *Call to Discipleship*, Extract from Karl Barth, *Church Dogmatics*, Fortress Press, 2003.

Bauckham, Richard, *Bible and Mission: Christian Witness in a Postmodern World*, Grand Rapids: Baker Academic, 2004.

Beale, G. K., *The Book of Revelation*, Eerdmans, 1990.

Beasley-Murray, G. R. *Jesus and the Kingdom of God*, Eerdmans, 1988.

Blauw, Johannes, *The Missionary Nature of the Church: A Survey of the Biblical Theology of Mission*, 1962, London: Lutterworth Press, 2003.

Blomberg, Craig L., *Matthew: An Exegetical and Theological Exposition of Holy Scripture*, The New American Commentary, B&H Publishing Group. Kindle Edition, 1992.

Bonhoeffer, Dietrich, *Life Together*, Harper Collins, 1954.

Bonhöffer, Dietrich, *The Cost of Discipleship*, SCM Press, 1959.
Bosch, David, *Transforming Mission: Paradigm Shifts in Theology of Missions*, New York: Orbis Books, 1991, 2011.
Boyd, Gregory A., *The Myth of a Christian Nation*, Grand Rapids: Zondervan, 2005.
Bright, John, *The Kingdom of God: The Biblical Concept and its Meaning for the Church*, Abingdon Press, 1957.
Bock, Darrell L., *Acts*, Baker Exegetical Commentary on the New Testament, Baker Publishing Group. Kindle Edition, 2007.
Brueggemann, Walter, *Theology of the Old Testament: Testimony, Dispute, Advocacy*, Augsburg Fortress, 1997.
Bruce, F.F., *The Book of Acts*, New International Commentary on the New Testament, Eerdmans Publishing Co., Kindle Edition,1988.
Caird, G. B., *The Revelation of St. John the Divine*, Harper and Row, 1966.
Carson, D. A., *Christ and Culture Revisited*, Grand Rapids: William B. Eerdmans, 2012.
Childs, Brevard, *Biblical Theology of the Old and New Testaments*, Augsburg Fortress, 1993.
Childs, Brevard, *Old Testament Theology in a Canonical Context*, Augsburg Fortress, 1985, Kindle Edition.
Coppenger, Jedidiah, "The Community of Mission," *Theology and Practice of Mission*, Ed. Bruce Riley Ashford, Nashville: B & H Publishing Group, 2011.
Cullmann, Oscar, *Christ and Time*, Westminster: John Knox, 1964.
Davies, W. D., and Dale C. Allison, *The Gospel According to Saint Matthew*, Edinburgh, T & T Clark, 1991.
Dodd, C. H., *Apostolic Preaching and Its Developments*, 1936, Grand Rapids: Baker Reprint, 1982.
Escobar, Samuel, *The New Global Mission: The Gospel from Everywhere to Everywhere*, IVP Academic, 2003.
Fair, Ian A., *Conquering With Christ*, ACU Press, 2012.
Fair, Ian A., *A Biblical Theology of Worship*, HCU Media, 2020.
Fee, Gordon D. and Douglas Stuart, *How to Read the Bible Book by Book*, Zondervan, 2002.

Ferguson, Everett, *The Church of Christ: A Biblical Ecclesiology for Today*, Eerdmans, 1996.
Flemming, Dean, *Contextualization of the New Testament: Patterns for Theology and Missions*, Downers Grove: IVP, 2005.
Frankl, Victor E., *Man's Search for Meaning*, Boston: Beacon Press, 2006. Original publication in German, 1959.
Hagner, D. A., *Matthew 1–13*, Vol. 33A, Dallas: Word, Incorporated, 1993.
Harvey, Barry, *Another City: An Ecclesiological Primer for a Post-Christian World*, Valley Forge, PA: Trinity Press International, 1999.
Hicks, John Mark and Bobby Valentine, *Kingdom Come*, Abilene, Texas: Leafwood Publishers, 2006.
Hirsch, Alan and Debra, *Untamed*, Grand Rapids: Baker Books, 2010.
Hirsch, Alan, *The Forgotten Ways*, Brazos Press, 2006.
Holloway, Gary, & Douglas A Foster, *Renewing God's People*, Abilene: ACU Press, 2006.
Hooper, Richard, *A Distinct People: A History of the Churches of Christ in the 20th Century*, West Monroe: Howard Publishing Co., 1993.
Hughes, Richard T., *Reclaiming our Heritage*, Abilene: ACU Press, 2002.
Hughes, Richard T., *Reviving the Ancient Faith*, Grand Rapids: Wm. B. Eerdmans, 1996.
Hughes, Richard; Nathan G. Hatch, David Edwin Harrell, *American Origins of Churches of Christ*, Abilene: ACU press, ca 2000.
Huitt, William G., "Maslow's hierarchy of needs," *Educational Psychology Interactive*. Valdosta State University, 2007.
Kaiser, Walter C., *Mission in the Old Testament: Israel as a Light to the Nations*, Grand Rapids, Baker Academic, 2000.
Keener, Craig, *A Commentary on the Gospel of Matthew*, Grand Rapids: Wm B. Eerdmans, 1999.
Kingsbury, Jack, *Matthew: Structure, Christology, Kingdom*, Fortress, 1975.
Kung, Hans, *The Church*, New York: Sheed and Ward, 1967.
Ladd, George Eldon, *The Gospel of the Kingdom*, Grand Rapids: Wm. B. Eerdmans, 1959.

Longman, Timothy, *Christianity and Genocide in Rwanda*, Cambridge: Cambridge University Press, 2010.
Malherbe, Abraham J., *Social Aspects of Early Christianity*, Philadelphia: Fortress Press, 1983.
Malherbe, Abraham J., *The Mission and Expansion of the New Testament Church*, Ian A. Fair Class Notes, Abilene Christian College, 1967.
Mathews, Kenneth A., *Genesis 1-11:26*: The New American Commentary, Nashville: Broadman and Holman Publishers, 1996.
McGuiggan, Jim, *The Book of Daniel*, Sunset Institute Press, 1978, 2011.
Moore, Russell D., *The Kingdom of Christ*, Crossway Books, 2004.
Morphew, Derek, *Breakthrough: Discovering The Kingdom*, Derek Morphew Publications, 2011.
Morphew, Derek, *The Future King is Here, The Theology of Matthew*, Derek Morphew Publications, 2011.
Morphew, Derek, *The Implications of the Kingdom*, Derek Morphew Publications, 2009.
Newbigin, Lesslie, *The Gospel in a Pluralist Society*, Grand Rapids: William B. Eerdmans, 1989.
Newbigin, Lesslie, *The Open Secret: An Introduction to the Theology of Mission*, Grand Rapids: William B. Eerdmans, 1978, 1995.
Niebuhr, H. Richard, *Christ and Culture*, New York: Harper and Row, 1956.
Orlov, Andrei, *The Glory of The Invisible God: Two powers in Heaven Tradition and Early Christianity*, London: T & T Clark, 2019.
Osborne, Grant R., *Revelation*, Baker, 2002.
Ott, Craig, Stephen J. Strauss, *Encountering Theology of Mission*, Grand Rapids: Baker Academic, 2010.
Packer, James I., *Evangelism and the Sovereignty of God*, Downers Grove; IVP Books, 2012.
Pannenberg, Wolfhart, *Theology and the Kingdom of God*, 1967/1968, ed., Richard John Neuhaus, Westminster, 1969.
Peters, George W., *A Biblical Theology of Missions*, Chicago: Moody Press, 1972.

Pocock, Michael, Gailyn Van Rheenen, and Douglas McConnell, *The Changing Face of World Missions*, Grand Rapids: Baker Academics, 2005.

Polhill, J. B., *Acts,* Nashville: Broadman & Holman Publishers, 1992.

Rossing, Barbara R., *The Rapture Exposed: The Message of Hope in the Book of Revelation*, Basic Books, 2005.

Rose, M., "Names of God in the OT," *vol. 4: The Anchor Yale Bible Dictionary,* D. N. Freedman, Ed., New York: Doubleday, 1992.

Schnabel, Eckhard, *Early Christian Mission*, 2 vols, Downers Grove: IVP Academic, 2004.

Schnabel, Eckhard, *Paul the Missionary: Realities, Strategies and Methods*, Intervarsity Press, 2008, Kindle Edition.

Senior, Donald and Carroll Stuhlmueller, *The Biblical Foundation for Mission,* New York: Orbis Books, 1983, 2000.

Skreslet, Stanley H., *Comprehending Mission*, New York: Orbis Books, 2012.

Slate, C. Philip, *Lest We Forget*, Winona: Missouri, J. C. Choate Publications, 2010.

Stetzer, Ed, *Planting Missional Churches*, Nashville: Broadman and Holman, 2006.

Stott, John, *Christian Counter-Culture*, Downers Grove: IVP, 1978.

Tennent, Timothy C., *Invitation to World Missions*, Grand Rapids: Kregel Publications, 2010.

Vicedom, Georg, *The Mission of God: An Introduction to the Theology of Mission*, St Louis: Concordia, 1965.

Von Harnack, Adolf, *The Mission and Expansion of Christianity in the First Three Centuries*, 1923, Nabu Press, 2010.

Wenham, Gordon J., *Genesis 1-15*. Word Biblical Commentary *Vol. 1*, 2002.

Willis, Wendell, Ed., *The Kingdom of God in 20th-Century Interpretation*, Hendriksen, 1987.

Wright, Christopher J. H., *The Mission of God's People*, Grand Rapids: Zondervan, 2009.

_____, *The Mission of God: Unlocking the Bible's Grand Narrative*, Downers Grove: InterVarsity Press, 2006.

Wright, N. T., *Following Jesus*, Eerdmans, 1994.

_____., *How God Became King: The Forgotten Story of the Gospels*, Harper Collins, 2012.

_____, *Jesus and the Victory of God*, Minneapolis, Fortress, 1996.

_____, *Justification*, IVP Academic, 2009.

_____, *Paul*, Minneapolis: Fortress, 2009.

_____, *Simply Jesus*, HarperOne, 2011.

_____, *The Last Word*, Harper Collins, 2005.

_____, *The New Testament and the People of God*, Fortress, 1992.

_____, *Paul and the Faithfulness of God*, London: Fortress, 2013.

Dictionaries:

A Dictionary of Christian Theology, "Kingdom" and "Eschatology," Richardson, Alan, SCM Press, 1969.

Anchor Bible Dictionary, "Kings, Kingship, and The Kingdom of God," Davis Noel Freeman, ed., Doubleday Dell Publishing Company, 1992.

Baker's Dictionary of Theology, "Kingdom of God," and "Eschatology," Everett F. Harrison, *et al*, eds., Baker Book House, 1960, 1983.

Dictionary of New Testament Theology, "King, Kingdom," vol. 2, Colin Brown, ed., Zondervan Publishing House, 1976.

The New Nave's Topical Bible, Swanson, James A. and Orville Nave, "Kingdom," Logos Research Systems, 1994.

Greek-English Lexicons:

A Greek English Lexicon of the New Testament, Bauer, Walter, William F. Arndt, and F. Wilbur Gingricht Cambridge, 1957.

A Greek-English Lexicon, Liddell, Henry George and Robert Scott, Claredon Press, 1843/1958.

Analytical Lexicon of the Greek New Testament. Baker's Greek New Testament Library, Friberg, Timothy, Barbara Friberg, and Neva F. Miller, Baker Books, 2000.

Dictionary of New Testament Theology, Brown, Colin, ed., 3 Vols, Zondervan, 1990.

The Complete Word Study Dictionary: New Testament, Zodhiates, Spiros, AMG Publishers, 2000.

Theological Dictionary of the New Testament, (TNDT), Kittel, Gerhard, ed., Eerdmans, 1977.

The Kingdom of Heaven in a Parable

You remember that Jesus taught many kingdom parables. He did this for a reason! Note Matt 13, *"And he taught them many things in parables, saying...the kingdom of heaven is like ... "* And then Jesus went on to explain his parable! Jesus' parables were intended to make a *practical spiritual* point!

Here is a parable, it is not as good as Jesus' parables, but it does contain an important point! Like Jesus' parables, it may need some explanation!

There was once a *jeweler* whose name was *Dei*.[1] He had a large *diamond* which he called *Creation*.

The diamond lived in *Dei's* presence, which *Dei* called *kingdom*. In the beginning the diamond was rough and without shape. But with the aid of his son *Iēsous Dei*, he began to polish his diamond into his own image and kingdom glory. *Creation* was beautiful, and reflected *Dei's* great giftedness and glory for all *his supporters* in *kingdom* to see and enjoy. The supporters were called *Angelos*.

There were many *facets* to the diamond that were intended to reflect the glory of *Dei*. One facet was called *Deceiver*, who turned out to be disloyal who endeavored to hide the glory of *Dei*. Two other facets of the diamond were called *Ish* and *Isha*. Other facets on the diamond were called *Creatures*. God gave *Ish* and *Isha* dominion over all the *Creatures*. In order for the diamond to be as beautiful in *kingdom* as *Dei* had planned, he gave the diamond certain gifts such as the *freedom* and *reason* to make good choices.

Electing to exercise their freedom, one of the facets of the diamond, the *Deceiver*, encouraged the two other facets *Ish* and *Isha* to exercise their freedom independent of the glory of *Dei*. The result was that they lost their kingdom freedom and elected to shine in a way that *Dei* had not chosen for them.

Because they chose to go their own way and not shine like *Dei* had planned for them, *Ish, Isha,* and *Deceiver* were punished and banished from *Dei's kingdom presence* to a place where they did not shine as they should.

---

[1] *Dei* is the Latin word for God or divinity. *Iēsous* is the Greek word for Jesus. *Ish* and *Isha* are Hebrew words for man and woman.

Because *Dei* loved *Ish* and *Isha*, he set about a plan to re-polish *Ish* and *Isha*, and renew *Creation* and *kingdom*. This project included a gift to re-polish *Ish* and *Isha* and cause *Creation* and *kingdom* to be restored to its original glory. *Dei* called this plan *Missio Dei*, which became known to lesser beings as the *mission* of *Dei*. Through his *Missio Dei, Dei* planned to restore *kingdom* to its original shining brightness.

This involved calling another *Ish* whom *Dei* renamed *Ab*. *Dei's* plan was to help *Ab* grow in his trust of *Dei* and eventually lead others forward in *Dei's Missio Dei*.

Dei gave *Ab* a commission and covenant promise which *Ish's* descendants called *mission*. *Ab's mission* was to be faithful to *Dei's* covenant and in so doing bring glory to all the other *Ishs* and *Ishas* in *Creation*.

Unfortunately, *Ab's* descendants did not like *Dei's Missio Dei* plan because it involved them becoming servants to the other *Ishs* who they thought were not clean like they were. They refused to fulfill *Dei's* covenant with *Ab* to become servants to all other *Ishs*, even those unlike them.

In time *Dei* had to send his son *Iēsous Dei* to fulfill His *Missio Dei kingdom* plan. Faithfulness to *Dei's Mission* cost *Iēsous Dei* his life. But *Dei* saved *Iēsous Dei* by raising him from the dead and anointing him *Messiah* over *Creation* and *kingdom* which had been *Dei's* original plan for *Ish* and *Isha* when he originally gave *them* dominion over his *Creatures*.

Iēsous Dei called new *Ishs* and *Ishas* to become his followers and built them into a new *community* of *congregations* which he called *ekklēsias*. *Iēsous Dei* gave his *ekklēsias* a charge or commission to continue the work he had begun in *Ab* of bringing new foreign *Ishs* and *Ishas* into *kingdom*. *Iēsous Dei* called this commission to tell his *evangelion message* to others in *mission*. The *mission* of the new *ekklēsias* was to go to the end of *Creation* and establish new *ekklēsias*, which *mission* involved various good *ekklēsia* deeds to the other *Ishs* and *Ishas* of *Creation* and *kingdom*. He called these good deeds *missions*, or additional personal *servant ministry* efforts.

So *Dei*, through his *Missio Dei*, was bringing *Creation* and *kingdom* back to its original glory so the *diamond* he had created would shine with even greater brightness and reflect his glory to all *Creation* and *kingdom*.

The new *kingdom ekklēsias* had a *mission* in *Dei's Missio Dei* to plant new *ekklēsias* and involve the new *Ishs* and *Ishas* in good *ekklēsia* deeds called *kingdom missions*, or good deeds of kingdom living. At all times the *Missio Dei* remained *Dei's Missio Dei*, but he charged his new *Ishs* and *Ishas* through *Iēsous Dei* to adopt his *Missio Dei mission* to restore fallen *Creation* to its former glory and brightness in *kingdom*.

The *Kingdom reflects* the original glory of *Creation* in which *Dei* lives in harmony with all his redeemed *Ishs* and *Ishas*. The theology of *Dei's Missio Dei* became known as *kingdom theology*. The *process* of joining with *Dei* and *Iēsous Dei* in the *Missio Dei* we call *kingdom mission*.

Kingdom theology is the *theological reason for doing what Ishs and Ishas do* in *kingdom living*. It is the *theological basis, reason,* and *power* for carrying out the *Kingdom Mission Dei*.

Ekklēksia's mission is *what Ishs and Ishas* do *because* of *kingdom theology*.

Kingdom and Ekklēksia's mission without due respect for kingdom theology is devoid of Dei's majesty, glory, and power.

Chapter 1
Introduction – Some Personal Reflections

As I have read, researched, pondered, lectured, and written on discovering kingdom theology I have wrestled over and again with the relationship between *kingdom theology, a theology of the kingdom, kingdom mission*, the *Missio Dei*,[1] and *kingdom living*.

I have pondered over whether I should title this study *a theology of the kingdom*, or as a study exploring the different nuances of *a kingdom theology*. I have also wrestled over the question whether *kingdom living* and *kingdom theology* are on the same theological level, or whether kingdom *living* is a *paranetic*[2] subset of kingdom *theology*. I hope to bring some light on these theological concerns and thoughts in this study.

It may appear from some conclusions I will make that I have a negative attitude toward the topic of kingdom living and the many ecclesiological programs of the church, but *this is not the case*. As I will emphasize as the study progresses, such topics are essential to understanding the full nature and expanse of *kingdom theology*.

My purpose will be to highlight and emphasize kingdom theology and the Missio Dei as the necessary and absolute foundation of all Church missions and kingdom living.

Perhaps I should insert a disclaimer or a clarifying comment or two at this point before you write me off! I am not opposed to kingdom living efforts such as benevolent and social injustice concerns of churches, orphan home support and individuals involved in such activities for they are to be admired and encouraged in their efforts, or in the churches delivering such benevolent kingdom living efforts. However, I am concerned over individuals or groups engaging in such activities outside of church sending programs since too often their missional theological motivation is either shallow or hardly evident!

---

[1] I have used the term *Missio Dei* in this study to refer to the mission of God, conceived in eternity before creation cf. Eph 1:3-10, to restore his sovereign reign over his creation after the fall of man as described in Gen 3. This is aptly described by some as God's Eternal Purpose.

[2] By *paranetic* I mean a practical or ethical result of a theological principle. Cf. my comment on this under fn. 3 below.

Mission efforts can begin in many different ways for a considerable array of reasons, many of them admirable. We are such a diverse people that it takes different reasons and concerns to motivate us into action. My primary concern is over the *theological reasons* or *foundation* for such concerns. A question to be asked is, *"are the reasons we have simply social concerns for suffering people, such as orphans or ethnic genocide, or are they theological concerns for their spiritual future?"*

Perhaps they are a combination of both! Another question I have is, *"are the end results, planting indigenous churches, in mind at the beginning or an accidental result of time?"* Another tricky question I have is, *"do we understand the Missio Dei as feeding the disenfranchised and impoverished, or de we understand the Missio Dei as God extending his kingdom to all nations as Jesus commanded in Mark 1:15 and Matt 28:18-20, and Acts 1:6-8?"*

Perhaps there is only a *thin line separating the differing excellent biblical ideologies inherent in the above reasons for our concerns*. In this study I want to explore and clarify that thin line!

It might be good to recall a statement I made above. This is a study of kingdom theology and not simply of one or more categories of kingdom living! Neither is this a study of church theology. Hopefully, it is a study of the overall kingdom theology[3] that will motivate the church.

As a former missionary in South Africa, and having taught in two schools of missions and been the dean of a university College that was home to a significant department of missions, and having been an active member of the Southern Africa Missiological Society, I have been increasingly concerned to bring into clearer focus the thin line of separation between the many church interests and activities in the *Missio Dei*, or *the mission of God*. In other words, identifying the thin yet important line that lies between kingdom theology and kingdom living and its related benevolent concerns, all of which are noble and good.

Over the past two decades there has been a legitimate growing concern among churches for the suffering of the many disenfranchised people, not only globally, but also in our own inner cities. Concern is expressed over the future of ethnic genocide survivors, for the condition of children and women in impoverished nations, and over our own growing

---

[3] Everett Ferguson has already plunged the depth of that study in his excellent book, *The Church of Christ: A Biblical Ecclesiology for Today*.

number of homeless people who struggle as a result of declining economies in our major cities. Concerns over social injustice have engaged most church outreach interests and mission thinking and discussions, and rightfully so. It should be obvious that kingdom theology and the church should be motivated to address these situations. *That should never be something that is debated or questioned.* What can and should be debated is *how* the church and Christians can be engaged in this concern, and *how* this fits under the category of kingdom theology.

Whereas there was once a clear line demarking traditional mission activity from benevolence and concerns for the poor, that line has now become blurred, very thin, or almost erased. My concern is that there should not be such a blurring of the difference between these two distinctive theological functions or important theological interests, for both are serious concerns of kingdom theology.

My concern is that the thin line that defines the distinctive nature of these initiatives, the *evangelistic missional outreach* of kingdom theology, and the *benevolent concerns* of kingdom living has faded to where the distinctive dimension of each has been lost.

I have personally been guilty of so finely defining each initiative that I have lost the *dynamic connection* between the two; Kingdom Theology as the *Missio Dei,* and Kingdom Living as benevolent service. As indicated below in an encounter with the two UNESCO[4] "missionaries" in Lesotho at the Blue Mountain Inn of Teyateyaneng, *my thinking was that we were doing kingdom theology missional planning and they were missing the point completely*! I still believe they were missing the *missional kingdom theology* point by detaching their motivation from the *Missio Dei* and being more concerned for the physical future of the people than their spiritual destiny! It seemed to our UNESCO friends that we were only concerned for the spiritual destiny of the people and not for

---

[4] UNESCO. The United Nations Educational, Scientific and Cultural Organization is a specialized agency of the United Nations aimed at contributing "to the building of peace, the eradication of poverty, sustainable development and intercultural dialogue through education, the sciences, culture, communication and information." Cf. https://www.britannica.com/topic/UNESCO.

their present suffering or physical which was the UNESCO missionaries' driving force!

But what if the missional dynamic of kingdom theology and the benevolent dynamic kingdom living are not that far apart, and are in fact part of the same whole?

Discussions and concerns along these lines have challenged me to dig deeper into the kingdom of God and refocus on what had become blurred. At the same time, this struggle has forced me to re-evaluate my own somewhat blurred focus, and broaden my horizons regarding the kingdom of God as the *Missio Dei*.

I was taught early in my Church journey (for which I am deeply indebted and grateful) to focus attention on the relationship of church and kingdom in the context of fierce premillennial debates and division in which in premillennial thinking the kingdom was defined as a future dimension and not yet part of the present life of the church. In response to this futuristic understanding of the kingdom I was taught that the kingdom and the church are the same present reality, with the kingdom arriving powerfully on the Day of Pentecost, Acts 2:1ff. Consequently, it was argued, if a Christian is in the church then the Christian is in the kingdom! I have no debate with the fact that the Day of Pentecost had a profound significance in the kingdom of God becoming an integral part of the church's experience, and in a striking manner. However, I have since learned that harmonizing the kingdom and church in order to answer the premillennial futurist emphasis of the kingdom is not the path to follow! Equating the church with the kingdom, notably the local church, has resulted in misunderstanding the nature of the kingdom as the *Missio Dei*, and the church as a subdivision of the *Missio Dei* with the responsibility of kingdom living and engaging in church benevolent ministries.

Likewise, the failure of the local church in our contemporary culture to manifest kingdom living responsibilities is no reason to defame the local church in comparison to the kingdom or kingdom living.[5]

---

[5] I am reacting to those who focus on the failures of the local church to reach some kingdom standards. As a result, the local church is disparaged. This should not result in a denigration of the local church in favor of a kingdom living option, and to see the church in contrast to kingdom living. This type of thinking would deny that the church in Corinth, due to its many weaknesses and failures, was not a kingdom church! I fully recognize that I and the local church have in too many cases failed to reach some

Let me express this differently, and hopefully more clearly! The church is an integral and essential component of the kingdom, but the kingdom is more than the church! The church as the agent of kingdom living is a ministry of kingdom theology, but there is a difference between ecclesiology,[6] discussing the church and church life, and kingdom theology.

Hopefully, I have matured theologically; some may question this, but I am mellowing slowly, to where I understand that there is much more to kingdom theology than it being equated with the church, church life, and kingdom living! Failing to distinguish the different *theological levels* of the kingdom and church produces a truncated theology of both kingdom and church. This also fails to understand that the kingdom was already in existence in God's *Missio Dei* long before it become part of the church's Pentecost experience, or even before Jesus' promise to build his church at Caesarea Philippi, Matt 16:18!

In my early learning experience little was said about kingdom theology other than that the kingdom had begun on Pentecost and was the same as the church.[7] I was taught that the kingdom was restored on the Day of Pentecost when the Holy Spirit fell on the Apostles, and now is a part of church theology. Not all bad theology, but unfortunately immature, truncated, and misleading!

Thus, for several reasons upon which I will shortly enlarge as the study proceeds, I prefer to refer to this study as *Kingdom Theology* rather than *A Theology of the Kingdom*. This latter expression, a theology of the kingdom, speaks more to the fact that there are several minor different theological emphases which could define our understanding of the kingdom theology. The pouring out of the Holy Spirit on the Day of Pentecost certainly is a theological topic that fits into kingdom theology and demands our serious understanding, but it does not define kingdom theology. We could profitably research and write a theology of the Holy

---

kingdom living standards, but this does not mean that the local church is not a kingdom church!

[6] Ecclesiology is the study of the church. The word ecclesiology comes from two Greek words, *ekklēsia* meaning "assembly" and *lógos* "word" - combined they mean "the study of the church." The church is the assembly of believers who belong to God. Everett Ferguson, *The Church of Christ: a Biblical Ecclesiology for Today*.

[7] I believe that a major reason for this reticence was fear of being defined as premillennial if we spoke too often about the kingdom.

Spirit as a subcategory of kingdom theology. It plays an important role in kingdom thinking, but kingdom theology goes much further than emphasis on that remarkable Pentecost experience and its impact on the early disciples.

In the expression *theology of the kingdom* one seeks to set the kingdom in a larger theological framework than simply the life of the church after Pentecost. We might profitably ask, "What does kingdom theology say about the church?" Or, to be more complete and accurate, we should ask, "What does kingdom theology say about the church, the Great Commission, the Apostle's ministry, evangelism, kingdom living, and Church missions?"

Each of these thoughts certainly would initiate a valid study, but in my mind the result comes up somewhat short of the big picture and narrative of *kingdom theology*! Stay with me and I believe and hope I will make this point clearer as we progress through this study!

In my mind the expression, *kingdom theology*, says that *the kingdom is theology* and that *the kingdom is not simply a subset of theology*! Thus, in this study I will seek to determine and unfold what I see kingdom theology to be.

A common brief definition to *kingdom* is that it is based on the meaning of the Greek word *basileia* which primarily refers to the *reign of a king*, in this case the reign of God in our lives. This obviously is a profound truth! My research has led me to the conclusion that although the *kingdom* of God indeed refers to the *reign* of God in people's lives on earth, kingdom theology proceeds beyond that initial *reign* emphasis and proclaims that *the kingdom is a theology* in itself which is far greater than our willingness to permit God through Jesus Christ to reign in our lives! That the sense of reigning is a vital emphasis in kingdom thinking is true. However, in *kingdom theology*, seen as God's plan and narrative of redemption and reconciliation, we are introduced to the thought that kingdom theology is profoundly *missional,*[8] or is *intricately involved with the redemptive mission of God,* which theologians call the *Missio Dei.*[9]

As a result of research in the field of kingdom and missiological studies I have been led to conclude that when one pays little attention to the *missional redemptive* dynamic of the *kingdom* in the sense of *what God was doing through Abraham* and *Jesus* to *reconcile* the world to himself, one misses the *theology* of the kingdom. Understanding *kingdom theology* as *God's missional purpose and activity* helps us understand that expanding the boundaries of God's kingdom through evangelism and *church planting* is a pivotal dynamic of the *Missio Dei* and the kingdom.

However, benevolence, addressing social injustice, feeding and housing the homeless, all excellent kingdom services seen as a ministry of the church, often ignore a vital and primary focus of kingdom theology – *kingdom theology is kingdom missional,* it is evangelistic, God expanding the kingdom which He planted in creation and has been recovering and restoring ever since the fall of man. He has invited us, the church, to join him in His *evangelistic missional kingdom journey and activity*!

A brief study of Jesus' commission to the apostles reflected in Acts 1:6ff connects kingdom issues with the evangelistic commission of Jesus:

> *⁶ So when they had come together, they asked him, "Lord, will you at this time <u>restore the kingdom to Israel?</u>" ⁷ He said to them, "It is not for you to know times or seasons which the Father has fixed by*

---

[8] As the study progresses I will enlarge on the term *missional*. At this point let me simply say that it implies *evangelistic outreach* and *establishing self-maturing and propagating congregations* who in turn take up the *Missio Dei*. In missiological terms it refers to the process of doing mission work by going out into the world, preaching the gospel message of Christ, establishing self-propagating congregations within the *Missio Dei* seen as the mission God has undertaken in favor of redeeming and recovering his lost creation through the call of Abraham and Jesus Christ. Key texts addressing this are Mark 16:15, Matt 28:18-20, Luke 24:44-49, Acts 1:6-8, and the missionary activity and missionary journeys of Paul and others.

[9] *Missio Dei* is a technical expression that will be discussed in greater detail in chapter 1. It refers to God's mission for this world. It refers to what God is doing in this world *to redeem his fallen creation*. It might refer to any mission that God has given to his servants but this is not how it will be used in this study. We will refer to the *Missio Dei* mission God has given to his servants by the English term *mission*. Mission refers to the church commissioned by God to carry the *Missio Dei* to the ends of the earth, Matt 28:19, 20, and Acts 1:8. I will use the term *missions* (plural) to refer to the various subsets of *mission* (singular) that the church carries on in the *Missio Dei*.

his own authority. ⁸ But you shall receive power when the Holy Spirit has come upon you; and <u>you shall be my witnesses in Jerusalem and in all Judea and Samaria and to the end of the earth</u>."

While the apostles were focused on the kingdom, on which Jesus had spent 40 days instructing them, Jesus did not tell them to go feed the hungry and address social injustice, he told them to go witness to him all over the earth. To understand what witness meant, follow the apostles in Acts and see them going all over the earth. What did they do? They taught, preached, made disciples, baptized them into Jesus, and instructed them further. This is precisely what Jesus had commissioned them to do in Matt 28:18ff, and Mark 16:15, 16.

We need to recognize that *missional, evangelizing* and *planting churches* is the key dynamic we must embrace in the *Missio Dei* and *kingdom theology*!

Permit me to emphasize once again! *Kingdom theology refers to <u>what God has done and is doing</u>* to reconcile the world to himself, through Jesus Christ, while *kingdom living* draws attention to what <u>we</u> or <u>the church do</u> in response to <u>what God has done and is doing</u>. This may seem to be a minor point on which we all readily agree, but the implication of this is profound in our understanding of *kingdom theology*.

Forgive me if I repeat the above emphasis! Definitively, *kingdom theology* speaks of God *reigning* in his kingdom in the lives of men, but it goes much deeper and further than that. *It involves a profoundly singular missional sense of Christians under the reign of God extending that kingdom reign in the lives of all men* through a commission to take that kingdom message to the end of the earth (Matt 28:19, 20). *Kingdom theology is fundamentally and intensely missional, all about expanding the kingdom first by missional evangelism among Israel and then among all nations.*

I will below spend some time discussing how the terms *mission* and *missions* are understood in missiological studies, and in relation to the *Missio Dei*. Suffice it to say at this point that mission in the single word *mission will be used when referring to the mission of the kingdom of God,* the *Missio Dei* and the plural word *missions will be used in referring to how in many excellent different ways the church can become involved in the kingdom mission* or *Missio Dei*.

In view of my somewhat negative comments above regarding kingdom living, a valid question one might ask is whether kingdom living and generic missions are not important! *They are obviously profoundly important; absolutely so*! Kingdom living and missions are intensely crucial as the practical and natural *paranetic*[10] effort vital to kingdom theology and effective Christian witness. However, I have been concerned over the fact that too often we have adopted an approach to practical topics that has zeroed in *first* on the practical living aspects of doctrines *rather* than digging in *first* to understanding the *theological or doctrinal basis* for the practice. We tend to zero in on the *paranetic missions* without first examining their role in the *theology* of *mission*![11]

In all biblical theological discussion, unless *paranesis* (practical exhortation and application) is deeply embedded in *theology*[12] the result is a truncated view of a practice which reduces *kingdom living* to what <u>we do</u> in the world, rather than setting kingdom living into the larger *theological* vision of missional kingdom theology and the *Missio Dei - what God is doing to redeem* our world, and how he expects us to respond appropriately.

Kingdom living is obviously vital since all Christians as disciples of Christ desire to be living as Jesus taught and lived, especially in his great Sermon on the Mount. In fact, without due care to good kingdom living evangelism is crippled and almost redundant, possibly even ineffective! Kingdom living is a vital door to evangelism, but is a key by which one opens the door that is often locked by social and cultural barriers.

---

[10] *Paranetic* or *Paranesis*; from the Greek *parainesis*, the moral, ethical or practical exhortation of fundamental doctrinal or theological principles.

[11] From our study of Pauline theology and practice we learn that *paranesis* without a *theological foundation* is that "cake half baked" as in Hosea's judgment of Israel's faith, Hosea 7:8 – see my reference to this below - while theology without a *practical paranetic* implication is "immature theology."

[12] *Theology and Theological*; from the Greek *theós* and *logos* meaning the discussion of those points where God engages human life. As I am using these terms in this book, *Biblical theology* discusses how Scripture describes and defines God's redemptive action, his *Missio Dei*. *Mission theology* describes how God's redemptive plan is expressed in the context of mission, or the reason for carrying God's redemptive purpose forward in human affairs. *Mission theology* must be defied by God's purpose as revealed in Scripture. *Kingdom theology* describes how the kingdom relates to God's purpose of reaching all men as a result of his covenant with Abraham and bringing them under his divine purpose and will.

Kingdom theology and God's *Missio Dei* will be almost totally ineffective if Christians do not live up to the ethical standards of the Messiah's kingdom. Kingdom living surely assists in unlocking the door to the evangelistic redemptive mission of kingdom theology, but if it is not seen in the context of the overall redemptive kingdom it becomes more social or ethical theology than kingdom theology. It is thus easy to focus on benevolence as a function of kingdom living to the exclusion of setting it within a kingdom theology redemptive goal, resulting more in benevolence and social justice than missional kingdom theology. For instance, when benevolence is based primarily on a benevolent spirit looking at a suffering world, which is obviously to be commended, rather than on an understanding of the larger *missional Missio Dei*, it remains a social principle rather than a *missional* kingdom principle. I hope that as we progress with this study the disparity within some kingdom living approaches and kingdom theology approaches will become more apparent.

Perhaps I should be more practical at this point by illustrating some concerns or issues that I have encountered in my missionary experience and working with some fine Christians, even great congregations. Good well-meaning Christians visit foreign nations and observe the financial and living struggles experienced by the locals, often food depravation, orphans, and the results of ethnic cleansing and genocide. Often these good, deeply spiritual benevolent Christians return home and raise funds to feed the struggling locals or build orphan homes to save the orphans. No reasonable Christian would oppose reaching out to such critical needs. The impetus for this activity is, however, more social injustice and benevolence than *missional* expansion of the kingdom through planting churches which will in turn take care of, or coordinate, social justice needs and local kingdom living concerns. Too often we have not realized that the most effective means of reaching out in such situations is through local indigenous churches. The answer is often that there are no local churches able to do this! Well, either plant a church that can, or enable the local churches to do so. Work through the local churches by enabling them to do so! A common response is often that the locals are not capable of doing so, reflecting a low esteem of the ability of locals to take responsibility in such matters!

A case in point occurred some years ago when I was an elder with a small church in Bayfield, Colorado. The congregation was challenged by their youth minister to raise $25,000.00 to assist an African Bible Institute purchase a vehicle to transport their students into the surrounding region for evangelistic outreach. In no time the goal was reached and I made the announcement to the congregation, with much celebration and thanksgiving, that we would be sending the money to the local native group leading the Institute. A visitor from a congregation in a neighboring state south of Colorado and east of Texas (that should take the heat off Texas!) approached me with the concern that he expected we were sending the money to a US missionary (most likely from his local state!) who would handle the funds appropriately. He was seriously disturbed and astonished when I responded that we were sending the funds directly to one of the local leaders in the church and Institute in the region. I informed him that there were more accountants in the Institute and local church in the particular mission region than there was in his own state-side congregation, or that had ever been seen in his local community! Obviously, I knew his congregation firsthand, and also the inability of some US missionaries to handle their own finances! Salty, but true! He had no real understanding of the ability of many African church leaders to handle such matters! They did not have an abundance of funds, but they certainly knew well how to handle what they had.

    I recall a survey visit I made with another missionary to the nation of Lesotho in Southern Africa. I discussed this experience above, but a reminder at this point will emphasize the difference between planting indigenous missional churches and doing benevolent social work. We were seeking to determine where would be the best location to begin an *evangelistic outreach with the intention of establishing local churches to minister to their own community needs*. Over lunch in the Blue Mountains Inn we engaged two "missionaries" in a discussion regarding what they were doing in Lesotho. They described themselves as missionaries who were likewise on a survey trip to determine the best location to establish a school as a base for addressing social injustice and the physical needs of the locals in the community of Teyateyaneng, a struggling community of Basotho people. This certainly was a noble and positive endeavor, albeit in my opinion shortsighted!

    The two men, in turn, asked us what we were doing in Lesotho. We explained that we were surveying the area with plans for planting churches in the region. Our program was a missional evangelistic effort. They asked what our plans were for educating and feeding the people. Our natural response was that was not our immediate purpose. We were concerned with planting self-propagating, self-governing, and self-supporting churches who could address the needs and social injustices of the Sotho people. The Lesotho government already had a good program of providing for the educational and physical needs of the locals.

We were severely admonished for only addressing the spiritual needs of the Sotho people, and not their obvious living conditions and physical needs!

It was obvious that we were following two different ideologies or programs for addressing the needs of the Sotho people. One, a socio-secular concern for the people, the other a theological missional benevolent program. Both were well motivated and excellent concerns, but each driven by different ideologies and principles.

Today, as a result of Church of Christ mission efforts in Lesotho there are numerous churches of Christ throughout Lesotho, each addressing the needs of their own people in a manner that they know are the most effective means of doing so. The driving force of the UNESCO "missionaries" was a short-term commitment and fix, whereas ours was a long-term indigenous solution.

To illustrate my point regarding the difference between the UNESCO plan and our missional indigenous plan was one of a short-term benevolent social injustice solution to a problem, and the other was a missional kingdom theology *Missio Dei* program. May I suggest, the one program, the UNESCO "missionaries," was more directed to kingdom living and social injustice, the other, our program, was and still is, *missional kingdom theological Missio Dei*. Both programs were serious attempts to address kingdom issues, the one was more *kingdom living*, the other *kingdom theology*.

Lest you draw a quick misleading conclusion from this discussion, let me assure you that I am in full support of kingdom living interests and efforts to address sociological issues as long as they are the outgrowth of kingdom theological missional churches, or church plantings which are more *indigenous*[13] than *external* sociological concerns and efforts. Perhaps I will be able to clarify this shortly!

Today, the UNESCO missionaries and their program in Lesotho are long gone! The churches established by local *missional indigenous* efforts are still there and functioning well!

The danger of a social injustice benevolent kingdom living program is real when the practice of kingdom living is not first anchored in an appropriate understanding of *missional* kingdom theology and the *Missio Dei*. By a failure to do this, that is, to embed kingdom living within kingdom theology, and then moving directly or rapidly to kingdom living, we have impoverished our understanding of the kingdom and its place in God's purpose, his *Missio Dei*. This failure has disadvantaged our evangelistic *missional* commitment of expanding the reign of the kingdom of God into all the world through converting people to God and Jesus rather than providing an external supply chain. My personal experience with such socio-economic kingdom living projects is that they too often have not produced long term thriving *missional* churches. They tend to address short-term fixes rather than long-term goals.

Socio-economic projects seldom, if ever, produce indigenous missional churches since their original theological focus is not rooted in the *Missio Dei*, whereas true *missional* indigenously focused efforts have rooted themselves in a keen understanding of the *Missio Dei*.

By speaking of the *indigenous*[14] *missional* nature of the kingdom I imply local church plantings engaging in the evangelistic outreach of the *Missio Dei* in a redemptive activity, converting those in their environment who are not in a covenant relationship with God and Christ, bringing them into such a relationship with Christ through faith, repentance, and baptism, building up the congregation in Christ, then taking care of their own people in a manner consistent with their own situation, needs, and ability. *Missional kingdom theology* focuses on planting indigenous missional churches that will sustain themselves and their people and expand the

---

[13] A brief definition of an indigenous church is one which is bedded in its own indigenous culture, self-governed, and motivated to be missional. It may receive external aid such as funding and instruction, but it is its own church!

[14] By *indigenous* I infer a movement or church produced, growing, living, or occurring natively or naturally in a particular region or environment. Merriam-Webster, *et al.*

missional commission of Christ. Again, I hopefully will clarify this in greater detail as we progress through this study.

It is obvious that a study of kingdom living is a most urgent, appropriate, and timely effort. However, exploring the dynamics of kingdom living in the absence of a sound theological foundation in kingdom theology results in an immature *"loaf,"* *"a cake half turned"* or *"a loaf half baked"*![15] Kingdom theology must become the primary entry and theological base for kingdom living and not only in the sense that we agree that the kingdom represents God *reigning* in our lives through Jesus and becoming the parameters to our behavior, but in a much larger, deeper, and profound *missional* sense of the fundamental principle of our kingdom and church's lives.

Understanding God's purpose in his eternal *Missio Dei*, that is, what he has been doing since the Fall in redeeming his disenfranchised people, is the driving force of the *Missio Dei* Kingdom theology effort. The *Missio Dei* is fundamentally and theologically prior to the need to practice kingdom living and benevolent activity. It is theologically and spatially[16] prior to kingdom living and addressing social injustice, as important as both of these ministries are!

Carrying forward God's *Missio Dei* in the Sinai desert was more important to Israel's future and God's *purpose* than giving them water and food! He could have sent them back to Egypt for food and water, which many thought was a good thing, but the primary *theological* lessons of faith and obedience to his Abrahamic *Missio Dei* covenant was profoundly essential—more essential than food! The key to God's redemptive purpose and what he had been doing since his call of Abraham and covenant promises, overrode the needs of food and water!

That is not to imply that such kingdom living provision of physical needs, as one finds in the Mosaic desert experience of God leading Israel in the kingdom purpose, were not important to God's working. They were simply not the primary purpose of God leading Israel out of Egypt, where they obviously already had food!

---

[15] Hosea 7:8. A kingdom not centered on God as YHWH is a kingdom half-baked and immature!

[16] By *spatially* in infer that which relates to space and the position, area, and size of things being discussed.

I fully recognize that the above thoughts may be disturbing to those who have a great heart for the hurting peoples of our world. I do not intend to leave them thinking that I am unconcerned for the needy, that is not what I am implying. Thinking like that is akin to the proverbial ostrich who hides his head under the sand so as not to see the danger approaching.

My primary intention is to stress that kingdom theology is incomplete if it does not lead to kingdom living and benevolent concerns! And to highlight the point that if kingdom living if not rooted in the *Missio Dei* of kingdom theology is not kingdom theology and the *Missio Dei*!

The *missional* nature of kingdom theology must first be set within a sound understanding of what God was doing (his *Missio Dei*) when he created man and set him in a position of nurturing service in his created order. *A sound understanding of being re-created in the image of God with a missional dynamic of being a servant to the original order is critical to understanding kingdom theology.*

It is also critical to understanding the *missional* nature of kingdom theology that one appreciate what it means for created man to have *dominion* over creation. Having dominion over creation involves *nurturing, caring for*, and *restoring Creation to its original relationship with God*. This process is more *missional redemptive* than paranetic ethical concerns, as important as they are. I will address this more fully under the next chapter, *A Necessary Introduction to Kingdom Theology*.

Influences that have shaped my thinking are several, but the following rise to the surface. They are not in any order of the importance to my thinking in the writing of this book, but each is vital to my understanding of the kingdom.

Perhaps this brief paragraph and few statements will clarify for you, and me, how I understand the principles of *kingdom theology* and kingdom living I am addressing.

Kingdom theology emphasizes *what God has been doing through Abraham and Jesus Christ* to reconcile the lost world to himself. It is *redemptive* and *atoning* in nature and is in fact *the major narrative of the Bible.*

Kingdom living is *what we do* in Jesus and the church as a result of what God has done for us through Jesus! This last statement regarding *what we do* does not ignore the fact that we should work with deep respect and awe for God and his purpose, *for God is at work in us to both will and work* as we complete what he has begun in us, and that as we work God strengthens us through his indwelling Holy Spirit.

Phil 2:12 reminds us that we should *energize* or *bring to maturity* the work that God has begun in us:

> [12] *Therefore, my beloved, as you have always obeyed, so now, not only as in my presence but much more in my absence,* <u>work out</u> [mature or complete][17] *your own salvation with fear and trembling;* [13] <u>*for God is at work in you, both to will and to work for his good pleasure*</u>.

And Paul at Eph 3:14-21 encourages us to remember that God strengthens us through his indwelling Holy Spirit.

> [14] *For this reason I bow my knees before the Father,* [15] *from whom every family in heaven and on earth is named,* [16] *that according to the riches of his glory he may grant you to be strengthened with might through his Spirit in the inner man,* [17] *and that Christ may dwell in your hearts through faith; that you, being rooted and grounded in love,* [18] *may have power to comprehend with all the saints what is the breadth and length and height and depth,* [19] *and to know the love of Christ which surpasses knowledge, that you may be filled with all the fulness of God.*
> [20] *Now to him who by the power at work within us is able to do far more abundantly than all that we ask or think,* [21] *to him be glory in the church and in Christ Jesus to all generations, for ever and ever. Amen.*

Summary

In this opening chapter I have attempted to express my understanding of the nature and content of kingdom theology. I expressed my concern for titling the study as either *Kingdom Theology*, *A Theology of the Kingdom*, or *Kingdom Living*. As I progressed I asserted that while I am deeply interested in the topic of kingdom living, that is, benevolent concern for those who suffer social injustice and physical deprivation which have left them impoverished, I am primarily concerned for the loss of the *missional* dynamic I see in many churches and individuals. I believe that kingdom

---

[17] "*Work out*" is a translation of the Greek κατεργάζεσθε from κατεργάζομαι, *katergázomai*, which means *to bring about, to complete, to accomplish*, or *to mature something* implied by the imperatival verb. Spiros Zodhiates.

living concerns should be seriously addressed by the Church living within and under the Kingdom of God and his *Missio Dei*.

However, it is my belief that too often well-meaning Christians have moved into the ministries of kingdom living, benevolence, and social injustice without fully understanding the real *missional* nature of the Kingdom of God.

I understand kingdom theology to be, as defined by the concept of God's *Missio Dei*, that which was planned before creation and carried out through God's call of Abraham and Jesus Christ's redeeming death and resurrection, and God calling mankind back to its original divine relationship through missional evangelistic effort.

Kingdom Theology is thus the *redemptive reconciling* story of the Bible expressed in God's eternal *missional* plan set in the context of his eternal love for his creation.

Kingdom Theology is inherently and intentionally missional!

Chapter 2 A Necessary Introduction to Kingdom Theology

What we will learn in his chapter

It is imperative that we keep all kingdom discussions firmly within several overriding and controlling factors. These are as follows:

Understanding the sovereignty of God expressed in his creation, his eternal kingdom purpose, and his redemptive plan in Christ Jesus.

Recognizing that the *missional Missio Dei*, that is, the mission of God, is primarily atoning, and reconciling, and intended as God's plan for *redeeming his fallen people* is a primary theme to Kingdom Theology.

Acknowledging that the *Missio Dei* is greater than *doing* mission work and benevolent deeds, as important as these may be, helps one maintain a focus of the heart of Kingdom Theology.

Realizing that the *kingdom Missio Dei* must be understood as God's *redemptive covenant with Abraham* to bless all nations, fulfilled in Christ, and carried out through his kingdom agents, the church.

Christians must distinguish clearly between *kingdom theology*, which is *theological*,[1] and *kingdom living* which is *paraenetic*.[2] Kingdom living refers to the practical ethical principles of living in God's kingdom, whereas kingdom *theology* refers to the *missional theological purpose* driving the *kingdom living*.

Kingdom *theology* is essentially *soteriological* and *missional*,[3] whereas *kingdom living* is essentially *practical paranetic*, doing good deeds, or being benevolent.

It is vital that Christians and churches understand the essential, dynamic priority of *kingdom theology* over *kingdom living*.

Each of the above terms and concepts will be defined and discussed in the development of this chapter.

---

[1] *Theological* in the sense of expressing the divine plan of redemption that explains and empowers all mission, benevolent, and evangelistic effort.
[2] *Paraenetic* is sometimes spelled *paranetic*. *Paranesis* explains the desired or planned response to the theological foundation of redemption.
[3] *Missional* in this study refers to going out into all the world, baptizing people, and planting churches in which they may be instructed and taught to be new disciples.

Scholarly thoughts regarding kingdom theology

I am particularly indebted to the following scholars and their groundbreaking works on the kingdom of God and missiology: John Bright, *The Kingdom of God: The Biblical Concept and its Meaning for the Church;* Wolfhart Pannenberg, *Theology of the Kingdom of God*; Eldon Ladd, *The Gospel of the King*dom; Russell Moore, *The Kingdom of Christ*; Derek Morphew, *The Future King is Here*; N. T. Wright, *How God Became King: The Forgotten Story of the Gospels*; Leslie Newbigin, *The Gospel in a Pluralist Society,* and *The Open Secret: An Introduction to the Theology of Mission*; David Bosch, *Transforming Mission: Paradigm Shifts in Theology of Missions*; Eckhard Schnabel, *Paul the Missionary: Realities, Strategies and Methods*; and *Early Christian Mission*; Christopher Wright, *The Mission of God's People*; and Timothy Tennant, *Invitation to World Missions*; Stanley H. Skreslet, *Comprehending Mission.*

A theological understanding of the creation account

Any study of the kingdom of God must be set in the overall context of God's eternal sovereignty, his initial creation, his sovereign purpose in creation, his consequent redemptive mission, his foreknowledge, and kingdom plan for rescuing his fallen creation.

Recall here the *Creation* narrative of our Creation Parable, *The Kingdom of Heaven in a Parable!*

Understanding the theology of God's *Missio Dei* in the creation narrative

A major problem we all inherit from growing up in churches with active bible class systems is that almost from birth we learn the wonderful Bible narratives like God's creation, Cain kills Abel, Noah and the Flood, Abraham commanded by God to offer his son Isaac as a sacrifice, David killing Goliath, Samson and Delilah, John the Baptist, the wonderful miraculous birth of Jesus, Herod out of fear for his throne trying to kill Jesus, Jesus walking on the water, Jesus' crucifixion and resurrection, and the amazing missionary trips of Paul the Apostle. The problem was that we were not taught how they each fit into the overall narrative of the Bible. Growing up in the Baptist church in Pietermaritzburg, South Africa, my wife and I as teenagers were blessed by wonderful bible class teachers. However, it was not until we had reached our "25 years" as parents of our own children that a minister invited us to study the Bible with him. Advancing technology in the early 1960s had blessed us with film strip projectors which were a "light years" advance over the old glass slide pictures. For the first time under the guidance of a program which became widely known as the Jule Miller Film Strips[4] we were introduced to the whole Bible narrative in a sequential manner. The Bible story came alive!

It is unfortunate that in spite of the wonderful resources we now have, we still tend to read these amazing Bible stories in a disjointed manner without connecting them to the overall biblical narrative of God's eternal redemptive plan, with each story highlighting what God was doing as he moved the narrative along from creation through the fall, the call of Abraham, the ministry of John the Baptist, Jesus' passion and resurrection, Jesus' great commission in Acts 1:6-8, the Holy Spirit on the Day of Pentecost, and the great missionary journeys of the Apostle Paul, and Peter's ministry to Rome.

Paul, in his great Epistle to the Ephesians, gathers these events into God's eternal plan of redemption, creation, the life and ministry of Jesus, and God's final goal of reconciling all things in heaven and earth together in Christ.
Eph 1:3-10.

> *³ Blessed be the God and Father of our Lord Jesus Christ, who has blessed us in Christ with every spiritual blessing in the heavenly places, ⁴ <u>even as he chose us in him before the foundation of the world, that we should be holy and blameless before him</u>. ⁵ He destined us in love to be his sons through Jesus Christ, according to the purpose of his will, ⁶ to the praise of his glorious grace which he freely bestowed on us in the Beloved. ⁷ In him we have redemption through his blood, the forgiveness of our trespasses, according to the riches of his grace ⁸ which he lavished upon us. ⁹ For he has made known to us in all wisdom and insight the mystery of his will, according to his purpose which he set forth in Christ ¹⁰ <u>as a plan for the fulness of time, to unite all things in him, things in heaven and things on earth</u>.*

---

[4] Some advanced Bible scholars took umbrage over what they perceived a slanted theology of kingdom and church, and they had a good point, but the first three filmstrips set the theme of God's redemptive work in a meaningful whole.

This magnificent text brings together the redemptive plan of God, his eternal mission, the *Missio Dei*, his kingdom theology restoration, and the role of the church.

In this sense, any study relating to kingdom issues must be set firmly within the extended framework of the original creation, God's sovereign power and purpose, the fall of man through disobedience to God (Gen 3), and *God's divine plan of redemption and reconciliation of his Creation.*

God's *redemptive kingdom plan*, which was advanced with his call and covenant with Abraham, and which reached fulfillment in Jesus' faithfulness, must play a pivotal role in any kingdom theology study or discussion.

N. T. Wright, in his remarkable study of justification, recognizes this principle, demonstrating that God's redemptive and justifying act of grace is the fulfillment of His promise to Abraham. Wright is careful to keep his discussion of justification and reconciliation deeply embedded in this Abrahamic covenant. In his exegesis of Gal 3:26-29 Wright observes:

> The problem of Gen 11 (the fracturing of humanity) is the full outworking of the problem of Gen 3 (sin), and the promise to Abraham is the answer to both together …
>
> It is impossible … to reconstruct the full implicit train of thought within which this makes the sense it does. But we may say cautiously … that Paul is working with the following idea (which is filled out quite a bit in the next chapter of the letter [Galatians]). God's purpose of calling Abraham was to bless the whole world …[5]

That interesting narrative of God's call of Abraham, in itself a miracle of God's divine intervention in the human story, his promises and covenant with Abraham to bless all nations, and the miraculous birth of Isaac, interesting as they each are in and of themselves, take on a cosmic dimension when perceived in God's kingdom theology. Paul grasped it when the Jews denied it, hence his comment at Gal 3:16ff that all nations fall into God's eternal purpose through Abraham. Wright brings that *kingdom narrative* into contemporary focus in his study of God's plan to justify all, both Jew and Gentile, who have faith in God's plan in Jesus.[6]

---

[5] Wright, *Justification*, p. 118.
[6] Wright, *Justification*.

The redemptive theology of the creation account seen as the activity of divine plurality in creation

Simply put, the theological nature and implications of the creation account indicate the all-encompassing redemptive activity of the Trinitarian godhead. Let's see how this unfolds!

In the beginning God created a world that he proclaimed was "very good" (Gen 1:31). Beyond the glory of the created earth God exceeded all other creation activity by creating *man*[7] (*ish*, remember our *Dei* parable) in his own image.

Several interrelated topics come together in a discussion of the kingdom; namely, creation, man in the image and likeness of God, the glory of God and man, man's relationship with God, sonship and adoption as *sons*,[8] and reigning with God as his vice-regent on earth. We will touch on each of these topics as we engage the topic of kingdom theology in greater detail.

The concept of being created in the *image* and *likeness* of God as recounted in Gen 1:26-28 introduces several interesting and challenging questions that flow out of the text:

> Then God said, "Let us make man in our image, after our likeness; and let them have <u>dominion</u> over the fish of the sea, and over the birds of the air, and over the cattle, and over all the earth, and over every creeping thing that creeps upon the earth." [27] So God created man in his own image, <u>in the image of God he created him</u>; male and female he created them. [28] And God blessed them, and God said to them, "Be fruitful and multiply, and <u>fill the earth and subdue it</u>; and have dominion over the fish of the sea and over the birds of the air and over every living thing that moves upon the earth."

Three major themes surface in this text; man created in the *image of God*, man in a *close relationship with God*, and man given *dominion* over creation.

---

[7] I use the term *man* in the sense of the generic Hebrew *ish* which stands for *man* as a representative of humanity, but essentially in relationship to God. This is similar to the Greek *anthrōpos*. Cf. Gen 1:26, 27, in the Greek *Septuagint* and Hebrew Bible.
[8] *Children*, cf. Eph 1:3ff.

To begin, we comment on the use of the plurals *elohim, us* and *our* in the creation narrative.

First, there are enigmatic plurals in "Let *us* make man in *our* image, after *our* likeness..." The plurals *us* and *our* have been interpreted in several ways. The background to the *plural* use of these two words must have some connection to the Hebrew word used for God in describing the creative activity of God in Gen 1:1ff. The name of God is also an enigmatic *plural* form of *Elohim* which can be both singular and plural.[9] Reyburn adds, regarding the use of the plural *Elohim*,

> *God* translates the Hebrew *'elohim*, the most commonly used of the general words for God in the Old Testament. *Elohim* is the only word for God found in this creation story. The Hebrew word is plural in form but functions grammatically as a singular noun.[10]

Wenham agrees with Reyburn regarding the plural form of Elohim for "God."

> The first subject of Genesis and the Bible is God ... The word is the second most frequent noun in the OT. It is derived from the common Semitic word for god *il*. As here, Hebrew generally prefers the plural form of the noun, which except when it means "gods," i.e., heathen deities, is construed with a singular verb. Though the plural has often been taken to be a plural of majesty or power, it is doubtful whether this is relevant to the interpretation of אלהים. It is simply the ordinary word for God: plural in form but singular in meaning.[11]

Martin Rose in the *Anchor Bible Dictionary* observes regarding the word *Elohim*;

> The striking feature of the OT texts lies in the use of this plural form "Elohîm" in order to designate the one God of Israel.

---

[9] *'Elohim*, the plural form of *'eloah*, is the most commonly used of the general words for God in the Old Testament. Although it is grammatically a plural formation, it functions as both a singular and a plural general name for "god." It most often refers to the God of Israel, but it can be used in the plural to refer to the "gods" of the other nations, William D. Reyburn, & E. M. Fry, *A Handbook on Genesis*. UBS Handbook Series #50, New York: United Bible Societies, 1998.

[10] Reyburn, *Genesis*, cf. Gen 1:1.

[11] Wenham, *Genesis 1-15*, p. 14.

One could think of a "plural of majesty"; however, it is most probable that this plural should be understood in the sense of an intensification and eventually as an absolutization: "God of gods," "the highest God," "quintessence of all divine powers," "the only God who represents the divine in a comprehensive and absolute way." In this function the term "Elohîm" can stand as a surrogate for the name of the biblical God; e.g., Gen 1 "In the beginning Elohîm created the heaven and the earth."[12]

The use of the plural form of *Elohim* in Gen 1:1 may cast some light on the plurals *us* and *our* in Gen 1:26. Some scholars have seen in the plurals *Elohim, us,* and *our* either reference to the *royal majesty of God,* or to a royal courtly heavenly council.[13] Others have seen a reference to a heavenly court comprised of the heavenly angels. The latter view raises some questions since that would include the angels in the creative activity of God, but this possibility does not lay outside the Old Testament references to angels in divine activity. However, if the statement was of God *informing* the heavenly court of his creative activity, the plural *we* and *us* holds some possibilities.

Others have seen in the plurals a reference to the royal sovereign plural of *majesty*. Still others have seen in the plurals a reference to the Trinitarian nature of God, but a Trinitarian concept would have been out of place to the original Jewish readers of the Pentateuch. That is not to deny that later texts attribute a creative role to Jesus as a person of divinity and creative power.

Andrei Orlov in a recent study in the field of Jewish mysticism, *The Glory of The Invisible God: Two powers in Heaven Tradition and Early Christianity*, finds early reference in Jewish mysticism to a plurality in understanding the plural name of God, *Elohim* suggesting that even before the Christian era Jewish thinkers were already finding a plurality of divine beings in heaven.[14]

---

[12] Rose, "Names of God in the OT," *Anchor Bible Dictionary*.
[13] For reference to the various resources regarding this topic cf. the scholars referenced under fn. 9 above.
[14] Orlov, *The Glory of the Invisible God, passim.*

Along similar lines of thought, some see in this a *plural* of self-exhortation.[15] Reyburn and Fry observe, "The usage is a 'plural of deliberation,' that is, when the speaker is conferring or consulting with himself."[16]

Kenneth Mathews comments on the above proposals.

They refer to:

(1) a remnant of polytheistic myth; (2) God's address to creation, "heavens and earth"; (3) a plural indicating divine honor and majesty; (4) self-deliberation; (5) divine address to a heavenly court of angels; and (6) divine dialogue within the Godhead.[17]

Mathews rules out (1) regarding a polytheistic myth.

It seems that a possible use of the plurals *us* and *our* in God's creative activity *resonates more with the royal sovereign plural of majesty or of divine deliberation*. One should not rule out the comment by Rose that the plural of *Elohim* points to the fact that this *god, Elohim, is the highest God who is to be considered above all other gods*, the "quintessence of all divine powers". In his divine sovereign majesty, fully within the understanding of god's in the Ancient Near Eastern vocabulary, *God refers to his own multifaceted and majestic nature*.

Furthermore, Mathews draws attention to the fact that the plural is sometimes used in *divine dialogue*:

"Subsequently in Genesis the plural "like one of us" occurs in 3:22, and the plural verb "let us go down" is attested in 11:7. Finally, in Isaiah's vision of the heavenly throne the prophet hears the divine request, "And who will go for us?" (Isa 6:8)."[18]

Consequently, it is my understanding of the plural use of *us* and *our* in Gen 1:26, that *God was speaking in his divine majesty in the context of divinity, possibly pointing to his sovereignty over all creation* in royal

---

[15] Thomas Whitelaw, *Genesis: The Pulpit Commentary*, Funk and Wagnalls Publishers: London and New York, various editions; Kenneth A. Mathews, *Genesis 1-11:26*, The New American Commentary, Nashville: Broadman & Holman Publishers, 1996; Gordon J. Wenham, *Genesis 1-15*, Word Biblical Commentary, Word, 1987; William D. Reyburn, & E. M. Fry, *A Handbook on Genesis*. UBS Handbook Series #50.
[16] Reyburn, & E. M. Fry, *A Handbook on Genesis*.
[17] Mathews, *op. cit.*, p. 161.
[18] Mathews, *Gen 1-11:26*, p. 161.

dialogue with his heavenly audience and creation. Reading this discussion in the context of the New Testament where Jesus is spoken of as the divine creative Word who was with God in the beginning, plural divinity can be seen in the plural *Elohim*.

Reading several New Testament passages regarding Jesus' role in creation back into this text to include a Trinitarian plurality in the dialogue *could be considered* a plausible solution to the plurality involved in the plural form of *Elohim*, the plural verbs *create* and *made*, and the plural forms of *us* and *ours*.

The plural form of *us* and *our* following on Moses' and Genesis' use of *Elohim* in the creative narrative of Gen 1 and 2 should, therefore, be taken as *a reference to God's <u>divine creative majesty, sovereign creative power,</u> and a sense of self deliberation in God's dialogue with his creation.*

These enigmatic plurals in the creation narrative emphasize the *all-inclusive divine power, glory, and majesty* of God in regard to the *all-encompassing theological nature of this creation narrative* and his *Missio Dei* kingdom. *Creation and kingdom discussions are all about the inclusive nature of God and his sovereign kingdom reign over all creation!* May we even add a Trinitarian dynamic to creation and the theology of the kingdom!

My point in this short divergence into the plural forms *Elohim*, *we*, and *us*, is intended to emphasize the sovereign *kingdom* nature of *creation* in the dialogue we are engaging. It must be the entrance point of understanding kingdom theology. Kingdom theology, as we pursue it in the biblical narrative, must return to creation, the fall of man, and God's plan to restore his image in man and return his creation to its original concept. Kingdom discussion is about the *Missio Dei* and the plural godhead's *missional redemptive* work, undertaken through the church that Jesus established primarily for that purpose.

Creation theology seen as the product of the *divine godhead* emphasizes the all-encompassing nature of kingdom theology.

God's creative kingdom theology program

In God's kingdom theology, fallen man, *ish*, is re-created and restored in the image of God in God's kingdom relationship. We will learn that the concept of the lost *image of God*, the *imago dei*, is *relational* and refers to the lost intimate relationship with God which man incurs through sin.

What was lost by man in God's kingdom is restored and renewed through an intimate relationship with Christ through faith in Jesus' death and resurrection.

Paul clearly draws on this in his theologically loaded opening pericope to the Christians in Ephesus and Asia at Eph 1:3-10. Briefly stated Paul writes,

> *³ Blessed be the God and Father of our Lord Jesus Christ, who has blessed us in Christ with every spiritual blessing in the heavenly places, ⁴ even as he chose us in him before the foundation of the world, that we should be holy and blameless before him. ⁵ He destined us in love to be his sons through Jesus Christ, according to the purpose of his will, ⁶ to the praise of his glorious grace which he freely bestowed on us in the Beloved. ⁷ In him we have redemption through his blood, the forgiveness of our trespasses, according to the riches of his grace ⁸ which he lavished upon us. ⁹ For he has made known to us in all wisdom and insight the mystery of his will, according to his purpose which he set forth in Christ ¹⁰ as a plan for the fulness of time, to unite all things in him, things in heaven and things on earth.*

We will explore this great text as we progress through this study.

The *Imago Dei*

The theology of the creation of man in the *image and likeness* of God has for centuries raised several challenges! Gordon Wenham[19] identifies five ways in which this thought-provoking expression has been interpreted, a) the *image* and *likeness* are distinct, each having a different implication, b) the *image* refers to the mental and spiritual capacity of man, c) the *image* refers to the physical nature of man (which to this writer does not seem a good choice), d) the *image* makes man God's representative on earth, e) the *image* represents man's capacity to relate to God.

Most scholars see the term *likeness* functioning as a synonym of *image* (Heb. *ṣelem*, LXX Greek *eikōn*). Likeness (Heb. *demut*, LXX Greek *homoiōsis*) merely enriches the meaning of *image*. In the Old Testament

---

[19] Wenham, *Genesis 1-15*.

the terms are used interchangeably.[20] Man, in some form was created to be *like* God and reflect God's *image* in and for creation.

The challenge of this discussion is reflected in the 2000 year long debate in Christian theology regarding whether man in the fall lost some or all of this image and likeness to God.

Mathews observes;

> In Genesis the terms "image" (*ṣelem*) and "likeness" *(děmût)* occur in just three passages (1:26–27; 5:1, 3; 9:6). Some contend that the theology of the "image of God" *(imago Dei)* had little significance among the Hebrews because of this paucity of references in the Old Testament. But this is fundamentally shortsighted, for 1:26–28 is the seedbed for understanding the promissory blessing of God for Israel's fathers and its realization in the life of the nation. We cannot look at 1:26–28 without viewing it through the prism of human sin, both in its beginning in the garden and its consequences for human life and humanity's relationship to creation. Theologically, it is essential for interpreting the Christian faith with its proclamation regarding human life, the universal sinfulness of mankind, and the sole resolution of sin through the incarnation, death, and resurrection of Christ.[21]

Irenaeus, ca. 185 CE, differentiated between *image* and *likeness* with *image* referring to man's ability to reason while *likeness* refers to a person's correspondence to God's spiritual attributes.

Augustine, ca. 400 CE, saw man in a trinitarian form of memory, knowledge, and will. The image of God referred to man's capacity to will and obey which capacity to obey was seriously impaired at the fall. Augustine saw the image of God, not in his abstract reasoning faculties, but in his power to use his reason to obtain knowledge of God.[22] Augustine held that without God's prevenial[23] enabling grace this capacity

---

[20] Mathews, *Genesis 1-11:26*, cf. the discussion in his Excursus at Gen 1:26.
[21] Mathews, *Genesis 1-11:26*, cf. Matthew's discussion of Gen 1:26.
[22] Hordern, "The Doctrine of Man," *A Dictionary of Christian Theology*, ed. Alan Richardson, p. 203, 1969.
[23] Prevenient grace (also referred to as prevenial) is a Christian theological concept rooted in Augustinian theology. It is embraced primarily by Christians who are influenced by the theology of John Wesley. Prevenient grace is divine grace which precedes human

to will and obey could not be restored. He maintained that man had been created perfect in the garden and thus able to do good. Sin resulted, and man's incapacity to obey God apart from God's enabling grace ensued.

    The 16th century Protestant Reformation continued Augustine's view that the *Imago Dei* was either destroyed or severely restricted at the fall. Without God's enabling grace and the operations of the Holy Spirit man was rendered incapable of fully believing in God to where he could obey God. It was man's spiritual nature that was destroyed or seriously diminished or lost in the fall. Some Reformation thinkers were, however, willing to understand *image* in terms of man's relationship and fellowship with God. The image of God in man, seen as a close relationship between God and man, had been perfect at creation, which relationship was seriously compromised or lost in the fall. Only by the gracious work of God through the Holy Spirit could that image be restored.

    Martin Luther, ca. 1500 CE, believed that man had seriously *lost* the image of God when he fell, not that it was simply destroyed. He argued that the image of God is not a set of static qualities but the complete orientation of man toward God. Thus the image of God is found in man only through a complete reorientation of man to God to where man reflects the love of God. This restored ability or orientation comes only by the grace of God and recreation by the Holy Spirit.[24]

    John Calvin, ca. 1540 CE, continued the Augustinian mindset. He leaned toward the Lutheran view but claimed that the divine image *was not annihilated* in the fall. He argued that the image of God was so *seriously corrupted* that whatever remained was a deformity of the image of God in man. Calvin held that the image of God was man's original righteousness in which he lived in a holy relationship with God. *In*

---

decision. It exists prior to and without reference to anything humans may have done. As humans are corrupted by the effects of sin, prevenient grace allows some to engage their God-given free will to choose the salvation offered by God in Jesus Christ or to reject that salvific offer. Whereas Augustine held that prevenient grace cannot be resisted, others believe that it enables, but does not ensure, personal acceptance of the gift of salvation. Calvinists believe that prevenient grace is offered only to those chosen by God for redemption.

[24] Hordern, *"The Doctrine of Man," A Dictionary of Christian Theology.*

Calvin's view the image of God was not lost in the fall but "horribly deformed."

Mathews suggests that Calvin further contended:
> that only from the New Testament could the original meaning of the "image" in Genesis be discovered since in Christ that pristine "image" is restored in the Christian believer (Col 3:10; Eph 4:24). For him the "image" in Adam was "the perfection of our whole nature," which was "destroyed in us by the fall." By "whole nature" Calvin meant foremostly knowledge, righteousness, and holiness, but he also admitted that the "image" included the human body: "Yet there was no part of man, not even the body itself, in which some sparks did not glow." This pristine state, while lost, was not totally absent in fallen humanity; there remained "obscure lineaments of that image." It was the remnant of that original gift that continued to distinguish the human from creatures. Reformed theology has traditionally held that mankind was created in the image of God, which was perfect in knowledge and righteousness, suffered irreparable destruction in the fall, and is delivered only through Christ's death and resurrection, whereby the image is being progressively transformed in the believer (2 Cor 3:18) until its state of perfection at the resurrection (Rom 8:29; 1 Cor 15:49; Col 3:9–10). Thus "the incarnate Son actualizes the perfection of the manhood which we have sinfully perverted."[25]

Although the debate over *the image of God* has continued in the Protestant Reformation, the primary view has been that what was lost in the fall related either to man's ability to reason and obey, or to his righteous relationship with God. Thus without the prevenient intervention of God's calling and grace working through the Holy Spirit this relationship could not be restored.

Karl Barth added an additional dimension to *the image of God in man*, seeing in the *image of God* man's ability to engage in a full relationship with God. Barth continued the Protestant Reformation concept of the divine intervention of grace operating through the ministry of the Holy

---

[25] Mathews, *Genesis 1-11:26*, cf. "Excursus on the Image of God," Gen 1:26; Cf. Calvin's *Institutes* and *Commentary on Genesis*.

Spirit. Barth saw in the *image of God* man's ability to sustain a real *I-Thou* relationship with both God and His creation.[26]

While the historical views of Christian theology have struggled to produce a consensus regarding the *Imago Dei*, it is apparent that several salient points have surfaced.

First, the image of God identifies in what manner man resembles the likeness, nature, and essence of God which carries a spiritual dimension. *Second*, being created in God's image and likeness enables man to function in God's place as the benevolent caretaker of God's creation. This does not necessarily define fully man's *function* which Genesis also discusses, but *function* is defined in what follows the discussion of *image* and *likeness*. Thus Gen 1:26-28 speaks of man *ruling* or having *dominion* over God's creation. We thus have in Gen 1:26-28 a discussion of the creation of man in the *image* and *likeness* of God, that is, his sovereign *power* and *nature*. Man's God given *function* to *rule* and have *dominion* over the natural creation results from his being created in God's image.

The terms *rule* (NIV) and *have dominion* (RSV, ESV) derive from the Hebrew *rādâ* which in the context of the Old Testament, as in Psalm 8, implies *kingly* or *sovereign rule*.

Note from the context of Psalm 8 how this reflects on God's glory and man's position of honor in God's creative order and kingdom:

> ^{1} O LORD, our Lord,
>   how majestic is thy name in all the earth!
>
> *Thou whose glory above the heavens is chanted*
> ^{2} *by the mouth of babes and infants,*
> *thou hast founded a bulwark because of thy foes,*
>   *to still the enemy and the avenger.*
>
> ^{3} *When I look at thy heavens, the work of thy fingers,*
>   *the moon and the stars which thou hast established;*
> ^{4} *what is man that thou art mindful of him,*
>   *and the son of man that thou dost care for him?*
> ^{5} *Yet thou hast made him little less than God,*

---

[26] K. Barth, *Church Dogmatics* III/Part One, ed. G. W. Bromiley and T. F. Torrance, Edinburgh: T & T Clark, 1958, 183–86. Cf. also see Claus Westermann, *Genesis 1–11*, 155–58, Wissenschaftliche Buchgesellschaft, 1993.

> *and dost crown him with glory and honor.*
> *⁶ Thou hast given him <u>dominion</u> over the works of thy hands;*
>   *thou hast put all things under his feet,*
> *⁷ all sheep and oxen,*
>   *and also the beasts of the field,*
> *⁸ the birds of the air, and the fish of the sea,*
>   *whatever passes along the paths of the sea.*
>
> *⁹ O LORD, our Lord,*
>   *how majestic is thy name in all the earth!*

In his discussion of rule and *dominion* at Gen 1:26 Mathews enlarges on this point by observing that:

> Psalm 8 ... focuses on human dominion, though without explicit mention of the "image" or "likeness." This is further indicated by the term "rule" *(rādâ)* in [Gen]1:26, 28, which is used commonly of *royal dominion*. Human jurisdiction over animate life in the skies, waters, and land corresponds to the "rule" *(māšal)* of the sun and moon over the inanimate sphere of creation.²⁷

It is not surprising that the writer of the letter to the Hebrews in our New Testament, when exalting the role of Jesus above angels and the whole world, made a *midrashic* reference of Ps 8 at Heb 2:5-10 to describe the glory and dominion of Jesus over angels:

> *⁵ For it was not to angels that God subjected the world to come, of which we are speaking. ⁶ It has been testified somewhere,*
>   *"<u>What is man that thou art mindful of him</u>,*
>   *or the son of man, that thou carest for him?*
>   *⁷ Thou didst make him for a little while lower than the angels,*
>   *thou <u>hast crowned him with glory and honor</u>,*
>   *⁸ <u>putting everything in subjection under his feet</u>."*
> *Now in putting everything in subjection to him, <u>he left nothing outside his control</u>. As it is, we do not yet see everything in subjection to him. ⁹ But we see Jesus, who for a little while was made lower than the angels, crowned with glory and honor because of the suffering of death, so that by the grace of God he might taste death for everyone.*

---

²⁷ Mathews, "Excursus on Interpreting the image of God," *Gen 1-11:26*, p. 168.

However, in order to get a more complete perspective of the *Imago Dei* one has to set such concepts not only in the Old Testament context of Genesis 1, creation, and Psalm 8, but *also in the New Testament context of the restoration or re-creation of the image of God in redeemed man.* Two texts in the New Testament refer to man having been renewed in the image of God with an obvious reference to Gen 1:26, 1 Cor 11:7 and Rom 3:13.

Notice where in the context of head coverings in prayer at 1 Cor 11:7 Paul discusses man being in the glory of Christ, and Christ being in the glory of God. The equation of glory and image should not be surprising since man being created in the *image of God* reflects *the likeness and glory of God*, and man bearing *the image of Christ* reflects *the likeness and glory of Christ*. The man being referred to by Paul in this context is man originally created in the image of God, and man recreated in the image of Christ.

This refers back to the creation recorded at Gen 1:26. This should not be interpreted to indicate that Paul is arguing that fallen man reflects the image and glory of God. The New Testament clearly teaches that *fallen man* needs to be *re-created* or *reborn*, and that only when he is reborn in Christ does he reflect the glory of Christ in whose image he now has been *recreated* (John 3:3-4, Eph 4:23, 24; 2 Cor 3:18). *To be recreated must imply that something has been lost*! What was lost was the *image of God*, the *Imago Dei* which is decidedly relational!

Paul quite clearly states at Rom 3:23 that "all have sinned and *fallen short of the glory of God*, but they can be justified by God's grace." Something had been lost! But by God's grace through faith in Jesus and God's redemptive power *man's fallen condition and lost relationship with God has been "put to right"*[28] and man can now be reconciled to God. In Pauline terms man is *redeemed, justified, restored, atoned for* and *reconciled* to God by God's grace and man's faith in Jesus Christ! Fallen man, the sinner, no longer reflects the glory of God, but redeemed and reconciled man created in the image of his creator now reflects the image of his creator!

At John 3:3-5 Jesus stressed to Nicodemus that unless he was *born anew from above* he could not *enter and enjoy the kingdom of God*. This

---

[28] N. T. Wright's favored expression, cf. his book *Justification*.

implies a new beginning, a new birth; one that originates with God and from God as in the beginning, and a new creation. Paul at Rom 6:3-11 explains that in baptism the sinner dies to his or her past life and is raised to walk in *newness of life*. This follows naturally on John 3:2-5 stressing that a new birth or new beginning has taken place. More specifically, at Col 3:10[29] Paul states that the baptized person has "put on the new nature, *which is being renewed in knowledge after the image of its creator.*" Again at Eph 4:22-24 Paul states that the Christian must *"put off your old nature which belongs to your former manner of life and is corrupt through deceitful lusts, ²³ and be renewed in the spirit of your minds, ²⁴ and put on the new nature, created after the likeness of God in true righteousness and holiness."*

Paul builds a similar argument regarding the renewal and regeneration of the image of God in man at Titus 3:3-7.

> *For we ourselves were once foolish, disobedient, led astray, slaves to various passions and pleasures, passing our days in malice and envy, hated by men and hating one another; ⁴ but when the goodness and loving kindness of God our Savior appeared, ⁵ he saved us, not because of deeds done by us in righteousness, but in virtue of his own mercy, by the washing of <u>regeneration and renewal</u> in the Holy Spirit, ⁶ which he poured out upon us richly through Jesus Christ our Savior, ⁷ so that we might be justified by his grace and become heirs in hope of eternal life.*

The Greek word translated *regeneration* in this text is *paliggenesía* which means *regeneration, restoration, renovation*, or *rebirth*.[30] Notice that Paul refers to the *washing* (*loutron, laver*) of regeneration; obviously, a reference to baptism in keeping with John 3:3-5. Paul refers to the action of the Holy Spirit in the *renewal* of man. The Greek for *renewal*, a synonym for *regeneration*, is *anakainōsis* which means *a renewing or a renovation which makes a person different than in the past*.[31]

At 2 Thess 2:13-14 Paul likewise spoke of the working of the Holy Spirit in the salvation and sanctification of man resulting in his obtaining the glory of Christ:

---

[29] Which builds on Col 2:12-13 and 3:1, 2.
[30] Zodhiates, *The Complete Word Study Dictionary: New Testament*.
[31] Zodhiates. *The Complete Word Study Dictionary*.

¹³ But we are bound to give thanks to God always for you, brethren beloved by the Lord, because God chose you from the beginning to be saved, through sanctification by the Spirit and belief in the truth. ¹⁴ To this he called you through our gospel, so that you may obtain the glory of our Lord Jesus Christ.

Paul repeats the point that *renewal* and *recreation* of the lost person into the image of God takes place at baptism through the work of the Holy Spirit.

Whatever had been the image of God or the likeness of God in man *at creation had been in some sense lost at the fall*. The renewal of his lost image and recreation in the image of his creator takes place in the new birth of the alienated sinner in his baptism.

Thus we learn that at the fall (Gen 2, 3), man's relationship with both God and creation changed. Rom 5:12 explains that Adam opened the door to sin and alienation from God, and because of this each lost sinner experiences the same alienation from God *through personal sin*, cf. Rom 5:12ff and 1 Cor 15:21f.[32]

Sin and death entered the world because Adam sinned, but all men do not die simply because Adam sinned and died. Paul stated that but *because all men sin, all men die!* There is a relationship to *all sinning* in Adam and *all men being reconciled* in Christ. This is not simply a *corporate* relationship, but a *personal* one! Rom 5:12:

¹² Therefore as sin came into the world through one man and death through sin, and so death spread to all men <u>because all men sinned</u>—[33]

---

[32] Rom 5:12ff has posed exegetical and hermeneutic problems for some but the reader should note that at Rom 5:12b Paul stresses that death spread to all men *because all men sinned*, not because Adam sinned.

[33] This is not the place to engage in an extended and complicated discussion of Rom 5 and Paul's argument on the Adam/Christ analogy. Paul here simply argues that all men die because all men have sinned. Likewise, all men are reconciled in Christ through faith and obedience to Christ. Some argue that it is in Adam that all men have sinned and not because of each personal individual sin. It is held by some that because Adam sinned all men inherit the consequences of Adam's sin and therefore die. Some doctrines stress that all men inherit sin and total depravity from Adam. Cf the discussion of this text in Douglas J. Moo, *The Epistle to the Romans*, The New International Commentary of the New Testament, Grand Rapids: Wm. B. Eerdmans, 1996, pp. 314ff; F. F. Bruce, *Romans*,

Due to their sinful behavior the lost or alienated sinner has *fallen short of the glory or image of God*, Rom 6:23ff, and has therefore *lost the image of God*. The alienated sinner needs to be *recreated in Christ* through the grace of God, personal faith, baptism, and the working of the Holy Spirit *into the image of his creator*. The story of the renewal of this lost image of God in man lies at the heart of the doctrine of atonement.

My point is that the *image of God*, lost in each individual through personal sin, has to be *recreated* in man by God and Christ through faith in Christ and the working of the Holy Spirit in a new birth from above. The tragedy of man's original fall (Gen 3) which changed man's relationship with God is repeated in each person's personal sin and alienation from God. Man, however, can be *put right again by God's grace through faith in Jesus*. This is Paul's story in Rom 5 and 6. As N. T. Wright puts it,[34] *in Christ God is "putting the world to rights again,"* or as we might express it, *in Christ God is making it possible for man to get right with God and be recreated in the image of the creator*.

This is the story line we will be following in our discussion of the *missional nature of the kingdom* and the *Missio Dei*.

A scripture that possibly defines more clearly the relationship of the image of God in man, sin, redemption, and being recreated in the image of God is 2 Cor 5:17.

Several related themes flow out of this text:

> "Therefore, if anyone is in Christ, <u>he is a new creation</u>; the old has passed away, behold, the new has come. [18] All this is from God, who through Christ reconciled us to himself and gave us the ministry of reconciliation; [19] that is, <u>in Christ God was reconciling the world to himself</u>, not counting their trespasses against them, and entrusting to us the message of reconciliation. [20] So we are ambassadors for Christ, God making his appeal through us. We beseech you on behalf of Christ, be reconciled to God. [21] For our sake he made him to be sin who knew no sin, so that in him we might become the righteousness of God."

Tyndale New Testament Commentaries, England: Inter-Varsity Press, 1985; Leon Morris, *The Epistle to the Romans*, Grand Rapids: Wm. B. Eerdmans, 1988.

[34] N. T. Wright, *Justification, passim*.

Notice how the *missional* message of the *kingdom* of God flows through Paul's magnificent text!

Being in God's image implies that man can have a unique relationship with God which is far deeper than man's relationship with the remainder of creation. *In fact, because of this divine image man was a suitable protector and caretaker of God's creation.* Being created in God's image and likeness *prepared man to function as God's regent in God's kingdom on earth* and in *God's missional sovereign care for creation.*

The image of God and man's dominion over God's creation

God's sovereignty over his kingdom was evidenced in his original creative activity. As sovereign creator, God created man in his image and likeness so that man could have an intimate relationship with God and *share in God's dominion over creation. This creative act prepared man in God's image for a role in sharing in God's missional kingdom and reign.*

This majestic story of man's *recreation* in God's image to share in God's *sovereign rule and kingdom mission* is the heart of the narrative *kingdom theology* and the *Missio Dei.*

Corporate personality[35] *relationships* between a king and his people may not be fully appreciated in today's postmodern individualistic culture, but the corporate personality relationship between a sovereign and his people would have been clearly understood by the original readers of Genesis. *Man was clearly created to share in God's image and sovereign reign over creation.* Note, Gen 1:25-31.

> "Then God said, "Let us make man in our image, after our likeness; and let them have dominion over the fish of the sea, and over the birds of the air, and over the cattle, and over all the earth, and over every creeping thing that creeps upon the earth." [27] So

---

[35] Corporate personality is a concept which in theology involves an organic relationship between an individual and a corporate body to which the individual belongs. As originally expressed in Scripture, it dealt with areas of the Old Testament where the relationships between individuals and a group of which they were part of were treated as a whole. For example, Achan's family as well as the nation were collectively punished for a sin that was viewed primarily as Achan's alone. Likewise the members of a kingdom were seen to be organically related to their king and shared in his reign. The message of the Book of Revelation relating to the martyrs receiving thrones with Christ and reigning with him is an example of this corporate personality concept.

> *God created man in his own image, in the image of God he created him; male and female he created them. ²⁸ And God blessed them, and God said to them, "Be fruitful and multiply, and fill the earth and subdue it; and have dominion over the fish of the sea and over the birds of the air and over every living thing that moves upon the earth." ²⁹ And God said, "Behold, I have given you every plant yielding seed which is upon the face of all the earth, and every tree with seed in its fruit; you shall have them for food. ³⁰ And to every beast of the earth, and to every bird of the air, and to everything that creeps on the earth, everything that has the breath of life, I have given every green plant for food." And it was so. ³¹ And God saw everything that he had made, and behold, it was very good. And there was evening and there was morning, a sixth day."*

Mathews, again in his *Genesis* commentary, discusses in some detail the relationship between the image and likeness of God and man having been created to have *sonship* and *dominion* over creation:

> The language of 1:26 reflects this idea of a royal figure representing God as his appointed ruler. This appears also to be the understanding of Psalm 8, which focuses on human dominion, though without explicit mention of the "image" or "likeness." This is further indicated by the term "rule" *(rādâ)* in 1:26, 28, which is used commonly of royal dominion. Human jurisdiction over animate life in the skies, waters, and land corresponds to the "rule" *(māšal)* of the sun and moon over the inanimate sphere of creation. Our passage declares that all people, not just kings, have the special status of royalty in the eyes of God. It is striking that God consigns jurisdiction to one of his creatures, since the major tenet of 1:1–2:3 is the sovereignty of God's creative word. It was this feature of creation that so astonished the psalmist; for him the Infinite One crowned human infancy with the glory of his rule (Ps 8:5 - 9). The supreme value God places on human life is also reflected in Ps 9:5–6. Whereas an animal may be wrongly brutalized, it is the taking of human life that merits the charge "murderer."[36]

---

[36] Mathews, *Genesis* 1-11:26, comment on Gen 1:26 and "dominion," p. 168.

.... The passage focuses on the consequence of that creative act, which is humanity's rule over the terrestrial world of life (1:28; Ps 8:6, 7). That lofty position merited the divine bestowal of "glory and honor" (Ps 8:5, 6) that one and at the same time acknowledged human creatureliness and yet honored mankind above all creatures as "human." Genesis 5:3 echoes 1:26 and indicates that the succession of the "image" and the blessing are realized through sonship. In the ancient Near East royal persons were considered the sons of the gods or representatives of the gods (cf. 2 Sam 7:13–16; Ps 2:7). Mankind is appointed as God's royal representatives (i.e., sonship) to rule the earth in his place.... In the New Testament these ideas of image, glory, and sonship are found closely related (e.g., 1 Cor 11:7; 2 Cor 3:18; 4:4, 6; Heb 2:5–10). By the grace of the Creator the new humanity is created in the "image of Christ" (cp. 1 Cor 15:49) and through his perfect obedience achieves life and glory for believers as his adopted children (e.g., Rom 8:17, 30; 9:23; 1 Cor 4:4, 6; Col 3:9–10).[37]

Wenham observes regarding man's rule over creation (Gen 1:26, 28) that his *dominion* was similar to that of a *benevolent king who ruled with concern for his people.*

"By upholding divine principles of law and justice, rulers promoted peace and prosperity for all their subjects. Similarly, mankind is here commissioned to rule nature as a benevolent king, acting as God's representative over them and therefore treating them in the same way as God who created them."[38]

In the case of man being created in the image of God, the benevolent creator, this implied that man created in the image of God would be a devoted benevolent ruler dedicated to the welfare of God's creation. Man's task would involve a *nurturing caring* concern for God's creation.

This concept lies at the very heart of the Missio Dei and kingdom theology!

---

[37] Mathews, *Genesis 1-11:26*, comment on Gen 1:26 and man's rule over creation, p. 164.
[38] Wenham, *Genesis 1–15*, p. 33.

God's purpose in creating man was that he should rule over the animal world (v 26). Here this injunction is repeated and defined more precisely. "*Let them have dominion* [rule] *over the fish of the sea, the birds of the sky and every living creature ... on earth.*" Because man is created in God's image, he is *a king over nature. He was intended to rule the world on God's behalf.* This thought presents no license for the unbridled exploitation and subjugation of nature. Ancient oriental kings were expected to be devoted to the welfare of their subjects, especially the poorest and weakest members of society (Ps 72:12–14). By upholding divine principles of law and justice, rulers promoted peace and prosperity for all their subjects. Similarly, mankind was here commissioned to rule nature as a benevolent king, acting as God's representative over them and therefore treating them in the same way as God who created them. Thus animals, though subject to man, are viewed as his companions in Gen 2:18–20.[39]

Unfortunately, man was not satisfied with his role of sharing with God in God's sovereign reign over creation and sought greater enlightenment, that is, to be like God knowing the difference between good and evil! Adam and Eve, contrary to God's decree, ate of the tree of knowledge and introduced sin and alienation from God into God's creation (Gen 3:1-7, cf. again Rom 5:12-14).[40]

In the story of Adam's and Eve's sin of disobedience God's sovereignty and reign were challenged and denied. Sin and alienation from God resulted and *the image of God's relationship with man being fractured.* God, however, in his infinite foreknowledge, love, and wisdom had already in eternity foreseen this and had prepared for this in advance, cf. Eph 1:3ff.

As indicated in the term *eternal*, God's kingdom plan had its origins in God's sovereign purpose before the foundation of the world and the beginning of time. Eternity refers to the state of God's personal existence

---

[39] Wenham, *Genesis 1–15*, p. 33.
[40] Genesis does not leave us with a complete understanding of the meaning of eating the tree of knowledge of good and evil (Gen 2:9) and the precise meaning of the details of this text remain obscure. We are left however with the knowledge that by eating of the fruit of this tree man disobeyed God, became alienated from God, and suffered the consequences of a broken relationship with their creator. Even the physical creation suffered from man's disobedience, cf. Rom 8:18-25.

before and during the created world. Thus, Adam and Eve's disobedience and sin set in motion God's great eternal redemptive mercy and sovereign grace. He had a plan for *restoring his kingdom sovereignty in man and over his created world*. Although beginning before the creation of everything, God's redemptive activity, his *Missio Dei*, reached its zenith in Jesus' ministry and faithful death and resurrection. Jesus inaugurated God's plan of redemption, his restoration of the image of God in redeemed man, and his restored *Missio Dei* kingdom. *This is the heart of kingdom theology!*

Paul reflected on God's eternal kingdom-purpose and God's *Missio Dei* plan as being carried forward *when the time was ready*, Gal 4:4, Eph 1:10, *in the fulness of time*, through His covenant people, the church. Cf. Eph 1:3-14:

> *Blessed be the God and Father of our Lord Jesus Christ, who has blessed us in Christ with every spiritual blessing in the heavenly places, ⁴ even as he chose us in him before the foundation of the world, that we should be holy and blameless before him. ⁵ He destined us in love to be his sons through Jesus Christ, according to the purpose of his will, ⁶ to the praise of his glorious grace which he freely bestowed on us in the Beloved. ⁷ In him we have redemption through his blood, the forgiveness of our trespasses, according to the riches of his grace ⁸ which he lavished upon us. ⁹ For he has made known to us in all wisdom and insight the mystery of his will, according to his purpose which he set forth in Christ ¹⁰ <u>as a plan for the fulness of time, to unite all things in him, things in heaven and things on earth</u>. ¹¹ In him, according to the purpose of him who accomplishes all things according to the counsel of his will, ¹² we who first hoped in Christ have been destined and appointed to live for the praise of his glory. ¹³ In him you also, who have heard the word of truth, the gospel of your salvation, and have believed in him, were sealed with the promised Holy Spirit, ¹⁴ which is the guarantee of our inheritance until we acquire possession of it, to the praise of his glory.*

This text explains that God's call and election of men and women to be his children in Christ was according to a divine *missional kingdom plan*

(*Missio Dei*) which He had "predestined"[41] before creation. It was a kingdom plan through which God intended to set his creation back on course through the faithfulness of Jesus, the Messiah.

Note carefully the *missional theological nature* of the *Missio Dei*, kingdom theology.

This plan, originally conceived in eternity, was triggered in Eden when man sinned through disobedience to God and in doing this rejected God's sovereign will. Through their disobedience Adam and Eve lost their favored place and relationship in God's created world. God's sovereign reign or kingdom on earth had been fractured by the disobedience of his creation, man.

However, as we have noted, even before creation, God had planned to redeem fallen man and restore him to his *special relationship*, his *imago dei*, with himself and with his plan for his creation. Theologically we call this relationship *reconciliation, justification*, and *righteousness*, or the condition of a being in *a right relationship with God* and his kingdom purpose for creation.[42]

This process of restoring God's relationship with man is the heart of kingdom theology and the Missio Dei.

Kingdom theology is thus both *redemptive* and *missional*. In his plan God actively seeks to *redeem* his fallen creation and *restore* what he had created in the beginning, which he will do in Christ.

What we have learned in this chapter

Kingdom theology, which we define as the *Missio Dei*, addresses God's plan in Christ for the recreation of *God's image* in man, his *imago dei*. The image of God relates to God's intimate relationship with man, who in Christ and through the Holy Spirit's sanctification is *restored in the image of God, his creator*. Note Paul's two comments in this restoration of the image of God.

Col 3:9, 10:

---

[41] At Eph 1:5, 12, Paul used the word *prohoridzō* which can be translated *predestined, pre-determined*, or *destined*. It primarily means *to decide beforehand*.

[42] For a definitive discussion of righteousness as being in a right relationship with God by being declared not guilty through grace and faith in Jesus, cf. N. T. Wright, *Justification*.

> *Do not lie to one another, seeing that you have put off the old nature with its practices* [10] *and have put on the new nature, which <u>is being renewed in knowledge after the image of its creator</u>.*

Eph 4:22,23:
> [22] *Put off your old nature which belongs to your former manner of life and is corrupt through deceitful lusts,* [23] *and <u>be renewed in the spirit of your minds</u>,* [24] *and <u>put on the new nature, created after the likeness of God</u> in true righteousness and holiness.*

The image of God in man, which refers to his being recreated in the image of his creator, primarily refers to his *distinctive renewed relationship with God*. This is what the *Missio Dei* is all about! It involves God's eternal plan of redemption, reconciliation, and recreation, wrapped up in his covenant with Abraham to reach out to all men. All of this is achieved in Christ for all men.

Kingdom theology is uniquely and intentionally *missional*, expanding the intimate relationship between God and man into all the world and all nations.

Chapter 3
Jesus and the Kingdom

What we will learn in this chapter

We will learn in this chapter that Jesus came preaching the kingdom of God and to inaugurate that kingdom.

We will note that the concept of the kingdom pre-existed and predated the church which Jesus established, and that the kingdom is more primary in kingdom theology than the church.[1]

However, we will stress that the church is an important aspect of kingdom theology.

It is our opinion that a truncated understanding of kingdom theology can lead to a distorted understanding of the *Missio Dei* and a divisive mindset among churches.

Significant Scriptures

Psalm 22:28: *"For dominion belongs to the LORD, and he rules over the nations."*

Psalm 103:19: *"The LORD has established his throne in the heavens, and his kingdom rules over all."*

1 Chron. 29:11: *"Thine, O Lord, is the greatness, and the power, and the glory, and the victory, and the majesty; for all that is in the heavens and in the earth is thine; thine is the kingdom, O Lord, and thou art exalted as head above all."*

Matt 16:13-20: *"*[13] *Now when Jesus came into the district of Caesarea Philippi, he asked his disciples, "Who do men say that the Son of man is?"* [14] *And they said, "Some say John the Baptist, others say Elijah, and others Jeremiah or one of the prophets."* [15] *He said to them, "But who do you say that I am?"* [16] *Simon Peter replied, "You are the Christ*[2], *the Son of the*

---

[1] In this study I speak of the church in its broader sense as spoken of by Jesus in Matt 16:18 and by Paul in Eph 5:23ff. Although I will address issues in my own fellowship, the Churches of Christ, I have no intention of entering the debate over which churches are the Church of Christ and which some may not consider to be so. I hope to set the church in a kingdom context and not in a denominational context. I am more concerned to see the church as a missional element or organ of the kingdom of God.

[2] The English word *Christ* derives from the Greek Χριστός, *Christós*, which in turn is the Greek translation of the word *messiah* which comes from the Hebrew *mashiach* and

*living God." * [17] *And Jesus answered him, "Blessed are you, Simon Bar-Jona! For flesh and blood has not revealed this to you, but my Father who is in heaven.* [18] *And I tell you, you are Peter, and <u>on this rock I will build my church</u>, and the powers of death shall not prevail against it.* [19] *<u>I will give you the keys of the kingdom of heaven</u>, and whatever you bind on earth shall be bound in heaven, and whatever you loose on earth shall be loosed in heaven."* [20] *Then he strictly charged the disciples to tell no one that he was the Christ.*

Introduction

Some years ago I heard that Professor James I. Packer, an internationally renowned theologian, was to give three lectures in Austin, Texas, on the kingdom. I had my secretary make reservations (the lectures were open to the public but only by reservation and the payment of a fee of $15.00). She wrote the necessary letter on Abilene Christian University, College of Biblical Studies stationery and included my personal check for $15.00. When I arrived at the appointed lecture hall in Austin and registered at the registration desk, the lady in attendance, on recognizing my name, informed me that Dr. Packer was anxious to meet me! I was surprised at this, but also intrigued, for after all, Dr. Packer was an internationally recognized theologian of some repute and I was simply a professor at Abilene Christian University and newly appointed Dean of the College of Biblical Studies! Why would he want to meet me?

I was directed to a room at the rear of the lecture hall where Dr. Packer was preparing for his lecture. On arrival, he greeted me warmly with the statement, "Dr. Fair, it is obvious that you are a Church of Christ theologian, but why would a member of the Church of Christ be interested in lectures on the kingdom? Church of Christ theologians have written much and well on the Church, but have written little of real depth on the kingdom."

Dr. Packer was not being derogatory, but merely making an insightful observation. Church of Christ theologians and ministers had written little of any depth on the kingdom, other than in the context of premillennial battles. Dr. Packer and I enjoyed a few minutes of warm discussion.

---

means "anointed one" or "chosen one" and was used of Israel's kings who were chosen and anointed by God. Cf. Saul and David.

His three lectures were "eye openers" that I will never forget, *The Theology of the Kingdom as it relates to Worship, to Evangelism, and to Christian Living*. Packer's comments made such an impact on me and the writing of this book that I will refer back to this on several occasions in the study!

In line with this thought on the importance of kingdom theology, Professor Wolfhart Pannenberg, specialist in Systematic and Biblical Theology, had in his study, *Theology and the Kingdom of God*, insightfully observed (1968) that "the message of Jesus centered in the proclamation of the imminent kingdom of God."[3] He went on to argue that without a proper understanding of the kingdom of God Christians would miss the heart of Jesus' message and ministry.

British theologian and former Bishop in the Church of England, N. T. Wright makes similar thought-provoking observations regarding Jesus' kingdom purpose.[4] He observes that to *separate the message of the kingdom from a central role in Jesus' ministry is to significantly diminish Jesus' purpose and mission*. This point will be the leading thought of this study of the kingdom.

Jesus and Kingdom Theology

Traditional Church of Christ emphasis on preaching the gospel has centered on preaching salvation and justification based on Jesus' death and resurrection as proclaimed by Paul at Rom 1:16, 17, and 1 Cor 15:1-4. No one with any knowledge of the Bible would debate that salvation by grace is good news. A gospel message that proclaims salvation for both the Jew and Gentile through faith in Jesus, and not by keeping laws, is certainly good news!
Cf. Rom 1:15-17:

> *I am eager to <u>preach the gospel</u> to you also who are in Rome.*
> *[16] For I am not ashamed of the gospel: it is the power of God for salvation to everyone who has faith, to the Jew first and also to the*

---

[3] Wolfhart Pannenberg, *Theology of the Kingdom of God*, p. 51.
[4] This is a central theme of Wright's observations regarding Jesus and his ministry. Cf. *Simply Christian*, HarperOne, 2006, pp. 91ff; *Simply Jesus*, HarperOne, 2011, passim; *Jesus and the Victory of God*, Minneapolis, Fortress, 1996, pp. 198ff.; *How God Became King: The Forgotten Story of the Gospels*, Harper Collins, 2012.

> *Greek. ¹⁷ For in it the righteousness of God is revealed through faith for faith; as it is written, "<u>He who through faith is righteous shall live</u>."*

Cf. 1 Cor 15:1-5:

> *Now I would remind you, brethren, in <u>what terms I preached to you the gospel</u>, which you received, in which you stand, ² by which you are saved, if you hold it fast—unless you believed in vain. ³ For I delivered to you as of first importance what I also received, that <u>Christ died for our</u> sins in accordance with the scriptures, ⁴ that <u>he was buried, that he was raised on the third day</u> in accordance with the scriptures, ⁵ and that he appeared to Cephas, then to the twelve.*

The question is, "does this tell the full story of the gospel as good news?" There was, however, certainly more to good news for the Jew than this great message of spiritual redemption. Living under the suppressive rule of Rome the Jews were longing for a new kingdom that offered freedom. They were looking for a day when God would restore his kingdom as proclaimed by Moses, David, and Daniel and deliver them from their oppressors. Any message offering such redemption would certainly be seen as "gospel," good news!

We acknowledge that in certain contexts the gospel, meaning good news of salvation, does take on more of a soteriological flavor (1 Cor 15:1-4), but context must always supply the richer meaning of the good news!

Jesus kingdom ministry, however, pressed deeper into the heart of the good news. The gospel message of Jesus was primarily a proclamation of the good news relating to the *restoration of the kingdom of God.*

The focus of Jesus' preaching was that in his ministry the kingdom God had promised to restore was already breaking into human history in Jesus' life and ministry. The point was that Jesus was *inaugurating* the *reconciliation of man with God in God's Missio Dei* kingdom. That this reconciliation and restoration of God's relationship with people in his kingdom pressed deeper than simply keeping the Law of Moses and placating the Romans was good news, not only for the Gentile, but essentially for the Jew.

Simply perceiving the preaching of the gospel as a message of salvation was not at all what John the Baptist and Jesus had in mind when

Matthew and Mark recorded that Jesus came preaching the gospel of the coming of the kingdom!

Matt 4:23; Mark1:14, indicate that the heart of Jesus' gospel message was that through Jesus' ministry and redemptive death, burial, and resurrection, the covenant promises of the restored kingdom and relationship with God made earlier to Abraham, then to Israel, *were in a real sense about to be inaugurated and break into human experience.* Right from the beginning of Jesus' ministry the gospel focused on *the imminent fulfillment of God's kingdom promises and his Abrahamic covenant.* All of this was to take place in Jesus' life, purpose, ministry, and death and resurrection.

Jesus' ministry centered on the restoration of God's kingdom as the fulfillment of God's covenant promises to Abraham. Jesus' preaching and teaching began to sharpen and *refocus* Israel's *understanding of the message of the kingdom*! Unfortunately, as recorded by John in his gospel message, Jesus' own people missed the point and rejected Jesus. Cf. John 1:9-13:

> *The true light that enlightens every man was coming into the world. ¹⁰ He was in the world, and the world was made through him, yet the world knew him not. ¹¹ He came to his own home, and his own people received him not. ¹² But to all who received him, who believed in his name, he gave power to become children of God; ¹³ who were born, not of blood nor of the will of the flesh nor of the will of man, but of God.*

The promised restoration of the kingdom was, however, indeed good news. It was much broader than a political kingdom in which Israel's enemies, essentially the Romans, would be defeated and a new political or regional kingdom established in Jerusalem. It included both a restoration of God's created kingdom including both redemption and reconciliation through the death of Jesus which was what God's initial *Missio Dei* was all about.

Mark and Matthew both proclaimed that Jesus' kingdom would be the restoration of the kingdom promises to Abraham. However, this promise and its good news demanded *repentance* and *belief in the sovereign reign of God in people's lives*!

Something radical about the reign or kingdom of God was about to break into the world of Israel and Rome! *But it was good news*! This kingdom restoration would not be rooted in political and military might which was the basis of all kingdom change in the ancient world. This kingdom restoration would be based on *dying to self, faith, repentance, baptism, and obedience to God through faith in the death of Jesus, the promised Messiah*! Now in any day and time, that is a radical understanding of good news!

This thought was a challenging one to the Israel of Jesus' day, even to his twelve disciples, for they were not expecting the kind of kingdom Jesus was introducing. They expected a physical kingdom like the one they had experienced in past centuries before the fall of the two divided kingdoms of Israel.

The kingdom in Jesus teaching and ministry

Matthew and Mark both record the words of John the Baptist setting the scene for Jesus' kingdom ministry. Matt wrote:

> ¹ In those days came John the Baptist, preaching in the wilderness of Judea, ² *"Repent, for the kingdom of heaven is at hand."* ³ For this is he who was spoken of by the prophet Isaiah when he said,
> "The voice of one crying in the wilderness:
> Prepare the way of the Lord,
> make his paths straight." [5]

In similar words Mark wrote:

> ¹ The beginning of the gospel of Jesus Christ, the Son of God. ² As it is written in Isaiah the prophet,
> "Behold, I send my messenger before thy face,
> who shall prepare thy way;
> ³ the voice of one crying in the wilderness:
> Prepare the way of the Lord,
> make his paths straight—"
> ¹⁴ Now after John was arrested, *Jesus came into Galilee, preaching the gospel of God,* ¹⁵ and saying, *"The time is fulfilled, and the kingdom of God is at hand; repent, and believe in the gospel."* [6]

---

[5] Mt 3:1–3.
[6] Mk 1:1–3, 14–15.

We will note below that the expression at hand carries a sense of imminent urgency and anticipation. From the above citations we can assume that John the Baptist and Jesus understood that they were *initiating or describing the imminent beginnings of a kingdom and kingdom ministry.*

Furthermore, both Matthew and Mark clearly stated that the kingdom of God, or the kingdom of heaven, *was at hand*, both referring to the same kingdom. The word *at hand* is the English translation of the Greek ἤγγικεν γὰρ ἡ βασιλεία τῶν οὐρανῶν[7] and ἤγγικεν ἡ βασιλεία τοῦ θεοῦ.[8] Zodhiates observes:

> The word ἤγγικεν is a perfect indicative active verb of ἐγγίζω, *eggízō*; which means *to bring near* and come near in a transitive context, and intransitive context it can mean to approach, as is often the case with verbs of motion such as *ágō* ... I lead. Usually in the New Testament it is used intransitively meaning *to come near, approach* ... *in the perfect tense éggika, it implies to have drawn near, to be near, to be at hand*; in the expression *éggiken*, is near, referring to the kingdom of God or heaven (Matt. 3:2; 4:17; 10:7; Mark 1:15; Luke 10:11). The verb has reference to space, meaning that something is here.[9]

The adverb ἐγγύς, *eggús*, related to the verb ἐγγίζω, *eggízō*, is found at Rev 1:3 as ὁ γὰρ καιρὸς ἐγγύς, *"the crisis time is at hand."* In my commentary on Revelation, *Conquering With Christ*, I demonstrate that several scholars, for example David Aune, Grant Osburn, and Elizabeth Schussler Fiorenza, argue for an *imminent expectation* in the use of ἤγγικεν/ἐγγύς when used in eschatological contexts. The following extract from my commentary will reference these thoughts:

> Greek has two terms for time. The one, *chronos* implies time that passes. The other *kairos*, used in this expression, stresses *urgent time, even crisis time. In the expression because the time is near, John uses the word kairos, that is, "urgent, significant, crisis time."* Osborne observes regarding *kairos* at Rev. 11:19 that the

---

[7] Nestle, *The Greek New Testament*, 27th ed., Matt 3:2.
[8] Nestle, *The Greek New Testament*, 27th ed., Mk 1:15.
[9] Zodhiates, *The Complete Word Study Dictionary: New Testament*, ἐγγίζω *eggízō*.

verse "is introduced by *ho kairos* . . . which occurs five times in the book (1:3; 11:18; 12:12,14; 22:10) and *refers not to chronological time but to eschatological time,* a period filled with the sense of God's judgment on those who do evil and his salvation for those who live for righteousness." John *urges immediate concern for deepening spiritual strength in view of imminent crises that were about to break in on the church.* Aune states that *hō kairos* "is an important technical term . . . which refers to *the impending crisis* that will overtake the world and that involves a traditional program of eschatological events." Beale describes the words *hō gar kairos eggus* as "*an exaggerated expression of imminence that includes a notion of present time.*" Schüssler Fiorenza observes: "Instead of a divine plan of historical events the author of Rev. introduces *the imminent expectation. . .* John does not intend to show as in Dan 2:28 (LXX) what must occur at the last day (ep eschaton ton hēmeron) but what must happen soon (ha dei genesthai en tachei; Rev. 1:1; 22:6). All the visions and images of Revelation—are determined by such an imminent expectation."[10]

From the kingdom messages of the Synoptic Gospel writers, it was obvious that Matthew, Mark, and Luke expected that the kingdom preached by Jesus was something on the point of breaking into human experience—an imminent expectation!

Matthew solidified this argument at Matt 12:22ff where Jesus explicitly stated that the kingdom had already arrived in his ministry. Jesus had just healed a blind man and is accused by the Pharisees of casting out demons by the power of Beelzebul, in Hebrew meaning *the lord of the manure pile*, or Satan! Notice the connection between the power of Jesus' ministry, the kingdom and the working of the Holy Spirit.

---

[10] Ian A. Fair, *Conquering With Christ*, ACU Press, 2011, pp. 79f. Cf. Aune, David E., *Revelation*, Vol 1, Dallas: Word, 1997; Fiorenza, Elisabeth Schüssler, *Invitation to the Book of Revelation*, New York: Doubleday & Company, 1981; *The Book of Revelation: Justice and Judgment*, Philadelphia: Fortress Press, 1985; Osborne, Grant R., *Revelation*, Baker Exegetical Commentary on the New Testament, Grand Rapids: Baker Academic, 2002.

Then a blind and dumb demoniac was brought to him, and he healed him, so that the dumb man spoke and saw. ²³ And all the people were amazed, and said, "Can this be the Son of David?" ²⁴ But when the Pharisees heard it they said, "It is only by Be-elzebul, the prince of demons, that this man casts out demons." ²⁵ Knowing their thoughts, he said to them, "Every kingdom divided against itself is laid waste, and no city or house divided against itself will stand; ²⁶ and if Satan casts out Satan, he is divided against himself; how then will his kingdom stand? ²⁷ And if I cast out demons by Be-elzebul, by whom do your sons cast them out? Therefore they shall be your judges. ²⁸ <u>But if it is by the Spirit of God that I cast out demons, then the kingdom of God has come upon you</u>. ²⁹ Or how can one enter a strong man's house and plunder his goods, unless he first binds the strong man? Then indeed he may plunder his house. ³⁰ He who is not with me is against me, and he who does not gather with me scatters. ³¹ Therefore I tell you, every sin and blasphemy will be forgiven men, but the blasphemy against the Spirit will not be forgiven. ³² And whoever says a word against the Son of man will be forgiven; but whoever speaks against the Holy Spirit will not be forgiven, either in this age or in the age to come.[11]

First, the expression *"But if ... "* at Matt 12:28 is in Greek a 1st class conditional sentence which carries the sense of *"Since it is by the power of the Holy Spirit ..."*[12] Jesus was making a firm statement of fact![13]

Second, the expression *has come upon you*, likewise in Matt 12:28, translates the Greek ἔφθασεν ἐφ' ὑμᾶς containing the aorist verb ἔφθασεν which makes a strong statement of fact, implying an act that has already taken place.

Craig Blomberg draws attention to the importance of this pericope:
> Jesus himself claims that *he exorcises by the power of the Holy Spirit, who descended on him at his baptism, marking the*

---

[11] Matt 12:22ff.
[12] The adverbial conjunction coupled with a verb in the indicative mood, εἰ δὲ ... ἐκβάλλω, implies a statement of fact not of possibility or probability Cf. Dana and Mantey, *A Manual Grammar of the Greek New Testament*, p. 289.
[13] Cf. Keener, Craig, *A Commentary on the Gospel of Matthew*, p. 364. Cf. also Davies, and Allison, *The Gospel According to Saint Matthew*, Edinburgh, p. 339f.

inauguration of God's reign, and who permanently empowers all disciples for ministry in the messianic age. Verse 28 is arguably the single most important teaching of Jesus on realized eschatology—the present aspect of the kingdom (on which see the discussion under 3:2). Debate continues on the meaning of ephthasen ("has come"), *but some sense of arrival seems inescapable here.* Matthew also uses the "kingdom of God" (rather than "kingdom of heaven") for the first time, probably to parallel the "Spirit of God" in the previous clause.[14]

Hagner concurs that this event signals the inauguration of the kingdom of God in the ministry of Jesus and the Holy Spirit.

The choice of the phrase "Spirit of God" already signals this difference. The exorcisms and healing miracles of Jesus are part of a larger whole and, unlike those of his Jewish contemporaries, are linked inseparably with both his person and *the proclamation of the dawning of the kingdom of God*. In this case, the powerful deeds of Jesus are considered *direct pointers to the reality of that proclamation. These deeds indicate that ἡ βασιλεία τοῦ θεοῦ, "the kingdom of God," is now directly present to the people of Israel* (Matthew uses "God" rather than "heaven" elsewhere only in 6:33; 19:24; and 21:31, 43 [cf. 13:43; 26:29]; here it is preferred probably to serve as the direct opposite of the reference to the kingdom of Satan in v 26). *The verb ἔφθασεν means "to come upon" and necessitates the conclusion that the kingdom of God has in some sense actually become present* (so rightly Davies-Allison)—a clearer statement than that made by ἐγγίζειν, "is near," of 4:17; 10:7. Admittedly this has happened without the fullest effects that one must associate with the kingdom; *we thus have fulfillment but fulfillment short of consummation.*[15]

---

[14] Blomberg, Craig L., *Matthew: An Exegetical and Theological Exposition of Holy Scripture*, pp. 202f.

[15] Hagner, *Matthew 1–13*, p. 343. Cf. Davies, and Allison, *The Gospel According to Saint Matthew*, p. 339f.

From the general discussion of Jesus' claim to have introduced the kingdom of God it is apparent that a clear appreciation of *inaugurated eschatology* is essential to understanding the full import of Jesus' claim. To speak here of realized eschatology is to miss the general point of biblical or New Testament theology even if realized eschatology indicates a more present reality of the kingdom than seen in futurist views of eschatology stressing the final end of time. In 1930 C. H. Dodd, Joachim Jeremias, and others introduced the concept of a *realized eschatology* to answer questions originating in a view that eschatology referred only to the future end of time. Futurists read into eschatology end time references of the final end of the world. Although Dodd's realized eschatology was helpful in restoring a balance to biblical eschatology, it overstressed its argument by not valuing the ongoing nature of an eschatology that had already begun in Jesus' ministry.

A directional adjustment to Dodd's and other views of realized eschatology was introduced by the works of Oscar Cullmann, 1956, *Christ and Time,* and Werner Georg Kummel, *Promise and Fulfillment*, 1957. They introduced the term and concept of an *inaugurated eschatology* which explained that although Jesus had *introduced* the eschatological kingdom of God in his Holy Spirit inspired ministry, he had in reality *opened* the eschaton, or *set in motion, inaugurated* the eschatological kingdom, in his ministry. Jesus, in his Holy Spirit inspired ministry, thus *inaugurated* the final end time age, the eschaton or eschatological age, or more expressively, the Christian or Kingdom age. This was not the final fulfillment of the Jewish eschatological age expectation which inaugurated age would continue throughout the apostolic age and church age in the ministry of Holy Spirit indwelt Christians. This inaugurated eschatological period would finally close when Jesus eventually returns in his *parousia* or second coming, cf. 1 Thess 4:13ff, 1 Cor 15:51ff.[16]

At the close of Jesus' earthly ministry the disciples were still struggling to get their arms around this life and world shaping kingdom concept. They fell back on their past limited Jewish understanding of the kingdom. In their closing moments with Jesus, after he had spent 40 days instructing them about the kingdom (Acts 1:3f), they asked Jesus whether

---

[16] *Baker's Dictionary of Theology*, "Eschatology," Frederick Fyvie Bruce, pp. 187ff ; Alan Richardson, "Eschatology," *A Dictionary of Christian Theology*, pp.113ff.

he was at that point going to *restore the kingdom to Israel* (Acts 1:8). They did not yet understand that Jesus' purpose and kingdom went far deeper and broader than their political expectations. Polhill observes:

> In Jewish thought God's promises often referred to the coming of Israel's final salvation, and this concept is reflected elsewhere in Acts (cf. 2:39; 13:23, 32; 26:6). Likewise, the outpouring of the Spirit had strong eschatological associations. Such passages as Joel 2:28–32 were interpreted in nationalistic terms that saw a general outpouring of the Spirit on Israel as a mark of the final great messianic Day of the Lord when Israel would be "restored" to the former glory of the days of David and Solomon.[17]

Regarding the impact of the command to witness Polhill adds:

> The future tense here has an imperatival sense: "you *will* [must] receive power"; "you *will* be my witnesses." Luke stressed this commission from the risen Lord at the close of his Gospel (24:47–49). All the same elements are there—the witness, the call to the nations, the power of the Spirit. The power they were to receive was divine power; the word is *dynamis*, the same word used of Jesus' miracles in the Gospels. It is the *Spirit's* power (2:1–21). The endowment with the Spirit is the prelude to, the equipping for, mission. The role of the apostles is that of "witness" (*martys*). *In Acts the apostles' main role is depicted as witnessing to the earthly ministry of Jesus, above all to his resurrection* (cf. 1:22; 2:32; 3:15; 5:32; 10:39, 41). As eyewitnesses only they were in the position to be guarantors of the resurrection. But with its root meaning of *testimony*, "witness" comes to have an almost legal sense of *bearing one's testimony to Christ*.[18]

Bruce adds an excellent context to the discussion of Jesus' instruction to the disciples regarding witnessing for Jesus and the kingdom:

> Whatever purposes of his own God might have for the nation of Israel, these were not to be the concern of the messengers of Christ. *The kingdom of God which they were commissioned to*

---

[17] Polhill, *Acts,* p. 84.
[18] Polhill, *Acts*, p. 86.

proclaim was the good news of God's grace in Christ. Their present question appears to have been the last flicker of their former burning expectation of an imminent theocracy with themselves as its chief executives. *From now on they devoted themselves to the proclamation and service of God's spiritual kingdom, which men and women enter by repentance and faith,* and in which chief honor belongs to those who most faithfully follow their Lord in the path of obedience, service, and suffering. Instead of the political power which had once been the object of their ambitions, a power far greater and nobler would be theirs. When the Holy Spirit came upon them, Jesus assured them, they would be vested with heavenly power—*that power by which, in the event, their mighty works were accomplished and their preaching made effective.* As Jesus had been anointed at his baptism with the Holy Spirit and power, so his followers were now to be similarly anointed and enabled to carry on his work. *This work would be a work of witness-bearing—a theme which is prominent in the apostolic preaching throughout Acts.* An Old Testament prophet had called the people of Israel to be God's witnesses in the world (Isa. 43:10; 44:8); the task which Israel had not fulfilled was taken on by Jesus, the perfect Servant of the Lord, and shared by him with his disciples. The close relation between God's call to Israel, "you are my witnesses," and the risen Lord's commission to his apostles, "you will be my witnesses," can be appreciated the more if we consider the implications of Paul's quotation of Isa. 49:6 in Acts 13:47.32 *There the heralds of the gospel are spoken of as a light for the Gentiles, bearing God's salvation "to the end of the earth"; here "the end of the earth" and nothing short of that is to be the limit of the apostolic witness.*[19]

Several critical thoughts surface in this profoundly important text, Acts 1:6-8!

---

[19] Bruce, F.F., *The Book of Acts*, Acts 1:7ff.

> *So when they had come together, they asked him, "<u>Lord, will you at this time restore the kingdom to Israel?</u>" ⁷ He said to them, "It is not for you to know times or seasons which the Father has fixed by his own authority. ⁸ <u>But you shall receive power when the Holy Spirit has come upon you; and you shall be my witnesses in Jerusalem and in all Judea and Samaria and to the end of the earth.</u>" ⁹ And when he had said this, as they were looking on, he was lifted up, and a cloud took him out of their sight.*

First, one would assume that this being the last physical communication Jesus had with his disciples that it would be profoundly important!

Second, it is intensely packed with missional *Missio Dei* themes.

Third, its association with the coming power of the Holy Spirit envelops it in eschatological import.

Fourth, the interesting question of the disciples regarding Jesus establishing the kingdom to Israel is immediately followed by a *Missio Dei* missional instruction, even a command, *you shall be my witnesses beginning in Jerusalem, and in all Judea, and Samaria, and to the end of the earth*!

Fifth, what followed in short order was the Jerusalem Christians and the Apostles going out preaching the message of Jesus and planting churches. The clearly understood that witnessing meant more than living good Christian, church, and kingdom lives, as important as this is!

As we seek to understand the *Missio Dei* missional dynamic of witnessing in both the Old and New Testaments, it is apparent that more was involved than living kingdom lives, as important as that must have been, the focus of witnessing was on the *proclamation of God's redemptive and atoning message* to all people, Jew and Gentile alike. Witnessing for Christ in Acts and the remainder of the New Testament was *intentionally missional*, preaching the message of Jesus' atoning death and resurrection.

We have traditionally struggled when speaking of the kingdom of God! We tend to focus on the root meaning of kingdom, βασιλεία, *basileia*, meaning God and Christ *reigning in one's life* which certainly is part of the meaning of and intent of kingdom, but this has tended to remove kingdom from the overall *Missio Dei missional* theological context of kingdom.

In a similar limited way, our simple equation of the church and the kingdom as synonyms demonstrates our inability to penetrate the depth of God's kingdom *Missio Dei* purpose, and Jesus' kingdom mission. The church certainly provides a vital dynamic in the kingdom, but to reduce the meaning and function of kingdom to that of a synonym for the church living exemplary kingdom lives and doing good deeds reduces the meaning of kingdom in the theological dynamic of the kingdom functioning in the missional nature of the *Missio Dei*.

The Kingdom and the *Missio Dei*

The key issue in this study has been to understand the depth and breadth of what Jesus meant by the kingdom of God, and how the church fits into this! In order to do this we find it necessary to examine how Jesus' life and ministry integrate with God's overall *Missio Dei*, or his plan to restore his creation to its original glory.

The kingdom gospel certainly has to do with the death, burial, and resurrection of Jesus, our personal salvation and redemption, living good Christian lives, and doing good deeds, but understanding the meaning of the kingdom lies deeper in the heart of God, and deeper than one's understanding of personal salvation and the pattern, structure, and form of the church, and certainly deeper than our understanding of *kingdom living*. The *Missio Dei* provides the theological *initiative* or *driving force* to the kingdom proclaimed by Jesus; *kingdom living* explains one "*consequence*" of the proclamation of Jesus' kingdom theology.

The dynamic of the kingdom must lie rooted in the meaning and program of God's *missional Missio Dei*, in His progressive restoration program traced through his call of Abraham, Israel's exile from Egypt, the occupation of the Promised Land, Israel's exile in Assyria and Babylon, and the Restoration of Israel to Judea. Focusing on the meaning of *basileia* as the *rule* or *kingship* of God and Jesus, which are essential components of kingdom theology, or as a synonym for the church, simply misses the point and diminishes the theological dynamic of the *Missio Dei*.

We learn that it took the faithfulness of Jesus to God's eternal purpose seen in his ministry and death to bring about God's *Missio Dei* and kingdom purpose. Israel's failure to understand and accept their role in God's *Missio Dei* kingdom and Abrahamic covenant *missional* promises eventually led to Israel's religious rebellion and broken relationship with God, and their consequent exile to Assyria and Babylon.

Likewise, the church's failure and reluctance to see its role in God's covenant *missional* kingdom purpose can lead to a similar lost relationship with God! Faithfulness to God's *kingdom missional* purpose for his chosen people, both for Israel and the church, is critical to understanding *kingdom theology*, and lies at the heart of this study.

The Jews' failure to understand the breadth of God's sovereign kingdom principle and their adamant focus on the Law as a boundary to who could be in a covenant relationship with God lay at the root of their disregard for their covenant *missional* kingdom ministry to the Gentiles. Israel's focus on *Torah kingdom living* was commendable, but when the Law was interpreted as the key to sustaining or providing appropriate boundaries to who could be in a covenant relationship with God, they missed the central theme of what God was doing by giving them a homeland, a national identity, and a doctrinal code of behavior. This corrupted and negated God's *missional* kingdom *purpose* which was greater than the nation of Israel and their legal rectitude and kingdom ethical living.

Israel's misguided understanding of the Law and consequent misunderstanding of who could share in the covenant promise to Abraham created a barrier between them and God's *missional* kingdom purpose which blinded them from recognizing the majesty of God's covenant with Abraham, and the Gentile conversion and inclusion in the kingdom. If there is one tragic story in the Old Testament that demonstrates this clearly it is the failure of Jonah to understand God's missional kingdom purpose in sending him to Nineveh (*The Book of Jonah*).

Another poignant story of Israel's stubbornness is reflected in Paul's statement at Rom 10:18-21 where he commented on Isaiah's remorse regarding Israel's covenant kingdom failure:

> [18] *But I ask, <u>have they not heard</u>? <u>Indeed they have</u>; for "Their voice has gone out to all the earth,*
> *and their words to the ends of the world."*
> [19] *Again I ask, did Israel not understand? First Moses says, "I will make you jealous of those who are not a nation; with a foolish nation I will make you angry."* [20] *Then Isaiah is so bold as to say, "I have been found by those who did not seek me;*

*I have shown myself to those who did not ask for me." *<u>*But of Israel he says, "All day long I have held out my hands to a disobedient and contrary people.*</u>*"*

The fault of the Jews that Jesus aggressively opposed was their misguided kingdom theology and legal and political understanding of the Law. They saw the kingdom as being *centripetal*,[20] that is, their *focusing on their own internal Jewish righteousness based in the Law to the exclusion of the Gentiles from God's covenant with Abraham.*

Israel used the Law to define boundaries as to who could be in a covenant relationship with God rather than as a *torah* guide, instructing Israel how to live in a covenant kingdom relationship with God. Israel's righteous living should have been their witness to their relationship with God and witness to the blessings of God's kingdom, but Israel took the Law and made it a boundary as to who could be in a righteous relationship with God.

Israel's consequent prerequisite was that the Gentiles should be like the Jews, strictly keeping the Law of Moses in order to be in a covenant relationship with God. This predisposed them to miss God's *centrifugal* missional purpose of *kingdom theology*. They, like many Christians today, mistakenly misunderstood kingdom *living* to be kingdom *theology*! Certainly, kingdom living is an essential *component* of kingdom theology, but only as a result of kingdom theology *missional* outreach, and not the *dynamic* of kingdom theology. Kingdom *living* is a valuable *method* or *instrument* of missional activity as it *demonstrates* to others outside the kingdom of God the value of living for God, but it is not the to be equated with the primary dynamic of evangelistic[21] *missional* outreach.

Israel became boundary *guardians* rather than *Missio Dei missional* redemptive boundary *extenders*!

We have already commented above on Jesus' correction of this misguided understanding of the kingdom when he responded to the centripetal kingdom question of his apostles at Acts 1:6-8, *will you at this time restore the kingdom <u>to Israel</u>,* and went on to define their new

---

[20] I use the term *centripetal* to imply an inward focus of a community as opposed to *centrifugal* which refers to an outward reaching dynamic. This point is a major concern of this book and my understanding of kingdom theology.
[21] By evangelistic I imply the *proclamation* of the good news of God's redemptive plan in his Messiah, Jesus Christ.

kingdom *Missio Dei missional* mission, witnessing from Jerusalem to the end of the earth. The typically Jewish centripetal thinking of the disciples was seen in their question as to whether Jesus was at that time going to *restore the kingdom to Israel*. As noted above, this question is interesting since Jesus had just spent 40 days instructing them on the kingdom! Jesus redirected their insular *centripetal* understanding of the kingdom and instructed them to see the *missional centrifugal* dynamic of kingdom theology. Specifically, they were to *begin* in Jerusalem with the kingdom message, then *spread out* to Judea, Samaria, and the ends of the earth, in a *centrifugal* mission.

It may seem to some readers that I have returned again to a theme previously discussed! That is true! I confess to the repetition! But although we have dwelt around this mountain, Mt Sinai, too long, we do need to have a clear understanding that there is more to the *Missio Dei* than staying locked in past persuasions of the value of the Law. Is that a pun? Perhaps, but one by intention![22]

This *Missio Dei* kingdom concern became the primary dynamic and driving force of the apostle Paul's early Gentile ministry. This is demonstrated in his three missionary journeys as depicted by Luke in Acts, and his Gentile/Jew relational concerns addressed in his epistles to the Galatians and Romans.

For Paul and the early apostles[23] kingdom theology was not about proclaiming scrupulous keeping of the Mosaic Law and kingdom living, but about taking the *Missio Dei* kingdom message to all nations. I particularly like Paul's closing *kingdom missional* thoughts to the Christians in Rome at Rom 16:14, and we should remember that Paul's Epistle to the Romans is in fact a missionary letter:

> "*I myself am satisfied about you, my brethren, that you yourselves are full of goodness, filled with all knowledge, and able to instruct one another.* ¹⁵ *But on some points I have written to you very boldly by way of reminder, <u>because of the grace given me by God</u>* ¹⁶ <u>*to be a minister of Christ Jesus to the Gentiles in the priestly*</u>

---

[22] For clarity! A pun is a humorous rhetoric that makes a play on words. A pun, therefore, makes use of words that have more than one meaning, or words that sound similar but have different meanings, to humorous or rhetorical effect.

[23] The term *apostle* makes a play on the Greek ἀπόστολος meaning *one sent out* as an ambassador or messenger!

service of the gospel of God, so that the offering of the Gentiles may be acceptable, sanctified by the Holy Spirit. [17] In Christ Jesus, then, I have reason to be proud of my work for God. [18] For I will not venture to speak of anything except what Christ has wrought through me to win obedience from the Gentiles, by word and deed, [19] by the power of signs and wonders, by the power of the Holy Spirit, so that from Jerusalem and as far round as Illyricum I have fully preached the gospel of Christ, [20] thus making it my ambition to preach the gospel, not where Christ has already been named, lest I build on another man's foundation, [21] but as it is written, "They shall see who have never been told of him, and they shall understand who have never heard of him."

Paul had earlier in his epistle to the Romans addressed his Gentile mission. At Rom 1:14, 15 he observed that he was *"under obligation both to Greeks and to barbarians, both to the wise and to the foolish: [15] so I am eager to preach the gospel to you also who are in Rome."*

At Rom 1:16, 17 he clarified the kingdom theology driving his mission, *"For I am not ashamed of the gospel: it is the power of God for salvation to everyone who has faith, to the Jew first and also to the Greek. [17] For in it the righteousness of God is revealed through faith for faith; as it is written, "He who through faith is righteous shall live.""*

The Jews' unwavering focus on the Law as a boundary to a righteous relationship with God demonstrated their lack of understanding the *Missio Dei* theology of God's purpose. This led to their related sociological withdrawal from the Gentiles in faith and practice which were *exclusivist* and *centripetal,* and not centrifugal *missional* in keeping with God's covenant *kingdom theological* purpose in calling Abraham.

Likewise, a real danger churches face today is their overbearing *centripetal* concern for *internal matters* such as maintaining the faith of their congregation and holding on to their members, especially during the time when their members walk the challenging road of maturing from childhood to adulthood. This certainly should be a time of pastoral concern. My comment is not intended to challenge churches to surrender serious concerns for the spiritual formation of their members, but when this becomes the driving force of a congregation's ministry, experience and recent missional church history point to the fact that kingdom missional plateauing and decline are inevitable. To get a check on this concern, simply refer to the church budget to find out where the primary concerns are in the church, are they on kingdom *living* or kingdom *evangelistic missional endeavor*?

Concern over the flight of members from traditional churches to alternate expressions of faith has not helped churches understand their primary role as missional churches. A primary motivation challenging church leaders is in many cases how to hold on to the members they have!

I am keenly aware that there are other pressing challenges facing the church in regard to the declining membership of churches reported in our media. An increasingly socialist culture and the postmodern inclination of its members are real challenges, but deeply imbedded in each of these is the challenge churches face regarding the *Missio Dei* nature of its purpose. Instruction on *kingdom living* in the life of the local congregation is a necessary and urgent defense against such challenges, but not at the cost of redefining, or degrading *kingdom theology* in favor of *kingdom living*! I am fully aware of the difficulties churches face today in America, but a study of many churches of Christ in Africa that are growing almost daily in number indicates that an emphasis on kingdom missional outreach need not result in declining emphasis on kingdom living and membership loss.

To measure the *centripetal* bias of a congregation all one needs to do is count the number of ministers in a congregation whose ministry is focused primarily on the local members' needs, and the number of ministers and missionaries whose ministry is clearly and unmistakably *Missio Dei centrifugal* kingdom *missional*! As an old traditional confession goes, we tend to put our money where our heart is! *Perhaps our hearts need a compass recalibration!*

In Churches of Christ, because of our heritage in the Stone-Campbell Restoration Movement, especially in the post-Campbell post-civil war side, we have focused our theology more on *the church* than on the *kingdom*. A primary concern has been to restore the New Testament church even though identifying the form of the New Testament church has led to a history of division. As indicated above, comments in a discussion with Professor James I. Packer, explain how many in the scholarly world, notably the evangelical world, perceive us to be in regard to kingdom theology. It appears to many that this is a topic which we have for decades seemingly ignored! We are recognized as *ecclesiological* leaders, but not *missiological* leaders.

A pastoral centripetal concern predisposes us to focusing almost exclusively on defining who we are and how we do church, which is *Missio Ecclesiae* or *kingdom living* and not *missional Missio Dei*. We have developed a non-denominational, non-synodal, non-conference allergy that *emphasizes local church autonomy and identity*. By doing this we have turned inward rather than outward in a kingdom missional dynamic. We have produced several excellent studies in the field of ecclesiology[24] but little if anything of a significant nature on the kingdom of God other than from a history of struggles with premillennialism especially in the 1940-1960 era.

I hope to demonstrate in this study that the kingdom is far larger in nature than the church, without diminishing or denigrating the importance of the church. However, our theological emphasis on the local church and preserving the biblical nature of the church has historically tended to be *centripetal* while the kingdom is primarily *centrifugal* and *missional*.

As a former convert of a missional outreach and church planting, having served as a missionary for fourteen years, having taught and mentored missiology for over 50 years, and having been the Dean of a university college that at one time had a fine mission program, I am fully aware of the great work many Churches of Christ and Christians have done in mission efforts. However, it would be a stretch of any imagination to argue or defend a proposition that Churches of Christ in the United States have been and are kingdom *missional* by nature, or have a strong *missional* DNA!

Like Israel, we have become *torah instructional* with the intent of preserving our identity and establishing the boundaries of who can be like us rather than understanding our true *missional kingdom Missio Dei* nature.

A significant reason for the *ecclesiological church* orientation among Churches of Christ in the American Restoration Movement germinated at a time when there was little unity among the young denominational

---

[24] *Ecclesiology* is derived from the Greek *ekklēsia* meaning *assembly, congregation, community,* or *church*. Ecclesiology is the study of church in the New Testament. Possibly the most important study of church among churches of Christ is Everett Ferguson, *The Church of Christ: A Biblical Ecclesiology for Today*, Eerdmans, 1996.

synodal Christian churches in America (ca. 1780). Establishing a nondenominational identity became a necessary and primary concern.

Concerned Christian leaders on the Eastern seaboard of America in the early stages of "colonial" settlement ca.1809, like Thomas Campbell, Barton W. Stone, Alexander Campbell, and others desired to create a sense of unity among Christians and churches by returning to Scripture as the only definition of faith, rather than holding on to denominational synodal creeds. This worthy principle was ensconced in a plea to speak where the Bible speaks and to remain silent where the Bible is silent. While commendable, this plea became in time a hermeneutical model which deteriorated into a divisive mechanism. This became clearly noticeable after the close of the American Civil War, ca. 1865-.

The movement which was defined as a Restoration Movement resulted in a passion to restore the New Testament church just as it was in the 1st century in contrast to the pattern of many Christian denominations in America. Identifying this New Testament church resulted in identifying a strict pattern by which one could measure the faithfulness of a church. Although new congregations were emerging, the concern was more *centripetal* than *centrifugal*! New churches were either the result of church splits or congregational migration.

The New Testament church pattern identified in this Restoration Movement became a *model*[25] of the church derived by pulling together different characteristics from the few churches that could be identified in the New Testament. As a result, through focus on the structure and form of the church, Churches of Christ became "specialists" in *ecclesiology*,

---

[25] I have on occasion used the word *pastiche* to describe this process, but that term is perhaps an overstatement of what I intend. However, literally, *pastiche* draws on "a musical, literary, or artistic composition made up of selections from different works." Merriam-Webster Dictionary. "*A picture or design made up of fragments pieced together similar to a musical composition made up of pieces from different sources.*" Cf. also the Oxford English Dictionary on *Pasticcio* and *Pastiche*. I have no intention of denigrating attempts to be Christians or churches after the style of the 1st century New Testament churches, or of attempting to be as biblical as possible. My purpose is merely to demonstrate that the New Testament itself makes no effort at defining exactly what a church should look like in pattern, form, or structure. We piece together several components of a church from several different contexts and form a pattern of what all churches should look like. An ecclesiastical *pastiche*!

that is *the theology of the church*. The result of this intense focus was underdeveloped understanding of *the theology of the kingdom*! Because of premillennial concerns Churches of Christ specifically in the South equated *kingdom theology* with *ecclesiastical church theology*! *Ecclesiological* church theology is fine, but not when confused with *kingdom theology*!

Unity, and a concern for being biblical, certainly are two noble commitments of the Restoration heritage among Churches of Christ. Unfortunately the two concepts have led to a divisive attitude among many Churches of Christ in America, and now globally. Furthermore, excessive stress on a "biblical" understanding of being a "nondenominational" church has distanced some from other Christian churches and has separated some churches within the Restoration heritage from many others in the Restoration Movement.

Although the post-Civil War history among Churches of Christ focused more on the life of churches after the tragic events of the Civil War, this resulted in the inhouse battles over doctrinal faithfulness. However, the history of the era following the turn of the 18th and 19th centuries indicates that church life was not silent regarding the numerous courageous Christians who ventured into foreign lands to plant churches far and wide. Dr. C. Philip Slate's excellent study, *Lest We Forget*, has provided mini-biographies of some 84 missionaries dating from 1886 who ventured forth with the gospel message in global missions. Although the post 1865 life of Churches of Christ was focused primarily on religious and political reconstruction, the *missional* aspect of the *Missio Dei* was apparently not altogether absent in church life, if not necessarily a missional driving force.[26]

Nevertheless, the extreme focus on restoring the *pattern*[27] of a perceived New Testament church in the years of reconstruction led to an

---

[26] Slate, *Lest We Forget*; Hughes, *Reviving the Ancient Faith;* Thomas H. Olbricht and Hans Rollmann, eds., *The Quest for Christian Unity in Thomas.*

[27] The concept of a *strict or tight pattern* among New Testament churches has been challenged by many who favor a cross-cultural form of "organization" among early 1st century churches. To argue that *all* churches in the 1st century adopted or manifested a strict pattern cannot be established from *within* the New Testament, and is an artificial construct projected back into the New Testament from an external hypothesis of a tight identifying pattern. There were certain identifying marks among some churches such as

unfortunate divisive mindset that opposed any serious concept of kingdom unity and kingdom theology.

During the premillennial "battles" among Churches of Christ in the 1940/50s the church developed a *kingdom doctrine* that argued that the *church* and the *kingdom* were terms that spoke of the same reality, for the church is the kingdom. It was argued if one was in the church one was consequently also in the kingdom, for the kingdom and the church are the same. In some measures this may be true but not precisely accurate! Nevertheless, this proved to be an effective argument against premillennialism since it argued that if the church was present then the kingdom must also be present and not a future kingdom of expectation. The premillennialism debates were hotly fought and resulted in bitter animosity between brethren and churches. The result was that rather than being united in the kingdom of God, churches divided over a shaky kingdom theology and came up woefully short of a true biblical kingdom theology.[28]

For several decades, in the mid-20th century life of churches of Christ in America, the topic of kingdom was neglected in fear of continuing animosity and withdrawals of fellowship. Addressing the topic of kingdom resulted in two Bible Department chairs in Christian colleges being disfellowshipped over false claims of being premillennial![29]

Professor James I. Packer was not far wrong in being puzzled over my interest in kingdom theology as against church theology! We were at that time more *church* people than *kingdom* people!

However, both views, seeing the kingdom as the church and the church as the kingdom may not be altogether or absolutely wrong! One could claim that if one were in the church then one was obviously in the

---

the observation of the Lord's Supper, prayer, the singing of hymns, a sermon, and a contribution, but to argue that these manifested a strict form found in all churches is an argument from silence or the absence of real evidence. The extreme sociological, economic, and ethnic differences of churches spread all over the Mediterranean world would have made such a structure untenable, as is demonstrated by the wide variety of church patterns today spread all over the world.

[28] For a survey of the premillennial discussions and withdrawals cf. Hughes, *Reviving the Ancient Faith*, pp. 137ff.

[29] Cf. Hughes, pp. 137ff.

kingdom, but this would also confine the kingdom to the church, and as I am contending in this study, the kingdom is larger than the church!

This is similar to arguing that the church does mission work rather than stressing that the church is a kingdom mission work of God! It may be more appropriate to say that the church is *Missio Dei kingdom missional* rather than saying that *the church does mission work.*[30] That thought may take considerable contemplation and unpacking before it sinks in, but in the course of this study I hope that it will become fully understood!

Here we are exploring how important the *missional* message of the kingdom is for understanding the Christian faith, and the nature and *purpose* of the church. We have above examined the implications of Jesus' proclamation that the kingdom was "at hand." We will shortly examine the inherent *missiological impulse* of the kingdom, and the full meaning of Jesus being the Messianic king in the kingdom of God, and the head of the church.

Americans with a radical democratic and constitutional political persuasion have never looked favorably on, nor understood the meaning of *being under a king or monarchy that has absolute authority over them.* The American democratic system of government "of the people, by the people, for the people" is *politically* excellent and apparently effective. But theologically, it breeds a fiercely independent people who manifest a rugged individualism with more emphasis on the personal civil rights of the individual than a *monarchial kingdom* mindset. For Israel this would not have been a problem, and neither should it be for people who understand the *sovereignty of God over all creation.*

We will learn below that the concept of kingdom is theologically opposed to a fiercely independent mindset!

The kingdom stresses *submission* of the *individual* to *God, Christ,* and *others*, and *putting others, even the perceived lost socially discarded,* before self. Our western culture is characterized by a strong drive for individual personal achievement. Individual effort in "climbing the ladder" to success over others is often the measure of personal accomplishment. The kingdom, however, is strikingly different! Jesus

---

[30] Cf. Alan Hirsch, "Defining Missional," *Leadership Journal.net*, article copyright 2008 by the author or Christianity Today, *International Leadership Journal*, 12.12.2008; Hirsh, *The Forgotten Ways.*

himself argued that the *greatest* in the kingdom is the *servant*, which certainly runs contrary to a socialistic mindset in which being a servant of others, especially the distasteful nations, is not highly esteemed! Cf. Luke 22:24-27:

> A dispute also arose among them, which of them was to be regarded as the greatest. ^{25} And he said to them, "The kings of the Gentiles exercise lordship over them; and those in authority over them are called benefactors. ^{26} But not so with you; rather let <u>the greatest among you become as the youngest, and the leader as one who serves</u>. ^{27} For which is the greater, one who sits at table, or one who serves? Is it not the one who sits at table? But I am among you as one who serves.

Furthermore, we will learn that the kingdom does not refer to something we do, that is, to our personal or church effectiveness. *The kingdom stresses what God through Christ and his Holy Spirit is doing in and thorough us.* Understanding kingdom theology introduces us to the sovereign will of God in our lives, but essentially in a submissive obedient *kingdom missional mindset*. Success in the kingdom comes through submission to God's missional kingdom working in and through Christians, and not through individual effort and achievement! Muslims have much to offer in their understanding that Islam means *submission* to the will and purpose of God! This is precisely what kingdom theology means, *submission to the kingdom will, missional purpose, and working of God*. Consider Phil 2:12ff:

> ^{12} Therefore, my beloved, as you have always obeyed, so now, not only as in my presence but much more in my absence, work out (*energize* or bring to maturity) *your own salvation with fear and trembling;* ^{13} <u>for God is at work in you, both to will and to work for his good pleasure</u>.

Understanding the missional nature of the kingdom is critical to finding one's place in God's eternal redemptive election, purpose, and plan. God indeed does have such a *missional kingdom plan* to which he has called us and which he is capable of achieving. However, he has invited, even charged us, to become part of that eternal kingdom missional plan and purpose. I have chosen a magnificent text from Paul's Epistle to the Ephesians, Eph 1:3-12, to highlight this. Pay particular attention to the sections emphasized in this text:

"*Blessed be the God and Father of our Lord Jesus Christ, who has blessed us in Christ with every spiritual blessing in the heavenly places, [4] even <u>as he chose us in him before the foundation of the world</u>, that we should be holy and blameless before him. [5] <u>He destined us in love to be his sons through Jesus Christ, according to the purpose of his will</u>, [6] to the praise of his glorious grace which he freely bestowed on us in the Beloved. [7] In him we have redemption through his blood, the forgiveness of our trespasses, according to the riches of his grace [8] which he lavished upon us. [9] <u>For he has made known to us in all wisdom and insight the mystery of his will, according to his purpose which he set forth in Christ [10] as a plan for the fulness of time, to unite all things in him, things in heaven and things on earth.</u> [11] In him, according to <u>the purpose of him who accomplishes all things according to the counsel of his will</u>, [12] <u>we who first hoped in Christ have been destined and appointed to live for the praise of his glory</u>.*"

We will learn that other important terms are used in scripture to describe the people of God, but that k*ingdom* is the *theological driving force behind each of these other terms*. Each term describes a particular dimension or facet of *the relationship of the people to God, to Jesus, and to one another*. *Kingdom* provides the *defining force* behind each of these terms. *Kingdom* tells us something crucial to our understanding of each of the other terms. Without a healthy understanding of God's *sovereign missional kingdom, kingdom unity* and *forgiving one another*, all essential elements of the unity of the family and church as the body of Christ, we will have difficulty practicing and maintaining kingdom perspective and obedience. Perhaps Jesus' prayer in the Garden of Gethsemane just before his arrest and crucifixion will demonstrate the kingdom mindset: "*And going a little farther he fell on his face and prayed, 'My Father, if it be possible, let this cup pass from me; <u>nevertheless, not as I will, but as thou wilt</u>'*…" (Matt 26:39). That is kingdom thinking!

Jesus' model prayer for his disciples, who he was about to send out on a kingdom mission plan opened as follows:
[9] Pray then like this:
Our Father who art in heaven,
Hallowed be thy name.

<u>¹⁰ Thy kingdom come.</u>
<u>Thy will be done,</u>
    <u>On earth as it is in heaven.</u>

The various terms that describe God's people appear historically in scripture at different points of God's dealings with his people, some early, and some later. However, the concept of *kingdom* and *kingship* predate and override each of these concepts or terms.

Chapter 4
Several Biblical Terms Used to Describe Kingdom People

The notion of the kingdom and sovereignty of God over all creation became a reality in the very beginning in the *creative activity of God*! In creation he established his sovereignty over all creation! However, in the process of time and the life of Israel and the Church, several terms were used in Scripture to describe the people of God.

The term **Israel** is used in Scripture to describe the particular people God called out of Egypt and formed into an elect nation after the Sinai experience and during their wilderness wandering. The name Israel was derived from the name God gave Jacob the father of twelve sons after whom the twelve tribes of Israel were named. We are introduced to Israel at Gen 32:28, after Jacob had experienced some form of encounter with an angelic being or *"man."*[1] The *"man"* spoke to Jacob and said, *"Your name shall no more be called Jacob, but Israel, for you have striven with God and with men, and have prevailed."* Israel thus refers to one who has *"struggled with God."* It was to Israel, the *new elect family/nation*, soon to be known as Israel, that God gave Moses, the law, judges, kings, prophets, and the kingdom. Being a *"called nation,"* or an *elect* people, was important to the psyche of Israel.

On this specific terminology, at 1 Pet 2:9 Peter Davids[2] observes:

> A chosen people, a royal priesthood, a holy nation, a people belonging to God (2:9). This image is more specific than a general reference to Old Testament priesthood. *Any of the readers familiar with the Old Testament would recognize the weaving together of Exodus 19:5–6 and Isaiah 43:20–21: "... out of all nations you*

---

[1] Most commentators recognize the difficulty of interpreting this man or the events surrounding this event. Later Jewish midrashic interpretations refer to the man as an angel of the Lord. The details while interesting are not as significant as the new name given to Jacob.

[2] Davids, *1 and 2 Peter, Jude, 1, 2, and 3 John*, kindle location 842ff. Italics IAF. Davids also references Rev 1:6; 5:10; 20:6.

will be my treasured possession. Although the whole earth is mine, you will be for me a kingdom of priests and a holy nation" and, "I provide water in the desert and streams in the wasteland, to give drink to my people, my chosen, the people I formed for myself that they may proclaim my praise." As other New Testament writers also do, Peter is calling these Gentile Christians by *the titles God gave to Israel in the desert.* For him there are not two covenants, one for the Jews and another for Gentile Christians, but one covenant, which the Gentiles, who once "were not a people," have been brought into and made "the people of God" (1 Peter 2:10), while those Jews and others who do not believe in Jesus stumble and fall from their natural heritage in the covenant.

Faithful Israel clung jealously to the belief that they were an elect people, called by God, belonging to God, and ruled over by God. In other words, *they were the kingdom of God. Eventually Israel forgot that it was God who was sovereign over all creation and who ruled in their lives.* Desiring to be like their neighbors rather than being a unique nation belonging to God, they forgot that they were expected by God to be different from their neighbors and to be a servant to the nations.

The term **Congregation of Israel** describes the community of Israel as they congregated around the tabernacle and offered sacrifices to God. At all times they understood they were a people in whose presence God was manifest in the tabernacle, the pillar of cloud and of fire.[3] Later, as the nation developed, the Temple became the center of their lives around which they congregated. The term used to convey this concept in the Septuagint, ἡ ἐκκλησία, *hē ekklēsia,* is the same term that describes the church community belonging to Jesus in the New Testament. In the New Testament era the people of God and Jesus were defined by the same term *hē ekklēsia,* that is, *the church.* Instead of Israel being congregated around God's presence in the Temple *hē ekklēsia* was used to refer to the *congregation* or *community* of Christians living under the lordship of Jesus, God's *Messiah. Ekklēsia* thus refers to *an assembly, a congregation, a meeting place, or a gathering for a meeting of people* in a united

---

[3] Ex 12:3, *passim.*

community.⁴ In the Septuagint it referred to Israel as a people who gathered in community around the Tabernacle as a cultic meeting place for sacrifice and worship. In the New Testament it referred to a community of *Messianic* believers belonging to the *Messiah* who gathered in congregations or churches to witness to Jesus the *Messiah*. The point of this discussion is to demonstrate that the *ekklēsia* of the New Testament, the *church,* has primarily the same meaning as in the Congregation of Israel in the Old Testament referring to a people who are congregated or gathered around God's presence and who belonged to God.

The expression **Kingdom of Israel**. After Moses and the Judges, Israel pleaded with God to give them a king like the other nations had kings. They forgot that the God who had saved them from Egypt by his power was their king and that they already were a kingdom with a divine mission. God through the prophet Samuel warned them against desiring a king like their neighbors, but they insisted on having a visible king who everyone especially their neighbors could see. When Samuel heard their desire for a king he interpreted it as their rejecting him as their leader. God explained to Samuel that the people were not simply turning against him but were rejecting God himself and God's personal reign over them. God warned Israel that the kings they desired would make extreme demands of them, take their lands and children, and make life miserable for them. But they persisted to their eventual regret!⁵ Not understanding the nature of the

---

⁴ It was a common term for a congregation of the *ekklētoí*, the called people, or those called out or assembled in the public affairs of a free state, the body of free citizens called together by a herald (*kêrux*) which constituted the *ekklēsía*. In the NT, the word is applied to the congregation of the people of Israel (Acts 7:38). On the other hand, of the two terms used in the OT, *sunagōgḗ* seems to have been used to designate the people from Israel in distinction from all other nations (Acts 13:43 [cf. Matt. 4:23; 6:2; James 2:2; Rev. 2:9; 3:9]). In Heb. 10:25, however, when the gathering of Christians is referred to, it is called not *sunagōgḗ*, but *episunagōgḗ*, with the prep. *epí*, upon, translated "the assembling . . . together." The Christian community was designated for the first time as the *ekklēsía* to differentiate it from the Jewish community, *sunagōgḗ* (Acts 2:47). The term *ekklēsía* denotes the NT community of the redeemed in its twofold aspect. First, all who were called by and to Christ in the fellowship of His salvation, the church worldwide of all times, and only secondarily to an individual church (Matt. 16:18; Acts 2:44, 47; 9:31; 1 Cor. 6:4; 12:28; 14:4, 5, 12; Phil. 3:6; Col. 1:18, 24). Spiros Zodhiates, *The Complete Word Study Dictionary: New Testament.*

⁵ 1 Sam 13:13; 15:28.

kingdom of God has always had devastating consequences for the people of God.

The term **Kingdom of God** (YHWH). The Psalms and prophets, notably Isaiah and Daniel, spoke of YHWH (God) as being the ruler of not only Israel, but *also of all creation*. YHWH was the absolute ruler of all creation and nations and would hold all accountable for their lives and commitment. Daniel spoke of a future *messianic* king whom God would send to reign over his people in a restored kingdom of God. This restored kingdom became the center for Jesus' *Messianic* mission.

The phrase **Kingdom of God and Heaven**. The New Testament, especially the Synoptic Gospels, Matthew, Mark, and Luke, speaks of a kingdom of heaven and a kingdom of God. There is no distinction in these expressions. Matthew[6] being sensitive to Jewish tradition of not using the term YHWH or God inappropriately spoke of the kingdom of *heaven* rather than the kingdom of *God* while Mark[7] and Luke not being oversensitive to Jewish concerns spoke in parallel passages of the kingdom of God. Jesus spoke of the kingdom breaking into history and human experience in his presence and ministry (Matt 12:28). Jesus understood himself to be the *messianic* king promised by Daniel. Paul in his epistles spoke of the kingdom of Christ, Eph 5:5, and in his preaching, Acts 28:21. He also spoke of Christians being transferred from darkness into the kingdom of "his (God's) dear son" Col 1:13. The kingdom of *Christ*, the kingdom of *heaven*, and the kingdom of *God* all speak of the same entity, the people over which God reigned through Jesus, the *Messiah*.

The **Church**. At Caesarea Philippi (Matt 16:16-18) Jesus promised to build (establish) his church (*hē ekklēsia, assembly, community, congregation*).[8] Interestingly, the English term *church* actually derives from the German term *Kirche*[9] which in turn derives from the Greek adjective *kuriakós*, meaning *belonging to the lord*.[10] For consistency and

---

[6] Matt 3:2, *passim*.
[7] Mark 1:15, *passim*; Lk 4:43, *passim*.
[8] Refer to my comments above under the Congregation of Israel.
[9] *Shorter Oxford English Dictionary*, church, Oxford, The Clarendon Press, 1972.
[10] "*Kuriakós* ... adj. from *kúrios, lord, master, belonging to a lord or ruler* ... 1 Cor. 11:20; Rev. 1:10 as belonging to Christ, to the Lord, having special reference to Him." Zodhiates, *The Complete Word Study Dictionary: New Testament*.

being sensitive to maintain the tradition of the Tyndale, Wycliffe, and King James Version our English translations have chosen to translate *hē ekklēsia* as *church* rather than *congregation* or *community*.[11] The English term *church* thus means a *congregation* or *community of people*. In the sense that Jesus used it at Matt 16:16 it referred to a *community of believers belonging to Jesus*.

At Eph 5:25 Paul explained that Jesus loved and purchased the church with his own blood (death). Thus, the church is a community of people *belonging to the Lord* whom Jesus purchased and built into a community of followers who believe in his death and resurrection, and who became his disciples. Paul's focus in his ministry was clearly on bringing the gospel of the kingdom to the Gentiles, but his *modus operandi* involved planting *churches* or *congregations* or *communities* belonging to the Lord in the Gentile world.

Having done this in one community Paul would move on to new areas, continuing his contact with the congregations he had worked with or knew from previous experience by writing letters to these *congregations*. *Paul's ministry was* thus both *kingdom theologically missional*, which involved planting new congregations in keeping with God's kingdom *Missio Dei*, and *congregationally pastoral in which he* continued his concern for *kingdom living paranetic* instruction.

Paul was certainly "church" or congregationally focused, but he clearly understood the significance of his *kingdom theological missional purpose to the Gentiles*! He never lost contact with the understanding that the "church" was God's or Christ's kingdom, an entity established in fulfillment of God's covenant with Abraham (Gal 3:10-18).

Thus, the word *church* in the New Testament, ἡ ἐκκλησία, *hē ekklēsia*, speaks of the people of Christ who assemble and function in congregations where they worship God and Christ, and carry out God's and Christ's *Missio Dei kingdom missional* activity, and the church's *Missio Ecclesiological* mission.

---

[11] It is interesting to note that the South African Afrikaans translation is at times *gemeente* meaning *congregation* or *community*, and at other times *kerk*, which derives from the German *Kirche*. The German and Dutch translations preserve the word *Kirche* from the Greek *kúrios* meaning *belonging to God*, the Spanish translation is *iglesia* preserving the Greek *ekklēsia*, *congregation* or *community*, and the Portuguese use *igreja* like the Spanish from *ekklēsia*.

The **Family of God**. The term ἡ πατριά, *hē patria, the family*, speaks of God's people as his own family. Paul's prayer at Eph 3:14, 15, *"For this reason I bow my knees before the Father, ^{15} from whom every family in heaven and on earth is named..."* recognizes that all families on earth actually belong to God, but in a special sense the church as the family of God refers to Christians being God's distinctive called and chosen family. God's people are his children whom he loves dearly (Eph 1:5). The stress is on the Fatherhood of God; the familial relationship of God's people with himself; the fact that God is responsible for their new birth (John 3:3-5; 1 Pet 1:23) in which he became their father in a new dynamic sense. It also stresses the familial relationship of Christians as brothers and sisters in God's family. Although God is the Father of all creation, Scripture speaks to Christians in the unique sense of God being *"our Father"* (Matt 6:9). At Rom 8:15 Paul explains that it is through the working of the Holy Spirit that Christians can cry out to God as "Abba! Father!"

The **Body of Christ**. Paul refers to the church as the body of Christ (Col 1:18; Eph 1:22, 23; 1 Cor 12:12-27; *passim*), emphasizing that Christians are all members of the one body whose head is Christ. Christians have all been *baptized by one Spirit into one body*, the church or the family of God (1 Cor 12:12, 13). In the one body of Christ each member is related to all the others, serves all others, and is no more important than any of the other members. Each member is expected to function in whatever capacity they have been gifted, Rom 12:3-8. In this unique sense, Christ is the head of only one body. He is the king of only one kingdom, emphasizing the unity of all Christians.

What we learned from this Chapter

From the above discussion we note that several definitive terms were used in Scripture to describe the people of God. Among them were: congregation of Israel, the family of God, the body of Christ, the church, and the kingdom.

Churches of Christ have traditionally focused more attention on the term *church* than on the *kingdom*. One reason is that Jesus promised to establish his *church* (Matt 16:18) and the term church features prominently in Acts and the Pauline Epistles.

It is not that Churches of Christ have ignored the term kingdom, but due to their heritage in the Stone-Campbell American Restoration

Movement, and the denominational divisions experienced in the early years of the 19th century in America, Churches of Christ have been dedicated to restoring the church as they perceive it to have been in the New Testament 1st century era of the church.

The intense religious debates and division over the present or future nature of the kingdom reflected in the premillennial debates cause Churches of Christ to eschew the term kingdom in favor of the term church.

Commitment to the restoration of the New Testament church, a noble concept, has consequently left Churches of Christ with an underdeveloped theology of the kingdom and predisposed to division.

The term kingdom should not simply be equated with the term church. Both describe different aspects of the life of Christians. We will learn in the next chapters that the concept of kingdom was present long before the term church was used to define the disciples of Christ.

Chapter 5
Kingdom Theology and Unity

A persistent concern for unity among churches, or the lack of it, has troubled me throughout the years of my work as a missionary and theologian. Surely in the kingdom of God there should be unity, or a passion for unity!

As a long standing student and "descendant" of the 19th century restoration movement that lay behind the beginning of Churches of Christ in both Scotland and America, I am proud of our tradition of seeking to be as biblical as possible. Maybe I should add, as biblically theological as possible.

I have come to realize that a primary ingredient in our failure to be as committed to "maintaining the unity of the Spirit in the bond of peace" (Eph 4:3) has been our model of biblical hermeneutic which is commonly described as *deductive proof texting* which results in a misconceived model of the New Testament Church and how things should be conducted in the church

By "proof texting" we have tended to identify a church model or form that has become standardized, and then to select our proof texts to support this. As a result, we have identified a model of what the church should look like and by which we identify what the restored New Testament Church should look like. This might sound as though I am not concerned with a commitment to the church being Scriptural "organized." That is as far as can be from the truth of my conviction regarding a sound biblical and theological foundation to the church! The danger has been that we have used a model of biblical hermeneutic that ignores the context of the text and forces it to support our particular model or need.

Some years ago I was invited to speak on a discussion panel between the Church of Christ practice of singing without a music instrument in worship and the Christian Church practice of singing accompanied by instruments in the worship assembly. The two persons speaking for the Christian Church were and still are fine Christians but we differed seriously on the topic which had for over 100 years divided the fellowship of these two divergent Stone-Campbell Movement groups. My fellow Church of Christ speaker, Dr. Philip Slate of Harding Graduate School of Theology, made a statement that had early in my conversion experience and early ministry not been fully recognized. He reminded us that our disunity over musical instruments in worship "is not the instrument, but our way of reading Scripture." The problem is that some read Scripture inductively while others read it deductively! I hope to clarify what this implies as we progress with this study. So let me set the stage here! A major problem in understanding unity in the kingdom of God is not simply our stubborn ecclesiological, sociological, or ethnic differences, but our misunderstanding of the kingdom of God and our misdirected approach to how we read and interpret Scripture, that is our difference in our approaches to exegesis and hermeneutics! More to come on that!

In addition, we have too often tended to make the model of a restored church the driving force of our mission outreach rather than a proper understanding of the kingdom as the *Missio Dei*. As a result, much of our earlier missionary church planting philosophy had focused almost exclusively on "restoring the New Testament Church" and by doing this we missed the heart of kingdom theology. By centering our attention on restoring some model of the church, mostly shaped by an American 19th or 20th century church structure, rather than seeking to restore God's and Jesus' intended kingdom theology and *Missio Dei*. We have lost contact with the diversity of church life obviously present in 1st century congregations spread over the Mediterranean world and a wide range of cultural, ethnic, and religious models. Remember, when the early 1st century church focused on Jewish and Gentile models, the church suffered. If this is questioned, read Paul's Epistle to the Galatians, and ask why Paul had so much to say about the issues between Jewish and Gentile house churches in Rome, and unity in Ephesians.

Clearly some diversity in form must be permitted within the broad global, cultural, sociological, and ethnic environments in which the church finds itself.

Before you write me off as some liberal or progressive radical, I am not suggesting that doctrinal fidelity has no part in kingdom theology, or that careful Scriptural exegesis and hermeneutic are irrelevant. Neither am I recommending that we should have radical freedom in regard to how the church should be understood, or how it should be organized in its ministry and witness. Reference to my recent book, *A Biblical Theology of Worship*, 2020, should correct any such loose assumptions!

However, by focusing too heavily on an arrangement of church supposedly based on a model of a New Testament church rather than on a broader kingdom theology, misses the point of an indictive biblical theology of church or ecclesiology. Permission to be diverse in form in church life is too often interpreted as digression from the *pattern* which some have identified defining a restored New Testament Church. For example, in our Church of Christ Restoration Heritage we have divided over whether preachers could be paid, over what the church building should look like, over what we should call the church, over song books, where the song leaders should stand, whether a song leader may be assisted by a group of singers among whom some are women, where the singers should stand, whether we should use one cup in communion, and on and on we can go! You might respond, well those things are from our immature past! Some surely are, but these are current tendencies and situations which we find in the Church or kingdom of God today! Our literature is replete with references to such divisiveness current among us in our contemporary "brotherhood." Check the footnote below for references that document such a history.[1]

Experience on the mission field in Africa, with its wide range of cities, villages, tribal regions, cultures, and languages soon inoculates a missionary and westerner against the concept that one model or form fits all!

A failure to appreciate church diversity within church unity has resulted in a divided fellowship and failure to identify the real meaning of kingdom theology. Hopefully, what I intend in this thought will become clearer as we progress in this study of kingdom theology.

In the post-civil war era in America (1861-65) the sectional animosity between the North and South colored any sense of kingdom unity that might have been present among Churches of Christ. Emphasis on what the church may or may not do in its Christian worship overshadowed any concept of kingdom theology and what God is doing in and through his church. This statement should not be intended to imply that there are no

---

[1] Cf. Hughes, *Reclaiming our Heritage*; Hughes, *Reviving the Ancient Faith*; Holloway & Douglas A Foster, *Renewing God's People*; Hughes, Nathan G. Hatch, David Edwin Harrell, J., *American Origins of Churches of Christ*; Allen, *Distant Voices*; Hooper, *A Distinct People: A History of the Churches of Christ in the 20th Century*.

biblical or theological principles that should guide Christian worship and practice, for it is my persuasion that Christian worship and Christian living should be guided and shaped along sound biblical and theological principles rather than on some preconceived biblical church form, but that is a study for another chapter, or even another book! Might I reference my book *A Biblical Theology of Worship*, in this regard?

By an over-emphasis on the correct *doctrinal form* of the "restored" New Testament Church, kingdom theology was overshadowed by faithfulness to doctrinal persuasions which bordered on a new form of Christian legalism. The result has been that the kingdom *missional* emphasis of the *Missio Dei* and kingdom theology has been *overshadowed by ecclesiological concerns*. As mentioned previously, it is my persuasion after some 50 years of church ministry, mission work, and theological reflection that our emphasis has been placed more on ecclesiological doctrinal fidelity than on any kingdom theology intended by God in His covenant with Abraham, for which Jesus came and died, and for which the Apostle Paul and others faithfully preached as the church expanded into new horizons in new cultures, languages, and ethnic groups.

But sadly for many in our Church of Christ tradition, our early mid-nineteenth century premillennial struggles, and our historic restorationist ecclesiological penchant has resulted in kingdom theology being moved to the back shelves of our theological diets!

If some of the thoughts in the above paragraphs regarding unity and my questioning our traditional fixation on defining doctrinal faithfulness in ecclesiology, that is, the church, and my comments on our lack of unity, gives you heartburn, take an antacid pill and read on, for you will find that I am totally committed to a sound inductive approach to Scriptural and doctrinal fidelity in all we do as Christians, especially in regard to worship.[2]

It was apparent from Paul's encounters with Jewish and Gentile Christians living and worshipping together in a multilayered culture that unity focused on ethnic or personal doctrinal preferences often resulted in division. A brief study of Paul's epistles to the Galatians, Ephesians, and Romans reveals that although doctrinal issues are important, living under

---

[2] For clarification of this I encourage you to carefully read my book on *A Biblical Theology of Worship*.

the vast possibilities within kingdom theology was essential to bringing balance into ecclesiastical life.

Paul's admonition in Ephesians 4:1ff to the churches in Asia makes a strong case for unity in the church and kingdom of God. From this long text, the first major practical or paranetic point Paul made in his letter to the Ephesian and Asian Christians, you get the idea that unity is of utmost importance in Paul's mind within the membership in the church.

> *^{1} I therefore, a prisoner for the Lord, <u>beg you to lead a life worthy of the calling to which you have been called,</u> ^{2} <u>with all lowliness and meekness, with patience, forbearing one another in love,</u> ^{3} <u>eager to maintain the unity of the Spirit in the bond of peace.</u> ^{4} <u>There is one body</u> and one Spirit, just as you were called to the one hope that belongs to your call, ^{5} one Lord, one faith, one baptism, ^{6} one God and Father of us all, who is above all and through all and in all. ^{7} But grace was given to each of us according to the measure of Christ's gift. ^{8} Therefore it is said, ... ^{11} And his gifts were that some should be apostles, some prophets, some evangelists, some pastors and teachers, ^{12} to equip the saints for the work of ministry, for building up the body of Christ, ^{13} <u>until we all attain to the unity of the faith and of the knowledge of the Son of God, to mature manhood</u>, to the measure of the stature of the fulness of Christ; ^{14} so that we may no longer be children, tossed to and fro and carried about with every wind of doctrine, by the cunning of men, by their craftiness in deceitful wiles. ^{15} Rather, speaking the truth in love, we are to grow up in every way into him who is the head, into Christ, ^{16} <u>from whom the whole body, joined and knit together by every joint with which it is supplied, when each part is working properly, makes bodily growth and upbuilds itself in love</u>.*

Regarding our poor history of maintaining the unity among churches within the kingdom of God, sometimes even within the local congregation, something caused us to take a wrong or unfortunate turn in our restorationist movement.

Let me explain! The result of our post-civil war sectional struggles was that kingdom theology and being united in Christ in his kingdom mission became a neglected focus. I became hidden behind a faulty proof text biblical hermeneutic, and a congregational or church-form doctrinal rectitude. The noble passion for unity reaching back to the early years of Thomas Campbell became a mission to restore a New Testament church which I believe we had defined by a poor proof-text hermeneutic. Unity became confused with uniformity!

Possibly our definition of what church should look like needs reinterpretation, but that is not the focus at this point of the study! We perhaps should leave that to the field of ecclesiology![3]

My purpose in this chapter has been to focus on the need for unity in the kingdom of God which inherently involves unity within the ecclesiological realm of the church.

However, we will need to move on in this study to address a more theologically and missiologically defined concept of the kingdom and the church as the agent of God's kingdom restoration or *Missio Dei*.

Furthermore, in many ways our definition of restoring the New Testament church has emphasized *what* we teach, *what* we do, and *how* we do it, rather than *why* we do it, and *what God has been doing and is doing today to fulfill his covenant with Abraham*! Restoring the New Testament church is a noble cause but unfortunately one which tends to focus more on *what* we do and *how* we do it than on God and *what God has been doing especially through his call of and covenant with Abraham. The Missio Dei is not an emphasis on what we do, but on what God has been doing ever since he called Abraham and entered a covenant with him and his descendants, whose descendants we are in the church!*

Unfortunately, like Israel we have turned God's covenant with Abraham inward, *centripetally* focusing on the details of how we should live in the community of Israel or the church, rather than the *centrifugal* aspect of God's covenant with Abraham and His *Missio Dei*. In contrast with the centrifugal nature of God's covenant with Abraham we have lost the kingdom missional dynamic of the church as the agent of God's *Missio Dei*.

This should not be interpreted to mean that kingdom living, that is, our behavior as disciples of Jesus, is not important. Kingdom living as disciples within churches is extremely important to maintaining our Christian example in our communities.

---

[3] Cf. Ferguson, *The Church of Christ: A Biblical Ecclesiology for Today*.

However, focusing on the kingdom of God and its *Missio Dei* theological dynamic points more to what God has been doing ever since creation rather than on what we are doing in restoring the New Testament church today. It has been my conviction for some time that we should be attempting to restore the kingdom rather than the church! But even here our understanding of the kingdom has in the words of Hosea been "a cake half turned or half baked"![4] Bear with me as we progress through this study and unpack this concept!

---

[4] Hosea 7:8.

Chapter 6
The Church as the Agent of the *Missio Dei*

I need at this point to insert a caveat regarding the concept of church. Church is not a bad word, concept, or term! It is thoroughly biblical and speaks directly to Jesus, what Jesus came to establish as part of his kingdom ministry, what Jesus has been doing in our lives ever since Pentecost, and the kind of people Jesus' disciples should be. Church speaks directly to the worldwide communities of "Jesus people" who are the agents of the *Missio Dei* and great commission. We should pay attention to the calling of the church as we follow Jesus the Messiah into his kingdom and serve in that kingdom *Missio Dei*.

We need to understand that although we all universally serve under the sovereignty of Jesus[1] in his united kingdom, we do so in local congregations spread out all over the globe in a diversity of nations and cultures who are identified as churches of Christ in the New Testament.

I hear negative statements from some that the term church is an emphasis on the human dynamic of religion which includes all of the failures of what churches have done or failed to do in society. The persuasion is that we should drop the term church from our vocabulary due to its negative connotations in contemporary society. In postmodernity the term church becomes a symbol of organized religion that constricts human freedom and has failed to reach the freedom desired by some. There is some validity to this charge, but it is not a death knell over the concept of church!

Furthermore, in our postmodern culture many react to and reject the term or concept of church because it speaks of a static form of religion bound by legalism and doctrine. Unfortunately, many Christians are persuaded by this mindset.

It is not uncommon for young people of the millennial cohort, and younger, to reject the concept of church and to claim to be followers or

---

[1] Cf Matt 28:18-20, *And Jesus came and said to them, "All authority in heaven and on earth has been given to me.* [19] *Go therefore and make disciples of all nations, baptizing them in the name of the Father and of the Son and of the Holy Spirit,* [20] *teaching them to observe all that I have commanded you; and lo, I am with you always, to the close of the age."*

disciples of Jesus, desire to be in a right relationship with him rather than in a relationship with a church. Sounds profound but is deeply misdirected! Jesus loved the church and died to bring it into being! It is interesting that when Jesus discussed his ministry with his early disciples he claimed to build his *church*, not simply good relationships with people. Paul in his epistle to the Ephesians, following a strident discussion of maintaining the unity of the church, argued that Jesus died for the church in order to bring it into being. Because of this Paul encouraged the Ephesian church to be subject to one another. Although he addressed this to husbands and wives, Paul explained that he was speaking of the *church! This mystery is a profound one, and I am saying that it refers to Christ and the church ...*[2]

Biblically the term church speaks of a living organism or body of people under Christ as their head who in an analogy to the human body function together, minister to one another, and carry out God's *Missio Dei in His kingdom mission*. Christians assemble in congregations (churches) for fellowship, worship, and edification. They love one another as Christ loved the church, and gave his life for them, the church (Eph 5:24-33). Living together in fellowship the church glorifies God and Jesus by the way they live and treat people. Living as disciples (followers) of Christ they seek to manifest in their lives the teachings of Jesus as in the Sermon on the Mount and in his kingdom parables, and witness to his death, burial, and resurrection and great power. This is Christian living, or disciples living under the kingdom reign of Jesus, or if you will, kingdom living. There is absolutely no difference between kingdom living and Christian disciple living.

However, I hear some say, and have even heard it preached from pulpits, that what I have just outlined in the above paragraph regarding the church is not what they were taught! For them, the church was all about doctrine and getting doctrine and worship right. If that is the case, "Where did you come from?" "Have you not read your Bible for yourself?" Admittedly, the Church of Christ I was introduced to 60 years ago did pay significant attention to doctrinal fidelity, but we were also taught to be good disciples of Christ and to honor the Sermon on the Mount, and to be missional. Perhaps we have forgotten much of the good of our heritage

---

[2] Eph 5:32.

and are listening more to a frustrated few who have had a negative experience in their church or Christian life. Sometimes it is easier to listen to negative persuasions, perhaps even popular to do so, than to think for ourselves or to remember the joy of our early Christian experience!

The problem is not with the concept or term church but with the fact that some simply were not taught biblically about the church, *or they have read into the church what they hear others saying about the church*! The correction is not to flee from the term church but to do some good personal study and teaching on the church and get a better understanding of the real church! *Kingdom living is not something new or different from church or disciple living.* Living as good honorable disciples in the church is what Christians have read or been taught over the past 100 years in Churches of Christ, which at least covers the lifespan and experience of most of us today!

Kingdom living, church doctrine, and Christian discipleship are inextricably integrated and profoundly important, but not to the denigration of the term church. If the problem is a poor understanding of the church as an organization, or the failure of some to meet the standards of Christian discipleship, then we should do some good personal study and teaching on the true nature of the church as the body of Christ, a people organized and living under Christ and his Word, and serving in the kingdom as God's agents in the *Missio Dei*.

The church is a great blessing and heritance and should not be denigrated for failed religion in the life of some.

The Coming and Arrival of the Kingdom

Studies in Revelation and the Gospel of Matthew have increasingly drawn my attention and my theological horizons to the impact of apocalyptic eschatology and concerns regarding the "arrival" of the kingdom. An understanding of Jesus' prayer at Matt 6:9ff brought home the impact of Jesus' concern for *the kingdom to be on earth just as it is in heaven*; a prayer that surely all Christians should pray fervently and certainly one which any Jew or Christian with apocalyptic sensitivity would understand. I use the term apocalyptic here as N. T. Wright expresses it in his excellent study, *Simply Jesus*.

Apocalyptic is a view or vision of heaven intersecting with earth and becoming an earthly reality.[3]

That the kingdom is not experienced and enjoyed in many places on earth in the present as it is in heaven does not mean that the kingdom has not already broken into the present during Jesus' ministry! It only means that the kingdom has not yet been experienced fully on earth and in our lives as it is in heaven.

Jesus' concern in his ministry was for the kingdom to become a reality and to be enjoyed and experienced on earth just as it was in heaven. Careful study of the four Gospels reveals that kingdom theology dominated Jesus' ministry and teaching. In our Gospels the kingdom is mentioned well over 200 times, whereas the church is mentioned only three times![4] This does not mean that the church is not extremely important! It only points to the fact that the kingdom was Jesus' overriding concern in his ministry, not the church. Furthermore, for Jesus the kingdom was decidedly missional, which point is the purpose of this study!

Pivotal to our study of the present reality of the kingdom is Jesus' own words at Matt 12:25-28! This discussion was in the context of Jewish Pharisees accusing Jesus of casting out demons by the power of *Be-elzebul*, or the devil.

> [25] *Knowing their thoughts, he said to them, "Every kingdom divided against itself is laid waste, and no city or house divided against itself will stand;* [26] *and if Satan casts out Satan, he is divided against himself; how then will his kingdom stand?* [27] *And if I cast out demons by Be-elzebul, by whom do your sons cast them out? Therefore they shall be your judges.* [28] <u>*But if it is by the Spirit of God that I cast out demons, then the kingdom of God has come upon you.*</u> [29] *Or how can one enter a strong man's house and plunder his goods, unless he first binds the strong man? Then indeed he may plunder his house.* [30] *He who is not with me is against me, and he who does not gather with me scatters.* [31] *Therefore I tell you, every sin and blasphemy will be forgiven*

---

[3] Wright, *Simply Jesus: A New Vision of Who He Was, What He Did, and Why He Matters*, pp. 92ff.
[4] Matt 16:18, 18:17.

> *men, but the blasphemy against the Spirit will not be forgiven.*
> *³² And whoever says a word against the Son of man will be forgiven; but whoever speaks against the Holy Spirit will not be forgiven, either in this age or in the age to come.*

Obviously in Jesus' mind he was busy inaugurating the kingdom of God. The kingdom had arrived in the ministry of Jesus and was formalized or certified in his death and resurrection. Jesus had conquered Satan and established his will and authority on earth! Obviously Paul agreed, for he wrote to the Colossians that God *had already delivered* them from the powers of darkness/Satan, transferred or transplanted, into the kingdom of Jesus. *¹³ He has delivered us from the dominion of darkness and transferred us to the kingdom of his beloved Son, ¹⁴ in whom we have redemption, the forgiveness of sins.*[5] Note, this transferal of the living Colossians was not something that would happen in the future, but had already occurred!

Because of Jesus' faithfulness, God's kingdom had already arrived on earth and was visible in the lives of the Colossians as they were being transformed into the life of Christ.

The Struggles within Churches of Christ over the Kingdom

A series of lectures by Professor James I. Packer in 1989, alluded to above, challenged me to think more seriously of the impact of kingdom theology on the life of the church, notably its worship, evangelism, and mission outreach. As you will read below in this study Dr. Packer was surprised that I, a member of the Church of Christ, would be interested in kingdom theology for we had shied away from kingdom discussion in the aftershock of premillennial debates and divisive battles in the 1940s/50s that had torn our fellowship apart. We consequently focused attention more on the safe harbor of the church than on the dangerous implications of kingdom theology!

The introduction of premillennial or dispensational theology into Church of Christ church life by Robert H. Boll and others, ca 1915 initiated a series of divisive debates with H. Leo Boles and others over whether the kingdom had arrived or whether it was still to become a reality shortly before Christ returned to fulfill God's kingdom promises.[6]

---

[5] Col 1:13-15.
[6] Cf. Hughes, *Reviving the Ancient Faith*, pp.141ff.

The normal response was that since the church and the kingdom were the same the kingdom had arrived with the establishment of the church. This was correct, but diminished discussion of the kingdom to discussion of the church.

The bitterness and divisiveness of these debates caused Church of Christ leaders to shy away from kingdom discussion toward a heavy emphasis on the church. In itself, this was good! The result of this caused Church of Christ scholars to specialize in ecclesiology and not write commentaries on the book of Revelation which merely opened the door to charges of premillennialism! We in churches of Christ became specialists in ecclesiology but not in eschatology! We will discuss this again in a later chapter.

The Covenant Promises and Theology of the Abrahamic Saga

My interest in the relationship of the kingdom, God's creation, and his redemptive and covenant promise to Abraham, has been piqued by Wright's writings regarding justification and Pauline theology.[7] *Setting man "to right"* (Wright's own unique and meaningful term) *is what kingdom theology and the mission of God are all about*!

In Wright's understanding of righteousness and kingdom theology it has been God's purpose ever since creation to bring man and *Creation* back into a right relationship with himself. Man sinned and broke that relationship with God, so God set about to restore that relationship.

God's redemptive mission, the *Missio Dei*, was both historically and theologically set in motion with God's call and covenant with Abraham recorded at Gen 12. Simply expressed, in this covenant God promised to bless Abraham, his descendants, and all nations.

The story of the Bible reveals how God brought this redemptive program to a climax through the faithfulness of Jesus, and His gracious promise to forgive and redeem man through faith in Jesus. Redemption, reconciliation, the sovereignty of God, and the kingdom mission in the Bible narrative serve as four points of a compass. As essential elements in God's putting man to right, they orient us in the direction of the *missional nature of the kingdom* and the *Missio Dei*. God's covenant with Abraham thus dominates the story of the Bible and God's kingdom theology and mission. It should become apparent that one may not separate kingdom

---

[7] Cf. the works by Wright listed in the bibliography.

theology from the covenant made with Abraham, the *Missio Dei*, and the *missional nature* of the church.

The Missional Nature of Kingdom Theology

I am impressed by Alan Hirsch's definition of the term *missional* in which he emphasizes that God is by nature himself *missional*! Mission is what God and the kingdom are all about! God is a God who actively seeks to redeem his lost creation. Jesus, God's Son and appointed Savior was *sent* on a *mission* to seek and to save the lost! He was not sent just to feed the lost! Both God's and Jesus' mission was *missional*! Hirsch's thoughts pose an interesting question *"Does the church do mission work, or is mission what the church is?"*

Hirsh astutely observes:

> "*Missional* represents a significant paradigm shift in the way we think about the church. As the people of a missionary God, we ought to engage the world with the same intensity and mission in the same way he does—by *going* out rather than merely *reaching* out. To obstruct this missional mindset is to block God's missional purposes in and through his people. When the church is in mission, it is the true church."[8]

The *Missio Dei*, the Church, and the Mission/Missions/Missional "Trifecta"[9]

In my research it soon became apparent that any study of the kingdom had to penetrate the concept of the *Missio Dei* and the role of the church and mission. Although this study was intended to be one developing only kingdom theology, as my research progressed I realized that careful attention had to be given to several local church ministries leading to thoughtful understanding of the terms *mission, missions, missional*.

I had attempted to integrate these interests and concerns in Chapter 3 of this study. As indicated above in my opening thoughts to this study it become apparent to me that my understanding of kingdom theology and

---

[8] Hirsh, "Defining Missional," *LeadershipJournal.net*, article copyright 2008 by the author or Christianity Today, *International Leadership Journal*, 12.12.2008. Cf. also www.christianitytoday.com. I have intentionally adapted Hirsch's comments in this paragraph.
[9] I use the term *trifecta*, originally a horse race term, to refer *to three necessary ingredients* to a proposition or point of view.

the *Missio Dei* discussion of mission and missions must incorporate the various ways or ministries in which the church can and should engage evangelism, church planting, social justice, care for the poor, spiritual formation, and benevolence. Hopefully, this study will clarify these thoughts and broaden our understanding of kingdom theology and the missional nature of the *Missio Dei*.

The Pivotal Role of God's Covenant to Abraham in Kingdom Theology

It is my prayer that a deeper understanding of kingdom theology and the missional nature of the church will lead us to understand more fully the relationship of the kingdom to God's covenant promise to Abraham that through his seed all nations of the earth would be blessed. Perhaps this Abrahamic connection will help us be more missional and missionary minded and better prepared to understand what God is doing in his world, and how we can join him in his *Missio Dei* and kingdom mission!

The Inaugurated Nature of the Kingdom

I am keenly aware of the dialogue found in most studies of the kingdom regarding the tension between the present nature of the kingdom and future aspects of the kingdom. This was reflected in C. H. Dodd,[10] and several other scholars' views of *realized eschatology*, and Oscar Cullmann[11] and others' views of *inaugurated and future eschatology*.[12] In many ways we are indebted to George Eldon Ladd's *The Gospel of the Kingdom* in which he set the tone for a renewed discussion of the kingdom especially in regard to the present/future dynamic of the kingdom.[13] It is not the purpose of this study to enter here into the detailed debate of the present and future aspects of the kingdom. However, one cannot discuss a theology of the kingdom without engaging Jesus' emphasis on the present nature of the kingdom in his ministry, while still holding to an unrealized hope that there is yet a future dimension of the kingdom to be actualized.

---

[10] Dodd, *Apostolic Preaching and Its Developments*.
[11] Cullmann, *Christ and Time*.
[12] Cf. the discussion of these features in Wendell Willis, Ed., *The Kingdom of God in 20th-Century Interpretation*. See further discussion of the term kingdom as realm in chapter 3 in this book relating to the translation and interpretation of *hō basileia*.
[13] Ladd, *The Gospel of the Kingdom*.

As observed previously in this study, both Jesus and Paul believed that the kingdom had arrived and was fully inaugurated in Jesus' ministry and victory over Satan on the cross, and in his resurrection, and in Paul's apostolic Holy Spirit empowered ministry of redemption.

Furthermore, although I am fully aware of the concept of a *physical realm* inherent in the term kingdom, it is my persuasion that this is a secondary concern in a kingdom definition. Such a *physical realm* understanding of the kingdom has unfortunately surfaced in many premillennial and dispensational emphases on the kingdom which hold to the future fulfillment of the kingdom that will take place in Judea and Jerusalem when Jesus finally returns to establish his unfulfilled kingdom and reign on earth. For more detailed studies on the issues relating to premillennialism and dispensationalism in kingdom theology I refer the reader to the several works referenced in my commentary, *Conquering with Christ: A Commentary of the Book of Revelation*,[14] and other works in the bibliography in this study.

Kingdom Theology, the *Missio Dei*, and Missional

Missional is a word that unfortunately has morphed in modern usage to mean *any new way of reaching the lost*, sometimes it is a reference to what has been called "the emerging church" being engaged in *social injustice, benevolence*, and *quasi political concerns* in the name of church.

The issues faced by the church in the recent 1994 failure of the church in Rwanda regarding genocide has refocused the thinking of many on addressing the social injustice issues of disenfranchised people. Certainly, this should be the concern of all Christians, but unfortunately, in this discussion the distinctive nature of the *missional* nature of the *Missio Dei* and kingdom theology has become hazy, and consequently confused with social justice and *kingdom living*.

Gradually, in place of evangelism and the planting of new communities as kingdom churches with the responsibility of addressing the benevolent needs of the disenfranchised, the fine definition of *mission* or *missional* has been reduced in a negative attitude toward evangelism

---

[14] Fair, *Conquering With Christ: A Commentary on the Book of Revelation*; Jim McGuiggan, *The Book of Daniel*; Barbara R. Rossing, *The Rapture Exposed: The Message of Hope in the Book of Revelation*; Aune, *Revelation*, pp. 1089f; Osborne, *Revelation*, pp. 696f.

and church planting. Rather than seeing the world as *lost* without Christ we have redefined the world simply as *disenfranchised* in the absence of social, physical, and temporal needs. The distinctive nature of the two kingdom terms, mission and missional, has been reduced to a thin line, or almost obliterated. Careful reflection in this shift, possibly a theological seismic shift, makes it necessary to refocus on the *missional* nature of the *Missio Dei* and kingdom theology!

Alan Hirsch has refocused the term *missional* to draw attention to *the missionary charge of the church in kingdom theology.*

A proper understanding of *missional* begins with recovering a missional understanding of God and kingdom theology. By his very nature God is a "sent one" who takes the initiative in redeeming his creation. This doctrine, known as *Missio Dei*—the sending nature and purpose of God—is causing many to redefine their understanding of the church. Because we are the *"sent"* people of God, *the church should be the instrument of God's redemptive mission in the world.*

As things stand, however, many people see it the other way around. They believe mission is an instrument of the church; a means by which the church is grown. Hirsch has pointed out that although we frequently say "the church has a mission," according to *missional Missio Dei* theology a more correct statement would be *"the mission of God has a church which serves as his agent."*

This definition of *missional* represents a significant shift in the way we think about the church. As the people of a missionary God, we ought to engage the world the same way he does—by *going* out rather than just *reaching* out. To obstruct or divert this missional redemptive movement is to block God's purposes in and through his people. When the church is *missional*, it is the true kingdom *Missio Dei* church.[15]

With the fall of man, God did not discard his plan for populating his creation with people with whom he could sustain a meaningful relationship. Neither did he abandon his plan to reign over creation through the ministry of man.

In due time, according to His predetermined plan, God inaugurated man's redemption and re-establishment of his kingdom on earth by calling Abraham from his home in the Ur of the Chaldeans, that is from

---

[15] Hirsh, *The Forgotten Ways*, and LeadershipJournjal.net, 12.12.2008.

Mesopotamia, sometimes called Babylon. God engaged a covenant with Abraham through which He, in and through Abraham and his descendants, would bless all men and inaugurate his predetermined plan for re-establishing his sovereignty and kingdom (Gen 11:27-31; Gen 12; 15; 17).

The missional point of this Abrahamic covenant is that God went out after Abraham, called, him, and sent him on a mission. We should carry God's redemptive plan forward by engaging in this Missio Dei! We must recognize that God's calling and covenant with Abraham was both *kingdom* oriented and *missional* in nature. Cf. Gen 12:1-3:

> "Now the Lord said to Abram, "Go from your country and your kindred and your father's house to the land that I will show you. ² And I will make of you a great nation, and I will bless you, and make your name great, so that you will be a blessing. ³ I will bless those who bless you, and him who curses you I will curse; and by you all the families of the earth shall bless themselves."
> Gen 17:1-8: "When Abram was ninety-nine years old the Lord appeared to Abram, and said to him, "I am God Almighty; walk before me, and be blameless. ² And I will make my covenant between me and you, and will multiply you exceedingly." ³ Then Abram fell on his face; and God said to him, ⁴ "Behold, my covenant is with you, and you shall be the father of a multitude of nations. ⁵ No longer shall your name be Abram, but your name shall be Abraham; for I have made you the father of a multitude of nations. ⁶ I will make you exceedingly fruitful; and I will make nations of you, and kings shall come forth from you. ⁷ And I will establish my covenant between me and you and your descendants after you throughout their generations for an everlasting covenant, to be God to you and to your descendants after you. ⁸ And I will give to you, and to your descendants after you, the land of your sojournings, all the land of Canaan, for an everlasting possession; and I will be their God."

The Kingdom, *Missio Dei*, and the Abrahamic Covenant

First, we should note that this covenant was initiated by God! It is God's covenant with Abraham. God appeared to Abraham and set out the terms of this covenant.

Second, this covenant was not made only between God and Abraham, or only between God, Abraham, and Israel (as Abraham's descendants would be called). It was between God and Abraham and all those who like Abraham would be people of faith, that is, both Jew and Gentile, Gal 3:6-29, note particularly vs 26-29:

> But now that faith has come, we are no longer under a custodian; *for in Christ Jesus you are all sons of God, through faith*. For as many of you as were baptized into Christ have put on Christ. *There is neither Jew nor Greek*, there is neither slave nor free, there is neither male nor female; for you are all one in Christ Jesus. And *if you are Christ's, then you are Abraham's offspring, heirs according to promise*.

Israel failed miserably to fulfill God's calling and *missional* intent of this covenant, and it was subsequently accomplished in and through the faithfulness of Jesus, God's *sent Messiah*.[16] God's *kingdom* and *missional* purpose included those of all nations, Jews and Gentiles, who through faithfulness to God and Christ would be justified and included in the kingdom heritage promised to Abraham.

The extent of the loss of the *missional* awareness *of kingdom theology* can be seen in the failure of Jesus' personal disciples, reflected in their question to Jesus at Acts 1:6-8:

> *⁶ So when they had come together, they asked him, "Lord, will you at this time restore the kingdom to Israel?" ⁷ He said to them, "It is not for you to know times or seasons which the Father has fixed by his own authority. ⁸ But you shall receive power when the Holy Spirit has come upon you; and you shall be my witnesses in Jerusalem and in all Judea and Samaria and to the end of the earth."*

When God's time was right (Mk 1:14, 15; Gal 4:4) the covenant promises to Abraham were extended to all men through Jesus' faithfulness to God's purpose, and the church's faithfulness in Jesus.[17] Through God's

---

[16] Note that the term Christ (Greek Χριστός, *christos*) is the Greek translation of the Hebrew *Messiah*. Messiah referred to an anointed one, a king anointed to reign, or in the context of biblical theology, the king of God's Kingdom. Cf. Acts 2:36.

[17] I find N. T. Wright's studies in *Paul* (2009) and *Justification* (2009) to be helpful in understanding the role of the faithfulness of Jesus in God's scheme of justification and righteousness, and covenant with Abraham.

covenant with Abraham and Jesus' faithfulness to God's purpose, God set man *"to right again,"* or set men of faith in a *right relationship with himself* again.[18]

Although Galatians 3:6-29 which I cited above is long, it is vital to following the thought of God's *Missio Dei* covenant with people of all nations and its role in our understanding God's preparation for inaugurating his kingdom through the Messiah. I highlighted significant sections of the text for emphasis. My purpose was to demonstrate that *one must keep kingdom theology thinking concretely within God's original purpose in creation, within his eternal purpose and plan to redeem his creation, and firmly within the context of God's covenant with Abraham and all of his descendants.* In addition, one must not miss the kingdom's *missional* purpose of God's plan of redemption for all nations.

Now Gal 3:6-29 speaks of kingdom *Missio Dei* theology in its purest form! The call of Abraham, kingdom theology, the faithfulness of Jesus and his church in extending the kingdom into all the world, is *kingdom theology*. It is *missional* at its very roots and in its ongoing mission to take the Gospel of Jesus into all the world.

The kingdom is both *theological*[19] and *missional* in that it represents *Missio Dei*[20] and not *Missio Ecclesiae*[21] or man's response to the theology and missional aspects of the kingdom, in the sense that it stresses God's sovereign purpose in creation and his *missional redeeming activity* rooted in his eternal love for his creation.

Kingdom *living*, or *Missio Ecclesiae*, speaks the Christian's *response* to God's sovereign reign in their daily lives, to kingdom theology's missional purpose by witnessing to God and Jesus through their Christlike

---

[18] Again, I like Wright's quaint yet precise expression that God put man *to right again*, that is, *justified him* through faith in Jesus and Jesus' faithfulness. Cf. the reference to Wright, *Paul* and *Justification* in the bibliography.

[19] Theological implies that a concept or activity relates to God's holiness, sovereignty, righteousness, and redemptive activity, and not to man's activity or impulse.

[20] The term *Missio Dei* is a Latin expression that literally translated means the mission of God. However in theological terms it refers to God's mission in this world and explains what God is doing in this world to set it right again to its created form. It explains what God's mission in this world is.

[21] *Missio Ecclesiae* speaks of the mission of the church and explains what the church is doing in this world to align itself with the *Missio Dei*.

living, concern for social justice, benevolence, and compassion for God's creation.

The kingdom is *theological* and *missional* in that it emphasizes God's calling and sending, and His covenant promise to Abraham which was realized in Jesus' faithfulness.

The full kingdom concept includes both the *Kingdom Theology, Missio Dei, missional*[22] dynamic, and the *Kingdom Living Missio Ecclesiae* ingredients. The *missional* dynamic of Kingdom Theology empowers the covenant promises to Abraham, promising that all men including the Gentiles would be blessed.

The Kingdom *Theological dynamic* of the kingdom *drives* the church's *Missio Ecclesiae*, the *living* personal *witness* of Christians demonstrated by their kingdom *living, concern for social justice, benevolence, and the marginalized peoples of the world.*

Kingdom *Theology* is *missional soteriological*[23] in that at its heart kingdom theology builds off the Abrahamic promises and the *redeeming* activity of God rooted in the faithfulness of Jesus and his death, burial, and resurrection, and the apostolic example of going out into all the world, preaching, and establishing Jesus communities wherever they went.

In all biblical discussions the theological distinction between *theology*[24] and *paraenesis*[25] must be carefully understood and maintained. Kingdom *living* is in some ways the equivalent of the paranetic response to kingdom theology.

Kingdom theology does not focus on practical paranetic ethical issues which lay emphasis on human effort. Ethical issues like *kingdom living* are important, but are *paraenetic* and not primary *kingdom theology*.

Kingdom theology is *what God has been doing* since the fall of man, through Jesus' faithfulness, and the missional *going, reconciling,*

---

[22] *Missional* relates to God's nature of seeking fallen man and the responsibility of the church to carry forward God's redemptive activity to all men. It carries the sense of being sent, seeking, or going out in redemptive activity to save the lost.

[23] *Soteriological* speaks of God's redemptive activity as he seeks for and justifies fallen man through the faithfulness of Jesus and man's faithfulness in return.

[24] *Theology* is understood here to refer to doctrinal or theological elements related to God and his sovereign will and activity.

[25] *Paraenesis* is understood here to refer to ethical and practical issues that are in response to theological or doctrinal elements.

soteriological character of the preached gospel, cf. Paul's comment to the Corinthians at 1 Cor 15:1-4:

> *¹ Now I would remind you, brethren, in what terms I preached to you the gospel, which you received, in which you stand, ² by which you are saved, if you hold it fast—unless you believed in vain.*
>
> *³ For I delivered to you as of first importance what I also received, that Christ died for our sins in accordance with the scriptures, ⁴ that he was buried, that he was raised on the third day in accordance with the scriptures ...*

Kingdom *living* is *what Christians have been doing* because of their understanding of the *Missio Dei* character of kingdom theology. Kingdom *living* represents the *witness* of the power of the gospel of Jesus reflected in the daily lives of Christians.

Kingdom *theology* is *sending, or being sent*, Missional. Kingdom *living* is *witnessing by living for Christ.*

Kingdom *theology* is reflected in kingdom *living* in the sense that kingdom theology predates the church and has been in existence since eternity and the fall of man, and kingdom *living* is seen in how the church responds and witnesses to that primary theology.

Kingdom *theology* relates to *what God was and is doing* in and through his covenant with Abraham, and through his covenant people, the church. Through the faithfulness of Abraham, the faithfulness to Jesus, and the faithfulness of the church to God's *missional* purpose, *God is bringing all mankind back into a right relationship with Him and his reign.*

God is *restoring* his kingdom. In Paul's terms, God's purpose was "*a plan for the fulness of time, to unite all things in him, things in heaven and things on earth,*" Eph 1:10.

Kingdom *theology* involves empowering the *Missio Dei* and God's kingdom *missional* purpose through the faithfulness of the church. *Kingdom theology is the church perpetuating God's covenant with Abraham by taking the Gospel to all men.*

Kingdom theology must always be the driving force behind the life and ministry of the church.

What we have learned from this Chapter

Kingdom *theology* relates initially to God's sovereign reign over all creation.

Kingdom *theology* involves the *mission of God to restore man's broken relationship with God* as a result of the sin and the fall of man.

Kingdom *theology* is expressed in God's eternal purpose to restore his creation to its original condition in Christ Jesus, cf. Eph 1:3-11.

Kingdom theology is seen in God's *missional* call of Abraham, and his covenant promise through Abraham to bless all nations.

The covenant with Abraham had global kingdom *theology* implications which were not fulfilled simply by *Torah* (Law) keeping, or *kingdom living* under the *Torah*, but were intended to be fulfilled by the faithfulness of Abraham, the faithfulness of Israel, and God's promised *Messiah*, Jesus.

Kingdom *theology* was intended to be *missional* through God's call of Abraham extending through the life of Israel, through Jesus, and then through the faithfulness of the church to God's missional purpose.

The kingdom is then essentially a *theological, soteriological*, and *missional* concept, and not simply a *paraenetic* ethical issue of *kingdom living* through keeping the Law, or through Christians living their lives in keeping with the moral implications of the Sermon on the Mount. The essence of kingdom *theology* is therefore not how Christians relate to one another and live ethical lives, but how Christians relate to God's *Missio Dei* in Abraham.

Kingdom *theology* emphasizes the commitment of Christians to God's covenant *mission* and *purpose* of *restoring* his sovereignty over all creation.

The essence of kingdom *theology* and its distinction from kingdom *living* is a thin yet profound line, and one whose understanding is essentially of understanding the difference in focus between kingdom *theology* and kingdom *living*. Kingdom *theology* is about the sovereignty of God and his people *carrying forward* God's *redemptive missional* purpose inaugurated originally through Abraham.

As a consequence, the kingdom dynamic obviously must include a secondary corollary, concerns relating to ethical kingdom *living*, for that is why God initially gave Adam and Eve certain laws to define how they should live faithful lives to God's eternal purpose in God's kingdom.

God's *Torah* Law (*torah* meaning *instruction*) to Israel through Moses thus defined for Israel the *implications* of *living faithfully* to God's kingdom and covenant with Abraham. God's *missional* sending covenant with Abraham provided the impetus to the *godly living* required in the ecclesial *Torah*!

From the inauguration of God's covenant with Abraham, Israel, and all nations (Gen 12), the kingdom involved maintaining a faithful and proper covenant *relationship* with God grounded in faithfulness to God and his *missional kingdom purpose.*

We will shortly learn how Israel lost faith in God's kingdom purpose, rejected his *missional* intention, and consequently were rejected by God as his *kingdom people*, losing their kingdom *relationship* with him.

Chapter 7
Kingdom Theology, the *Missio Dei*, Kingdom Living, the Church, and Church Ministries

The interrelationship of the kingdom, the *Missio Dei*, and the local church is vital to understanding how church ministry through its varied ministries integrate in kingdom theology and relate to what God is doing in our world, and what the church should be doing.

God has a *mission*, His *missional Missio Dei*. The church has a *ministry* in this *Missio Dei* as the agent of God's *Missio Dei*.

In four figures below we will explore several possibilities as to how the interrelated concepts of kingdom, mission, and church relate to the *Missio Dei*, and the ministries available to the church as it carries out its kingdom *mission* in the world.

Introduction

Although this book is intended to focus on kingdom *theology* it is in the very nature of kingdom *theology* to explore the theology of church and mission since the *Missio Dei* encompasses all three: kingdom theology, church theology, and mission theology. Hence this chapter will explore all three dimensions of the *Missio Dei* in an introductory manner.

Craig Ott, Stephen J. Strauss, and Timothy C. Tennant make the following profound observation in their Preface to *Encountering Theology of Mission*;

> Our conviction is that the church as community of the kingdom is both the primary agent as well as the chief fruit of the *Missio Dei* in this age. Furthermore, only a theology of mission that is rightly framed eschatologically will give proper place to the kingdom of God. The church as God's people lives as instrument, witness, sign, and anticipation of the kingdom that is already present but only to come in fullness upon Christ's return. The cross remains the fulcrum of history, the gospel the message of hope, and the Spirit the power of mission.[1]

---

[1] Ott, Stephen J. Strauss, and Timothy C. Tennent, *Encountering Theology of Mission: Biblical Foundations, Historical Developments, and Contemporary Issues*, kindle locations 29-32.

In this study I am using the term *Missio Dei*[2] to refer to the mission God has been on in our world since creation and the fall of man to restore his kingdom relationship with man by reaching out to fallen man, in fact by *going out* on a mission to reach fallen man. We see this specifically in call to, sending out, and covenant with Abraham, Gen 12, 15, 17, *et al.*

I see in the call of Abraham a *missional* dynamic, of sending Abraham out since Abraham's home was the Ur of Chaldea in Babylon. For Abraham to achieve his missional purpose he had to leave his home and go out!

God's Missio Dei covenant with Abraham reached a high point in *sending* the ministry of Jesus which covenant was carried out through Christians going out into all the world as the suffering servants of God, the church.

Missio Dei thus refers to what God has been doing in our world to redeem his fallen creation. *Missio Dei* is what God and the kingdom are all about! Hence the *Missio Dei* is what the church *is all about* rather than *what* the church is doing! I hope to explore this in greater detail as this chapter progresses.

It is often difficult to understand the intricate relationship between theology, ministry, and missiological practice. Either the biblical foundation of mission or the theology of mission has not been clearly defined and understood, possibly even neglected, or simply assumed, or as I have sensed or experienced too often, it has been ignored with the entrance point into ministry or mission being more *practical* than *theological*. We *do* mission work because the church is supposed to *do* mission work rather than understanding that mission work is what the church is! Not fully understanding this point results in mission being perceived as *one of the ministries of the church* which would be nice for the church to accept rather than seeing that the *very nature of the church is missional*.

Too often mission effort is engaged out of the goodness of a Christian spirit and concern for either the perceived lost, or for mission efforts needing some form of financial or personnel assistance. Much time and effort have been lost due to *hasty engagement* before *clear theological or strategic thought* has been given to the ministry of mission. My purpose in

---

[2] The missiological term *Missio Dei* as a technical theological term was discussed in some detail in chapter 1.

this chapter is to highlight some of the essential relationships between the biblical foundation of the *Missio Dei*, kingdom *theology*, and the church in its varied ministries, and finally kingdom *living*.

I have frequently labored over expressing in the clearest terms the integration of the different emphases of a traditional mission practice with the post-Lausanne 1974 Covenant[3] on mission. Both of which have decided biblical emphases, but also in my opinion, both manifest clear biblical shortcomings.

Traditional Mission Theology and Practice

By traditional mission theology I have in mind the often misguided mindset of my own heritage[4] which defined mission work simply as going overseas and planting or *restoring the New Testament church* in some distant land.

The emphasis was heavily on evangelism and the spiritual side of man. *The driving thrust was supposedly on restoring the New Testament church in a world or culture divided by denominational differences, Synods, and Creeds.*

In many cases within my early 1950/60 experience in South Africa the result of what was planted was not a New Testament church but a church shaped and defined by the practice and forms of the home sending church, mostly an American Southern Bible Belt church. Heavy emphasis was placed on maintaining doctrinal fidelity.[5] Consideration of the social needs or cultural differences was often ignored with little understanding of an *indigenous or culturally contextualized church*.

One of the first churches planted in South Africa ca 1953 was the Turffontein church in a Johannesburg suburb. A church building was built,

---

[3] Briefly I summarize the mindset of the Lausanne 1974 Covenant as emphasizing concern for a holistic view of mission which emphasizes the socio, social justice, and physical dimension of mission as well as the spiritual dimension. Traditional approaches of mission have in the past focused on the spiritual dimension of humanity and have given a lesser or minor role to social injustice.

[4] For those who do not know me I have for over 50 years been a member of the Stone-Campbell Restoration Movement and Churches of Christ. Although in some cases I am critical of some of the directions my heritage has taken I am proud of our strong biblical commitment and concern for evangelism and church planting.

[5] As indicated in the previous footnote I am proud of our biblical and doctrinal focus albeit that we sometimes placed more emphasis on doctrine than on Christ as the center and fulcrum of our faith.

using American finances, which looked more like a church in Tennessee than any church building in South Africa. We had to make a statement that our restored church was different from other churches! The first hymn books, and tracts written by American preachers and church leaders placed on a tract display were imported from the USA. The Christians sat when they sang, contrary to South African practice, and prayers were led while the congregation was seated. In 1950s South Africa this was a bold statement, made more in ignorance of any indigenous practice, but we were making a statement that the restored church was different from other churches in South Africa. Adverts were placed in local newspapers under the heading of "Ask Your Preacher!" The intention was intended to be dramatic but resulted in the new churches being identified as American churches, considered in South Africa as a derogatory comment.

Forgive me if I have overstated this point, but I think clear thinking Christians will understand my point. If you are not comfortable with my point of view, I encourage you to read some of our church papers over the past century!

Although this book is not intended primarily to be a detailed study of the church of Christ, our mission method, or our evangelism, it will be necessary to discuss these terms in some detail in order to understand the term *mission* as it refers to the church carrying out God's Mission, the *Missio Dei,* in his world.

Mission

Although the terms *mission* and *missions* will be referenced under the discussion of figure 4 below, and since the difference is considered by some to be a mere technicality, but nevertheless a significant technicality, I will explain how I and most missiologists today interpret and use these terms. Eckhard Schnabel writes:

> Before explaining what I mean when I speak of missionary strategies and methods, I need to define what the term *mission* means. In the context of historical and sociological studies of Christianity and also of other religions, the following definition of *mission* (or *missions* in terms of "missionary work") includes both general criteria and particular activities. The term "mission" or "missions" refers to the activity of a community of faith that distinguishes itself from its environment in terms of both religious belief (theology) and social behavior (ethics), that is convinced of

the truth claims of its faith, and that actively works to win other people to the content of faith and the way of life of whose truth and necessity the members of that community are convinced …

First, since the English term *mission* is derived from the Latin words *missio* ("sending") and *mittere* ("to send"), it seems obvious that intentionality and movement should be integral parts in the definition of *mission* if we continue to use this term. Mission proceeds from an authority that sends envoys and a message to other people and to other places. There is no reason to abandon either intentionality or geographical movement in the definition of *mission*. Intentionality refers to the purpose of the mission as designed by the initiator or sender of the messenger as well as to the purpose of the mission as understood by the messenger. Geographical movement is movement from point A to point B.[6]

I am comfortable with Schnabel's definition of *mission* and *missions* with the one caveat; I will use *mission* to refer to the *mission of the church* to carry out God's *Missio Dei,* and *missions* to refer to the *variety or ways or ministries in which the church does this*. I will understand the *mission* of the church in the technical sense of Acts 1:8 and Matt 28:19, 20, and Paul's missionary activity as recorded in Acts and reflected in his Epistles, that is, going out into the world, witnessing to the death and resurrection of Jesus, planting churches, and maturing them in the life of the Holy Spirit.

Jedidiah Coppenger in a penetrating discussion on mission and missions makes the following observation:

> Of course the difference between missions and mission is significant. The former is the activity of the church, and the latter is the reason we have a church. Missions are rooted in our ecclesiology, while our ecclesiology should be rooted in mission.[7]

In Coppenger's thinking the church should be about the *mission* of God, the *Missio Dei*. The church carries its *Missio Dei* mission out through various activities or *missions*. Coppenger opens his discussion by

---

[6] Schnabel, *Paul the Missionary: Realities, Strategies and Methods,* kindle locations 337-350.
[7] Coppenger, "The Community of Mission," *Theology and Practice of Mission*, kindle location 1611.

stating that a major problem of evangelical churches is that they tend to focus on ecclesiology, separating it from the kingdom and missiology. That is, they tend to neglect missiology when discussing who the church is and what the church does. Ecclesiology focuses on the *form* of the church and what it does such as worship, missions, etc. Missiologically relates to *what the church should do* as it conducts *mission* as an extension of God's *Missio Dei*. Coppenger states;

> One of the great tragedies in evangelicalism has been the separation of our ecclesiology from our missiology. It is difficult to talk about the mission of God without people thinking we are talking about missions for God...
>
> In order for evangelicals to recover a missional ecclesiology, they must grasp how the church fits into the overarching kingdom mission of God. This chapter contends that God's kingdom mission is the storyline of scripture.[8]

According to Coppenger's understanding, the church fits into the *Missio Dei* when it conducts mission as an extension of God's mission but not as an extension of church ministry.

Missiologically and theologically the reason, therefore, that we have church is to conduct mission as an extension of God's mission.

Christopher Wright makes a similar point regarding *mission* being an extension of God's *Missio Dei* in that God called the church to conduct mission. He observes;

> Finally, the biblical narrative introduces us to ourselves as *the church with a mission* ... Mission then in biblical terms, while it inescapably involves us in planning and action, it is not *primarily* a matter of our activity or our initiative. Mission from the point of view of our human endeavor, means the committed *participation* of God's people in the purposes of God for the redemption of the whole creation. The mission is God's. The marvel is that he invites us to join in.[9]

---

[8] Coppenger, *Theology and Practice of Mission*, kindle location 1615.
[9] Christopher Wright, *The Mission of God, Unlocking the Bible's Grand Narrative*, pp. 67f.

Addressing the difference between the singular *mission* and the plural *missions* Wright has several profound observations. I have brought these together in this one block of material developing Wright's thoughts, bringing to the table the discussion of the differences, yet relationships, of *mission* and *missions*.

> There is no doubt that the Bible shows God sending many people "on a mission from God," and the missionary movement in the book of Acts begins with a church responding to that divine impulse by sending Paul and Barnabas out on their first missionary journey ... So, even if we agree that the concept of sending and being sent lies at the heart of mission, there is a broad range of biblically sanctioned activities that people may be sent by God to do, including famine relief, action for justice, preaching, evangelism, teaching, healing and administration ... *It is not so much the case that God has a mission for his church in the world, as that God has a church for his mission in the world* (emphasis IAF).
>
> Mission was not made for the church; the church was made for mission – God's mission ... So when I speak of mission, I am thinking of all that God is doing in his great purpose for the whole of creation and all that he calls us to do in cooperation with that purpose ... But when I speak of missions, I am thinking of the multitude of activities that God's people can engage in, by means of which they participate in God's mission.[10]

It is apparent that Wright sees the plural missions to describe "the multitude of activities that God's people can engage in" as they engage in God's *Missio Dei*. The singular *mission* he contends refers to the church engaging in God's great purpose for the whole creation, that is redemption and restoring God's creation to its right relationship with himself. I am not in disagreement with Wright but prefer to focus *mission* more on the *specific sending of the church* to bring about this redemption which takes place through evangelism, telling the story of God's redemption, and church planting.

---

[10] Wright, *The Mission of God's People,* kindle location 149ff.

With remarkable biblical theological insight in his book *Bible and Mission: Christian Witness in a Postmodern World*[11] Richard Bauckham observes that a healthy understanding of mission must begin with God's calling and covenant with Abraham as reflected in Gen 12 and Gal 3, and extending into the continuing life of the church. What God began in his *Missio Dei* in Abraham and brought to maturity in Jesus he passed on to the church. This is the very fiber or "warp and weave"[12] of mission. In a section under the heading *"From Abraham to all the families of the earth"* Bauckham observes,

> While God's promise to Abraham is only rarely echoed in the Old Testament outside Genesis it finds significant echoes in the New Testament. Here Paul interprets the promise to mean that one specific descendent of Abraham, Jesus Christ, will bring blessing to Israel and to all the nations (Gal 3:6-9; 16) indeed, Paul identifies this promise as actually the Gospel.
>
> The scripture, foreseeing that God would justify the Gentiles by faith, declared the gospel beforehand to Abraham, saying, "All the Gentiles shall be blessed in you." For this reason, those who believe are blessed with Abraham who believed. (Gal 3:8-9, NRSV)
>
> Less often noticed is the way the Gospel of Matthew interprets the promise to Abraham in the same way that Paul does. Matthew frames the whole story of Jesus between the identification of him as a descendant of Abraham in the opening verse of the Gospel and in the closing words of Jesus at the end of the Gospel, the commission of the disciples of Jesus to make disciples of all nations ... However, for Matthew, Jesus is the Messiah not only for the Jews but also for Gentiles. He is the descendant of Abraham through whom God's blessing will at last reach the nations ...[13]

---

[11] Bauckham, *Bible and Mission: Christian Witness in a Postmodern World*. The book is actually the printed version of lectures Bauckham delivered to two mission organizations, one in England, the other in Ethiopia in 1999 and 2001.

[12] The expression *warp and weave* is my interpretation of Bauckham but expresses the essentiality of setting mission in God's redemptive story or *Missio Dei*.

[13] Bauckham, *Bible and Mission*, pp. 32f.

Timothy Tennant proffers several thoughts on the meaning and relationship of the terms *mission* and *missions*. His primary observation stresses the Trinitarian or divine activity of mission as the *Missio Dei*, rather than referring to what humans in the church do about the *Missio Dei*;

> In this book the word mission refers to God's redemptive, historical initiative on behalf of His creation. Mission is first and foremost about God and His redemptive purposes and initiatives in the world, quite apart from any actions or tasks or strategies or initiatives the church may undertake. To put it plainly, mission is far more about God and who He is than about us and what we do.[14]

Tennant stresses that the church is commissioned to carry out *God's Missio Dei* in our world. He underscores the point that the mission of the church is to *further God's mission* in the world, thus not eliminating a role of the church in God's *Missio Dei* but identifying the church as the *means* by which God furthers His *Missio Dei*. He quotes with approval the landmark book and conclusions of Georg Vicedom, *The Mission of God: An Introduction to the Theology of Mission*.[15]

Note Tennant's comment:

> The phrase *missio dei*, or the "mission of God," was later popularized by Georg Vicedom as a key concept in missions with the publication of his 1963 landmark book, *The Mission of God: An Introduction to the Theology of Mission*. Vicedom insightfully conceptualized mission as our participation in the Father's mission of "sending the Son." Vicedom declared that "the missionary movement of which we are a part has its source in the Triune God Himself."
>
> The idea of understanding mission through the lens of the *missio dei* is fundamentally sound, and it will be the foundation of the Trinitarian missiology that this book proposes. The problem with the twentieth-century ecumenical notion of *missio dei* was not so much in the concept itself as in the application of the concept and how it was actually understood and practiced. Certainly in his

---

[14] Tennant, *Invitation to World Missions*, kindle edition.
[15] Vicedom, *The Mission of God: An Introduction to the Theology of Mission*.

classic articulation of the *missio dei*, Vicedom in no way intended for God's mission to be separated from the church's proclamation and activity. When Vicedom declared that we can no longer speak of the "mission of the church," he meant that the church should not see its work in the world apart from its source in the *missio dei*. Nevertheless, a flaw occurred in the application of the *missio dei* in the last century because of the undue separation of God's mission from the church.[16]

Tennant's concern is that in 20th, and 21st century evangelical mission philosophy the tendency has been to focus on the *church's sociological* aspects of mission as in the Church Growth Movement[17] rather than on the divine *involvement* and *empowerment* of the *Missio Dei*. He also expresses concern over the view that God works only in the kingdom or *Missio Dei* through the ministry of the church,

> Of course, this is not to imply that we should affirm that God works only in and through His church. Indeed, God often works both beyond and despite of the church to accomplish His redemptive plans. Nevertheless, central to a biblical vision of God's mission is that God does, in fact, work in and through His church and that it is central, not ancillary, to His mission. Indeed, the church is the only community Jesus Christ has specifically instituted to reflect the Trinity and to participate in His mission in the world.[18]

I particularly like Tennant's conclusion to the discussion and clarification of the difference between *mission* and *missions* which is the position I am taking in this book.

> So, a biblical missiology must be built firmly on the foundation of Trinitarian [divine] theology. Furthermore, it must be simultaneously God centered and church focused. In order to capture both of these realities, we need to make an important distinction between the words *mission* and *missions*. In this book, as noted earlier, *mission refers to God's redemptive, historical*

---

[16] Tennant, *Invitation to World Missions*, Kindle location 495ff. I have intentionally italicized *missio dei* in this quote from Tennant.
[17] Donald McGavran, et al, Fuller Theological Seminary in Pasadena, California.
[18] Tennant, *Invitation to World Missions*, kindle location 529f.

initiative on behalf of His creation. In contrast, *missions refers to all the specific and varied ways in which the church crosses cultural boundaries* to reflect the life of the triune God in the world and, *through that identity, participates in His mission*, celebrating through word and deed the inbreaking of the New Creation. Missions is made possible only at God's invitation. The title of this book, Invitation to World Missions, refers to God's gracious invitation to the church to participate in His mission in the world.[19]

Returning to my discussion of the singular *mission* and plural *missions, mission* as I understand the term can include both God's redemptive activity in the *Missio Dei*, and the sending church as it responds by sending missionaries out in the context of God's redemptive story from Abraham to Jesus in an evangelistic outreach to those not in covenant relationship with God. It can also include individual Christian's carrying out the *Missio Dei* through planting churches in the power of God and His Holy Spirit.

The plural *missions* I will use to refer to the various *ministries* of individuals or churches that are not specifically defined by church planting but are delineated by various significant ministries encapsuled in the *Missio Dei* such as benevolence, taking care of orphans, ministering to the homeless and becoming involved in social concerns without specifically engaging in planting churches and evangelism.

In other words, I understand *mission* in the singular in missiological terms to refer to God's redemptive work and the church's *mission* to extend that redemptive work through evangelism and the planting of communities of believers in Jesus, hence planting churches. I understand *missions* to refer to what Christians do by witnessing through good deeds such as benevolence, taking care of orphans and the homeless, and becoming involved in social services. They do this to witness to God's love extended through His *Missio Dei*.

My point will be that we should distinguish between *mission* and *missions*; mission refers to *Missio Dei* missional church evangelistic planting, and *Missio Ecclesiology* to *kingdom living* and good deeds such as benevolent work; all of which are encompassed under the Kingdom Theology *Missio Dei* but each with a distinct intention.

---

[19] Tennant, *Invitation to World Missions,* kindle location 537f.

Thus, benevolent work as important as it is we will define as *missions*, but technically not *mission*!

Hang in with me and this will become more distinct as we develop this study!

Evangelism

Since the last chapter introduced *Missio Dei* evangelism it would be appropriate at this point to examine what evangelism might look like in a postmodern environment.

Postmodern concerns and issues have challenged Christians to re-evaluate their approach to telling the story of Jesus.

Postmodern rejection of absolute truths and consequently church doctrine has forced Christians to find new and effective ways of communicating the story and truth about Jesus.

The story of Jesus in a postmodern context consequently is not best told through doctrine, but must be demonstrated first through transformed and concerned lives! That is, *kingdom living*! Kingdom living creates the *environment* in which the truth about Jesus can be encountered in a practical way. This can then be confirmed by gospel teaching.

Evangelism essentially relates to the root words *euaggelízō* meaning *to proclaim good news* and *euaggélion, gospel* or *good news*. The words have a long, broad, and deep history in several contexts in Greek history and culture.[20]

Evangelism could have referred to proclaiming the good news of the arrival of a new king, or merely proclaiming good news of a victory, or any other significant event. In the New Testament sense it was used of proclaiming the good news (*euaggélion*) regarding Jesus' present but not yet eschatological kingdom, or telling the story of God's saving activity in the death and resurrection of Jesus which consequently has deep kingdom implications. It is used in such a kingdom and atoning sense in Mark 16:15 *"Go into all the world and preach the gospel to the whole creation. He who believes and is baptized will be saved but he who does not believe will*

---

[20] Cf. the discussion of *euaggelízō* and *euaggélion* in the major Greek-English Lexicons and Dictionaries such as Zodhiates; Kittel; Bauer, Walter, William F. Arndt, and F. Wilbur Gingricht; *et al.*

be condemned."[21] The gospel message, the good news, was that Jesus had already introduced God's kingdom and in his death and resurrection had established God's kingdom with both present and future implications.

In previous years, which we might define as in an age of *modernism* in which rationalism and progress carried the day, evangelism focused on *teaching certain doctrines* relating to salvation and the church in an effort to convince people of the importance and truth of the doctrines.

Although I am well aware of the discussions relating to a postmodern reaction to a rational approach to faith I am not at all convinced that one has to jettison reason and teaching good news from faith development as is the desire of some. A postmodern persuasion should not be interpreted to mean that there are not certain Scriptures and doctrines that Christians should learn, honor, respect, and obey (Rom 6:17) in spite of the persuasion of some.

Nevertheless, for those who reject a doctrinal Scripture approach to life, new ways of communicating this good news must be discovered and developed. Failure to do this will result in our closing the kingdom to those who do not think like we do! As I mentioned above, this approach does not reject the role of Scripture and reason in the development of faith, but merely places it in a different order of communication.

Instruction in biblical *doctrine* (the Greek word for doctrine is *didaskalía* which means *teaching* or *instruction*[22]) goes far beyond fundamental instruction in the *form* of rules and regulations, or regulated *function* that the church should take, and how it should worship. A failure to understand *doctrine* simply as Christian *instruction* on how to live in the kingdom or church, rather than rules and regulations, is a truncated and misleading understanding of doctrine. Consequently, limiting doctrine to that which defines church structure and church liturgy has caused some to react to church as an outdated cultural structure and one which can summarily be jettisoned.[23]

---

[21] I am fully aware of the scholarly discussion on the short and long ending of Mark but am not convinced that this saying is not in keeping with the invention and preaching of Jesus.

[22] Zodhiates, *The Complete Word Study Dictionary: New Testament.*

[23] The reader should read Gerhard Delling, *Worship in the New Testament* and Fair, *A Biblical Theology of Worship,* in which Delling, along with Fair and others, stresses the essential role of doctrine and Scripture in an appropriate theology of the worship of God.

This point should not be interpreted to mean that the church does not need to mature in some of the ways in which it operates. In order to reach out to an unchurched population that has no feeling for, or at least has a misshapen understanding of what the church really is, the church has to first demonstrate that it is a loving concerned community of people whose desire is to be of service to the community in which it lives.

As we will shortly observe, the concept of church goes far beyond doctrine, form, and liturgy! Teaching biblical doctrine or *instruction* should involve spiritual formation in which disciples of Christ are instructed in the Christian faith, and how to live in such a manner that will bring glory to God in Christ (Eph 1:12; 1 Tim 4:1-5; 2 Tim 3:14-16; Heb 5:11-14) and be servants to the world.

Perhaps we should explain to those sensitive of, and negative toward, doctrine that *doctrine* in Matthean terms is *"teaching them to observe all that I have commanded you ..."*[24] Such teaching involves *basic guidance* regarding what it means to believe in Jesus, what the true meaning and purpose of baptism is in being united with Christ and his purpose, and becoming a disciple of Christ (Matt 28:20), of loving ones neighbor, and ministering to the hurting. In some religious contexts the instruction in doctrine is termed *catechesis,*[25] the *instruction* of new or young Christians in the *teachings* of their faith.

It is important that doctrine be more fully defined as instruction in the faith and life of followers of Jesus, and not simply church rules and regulations.

The tragedy is that much evangelistic instruction in Churches of Christ in the last century (the 20th century) related to doctrine defining the restoring of the "true" New Testament church as opposed to other churches; focusing more on church *form* doctrinal structure of the church than on Christ and his power to transform lives and give hope to a struggling community. Evangelists became expert in converting people from what was perceived to be a false form of church to the "true" New Testament church. The approach was based on rational debates or discussion on doctrines relating to the "true" church *form*. People were converted from one church to another church, albeit to what was perceived

---

[24] Matt 28:18-20.

[25] Catechesis and catechism. The terms and practice are most often used by Anglican, Lutheran, Methodist, Orthodox, Reformed/Presbyterian, and Roman Catholic Christians.

to be the "true" New Testament church! This worked as long as people in other churches would listen, but once that well dried up evangelism dried up!

Church of Christ failure to successfully reach out to non-churched groups who were postmodern in persuasion resulted in a demise in evangelism as a ministry in many churches in favor of preserving sound doctrine and the church membership through an emphasis on *indoctrination* of the local membership. The church became fixated on retaining its members rather than reaching out to the unchurched. The church turned inward, *centripetally* preserving its identity rather than *centrifugally* reaching out to the unchurched. Churches became experts in preserving sound doctrine and judging the false doctrines of others rather than proclaiming the glory of Christ to a lost world that did not think like Christians.

If the reader is uncomfortable with this point, all they need to do is count the number of people converted and baptized into Christ from the unchurched population. We have been fairly successful in baptizing our own children or teenagers, and that is commendable, but hardly evangelism as defined by Jesus in Matt 28:19, 20 and Acts 1:6ff. Such baptisms are more the result of *catechism* than *evangelism*!

The decline in church membership in Europe and the West over the last two decades[26] cries out for a renewal in *biblical evangelism* and a review of how Christians tell the story of Christ, rather than proclaiming and defending the form and structure of the church.

Whether we like it or not we are living in an increasingly secular non-rational postmodern age in which people have great distrust of universal truths arrived at through rational processes, and of an institutional form of church. Emotion and feeling become the criteria in determining what is

---

[26] Cf. John V. Rutledge, *A Church Has Gone To Hell: Southern Baptists: A Denomination in a Decade of Decline*, 2017. This report was written by a member of the Baptist church. Polk Culpepper, *Decline and Dysfunction in the American Church*, 2015; James A Haught, *Religion is Dying: Soaring Secularism in America and the West*, 2014. Haught writes nearly 400 Gazette editorials a year, plus occasional personal columns and news articles. Haught has won 21 national newswriting awards and is author of ten books and 85 national magazine articles. Thirty of his columns have been distributed by national syndicates. He also is a senior editor of *Free Inquiry* magazine. He is listed in Who's Who in America and Contemporary Authors.

true! However, in a biblical theological understanding, truth is more than rules and regulations. It is an emphasis on that which is truly genuine. Christians hold that it is Jesus who is ultimately genuine and should be the center of the gospel we proclaim, not the "true" identity of the New Testament church, as important as a genuine understanding of what church really is.

Postmoderns reject *doctrine* as final truth and that which is genuine, and look rather to a genuine life, however that may be defined! Christians need to explain to the postmodern culture or mindset that Jesus is indeed that which is genuine even when the church is perceived as not being truly genuine. Christians do this by demonstrating that genuine followers of Jesus are live genuine, caring, and trustful lives!

In a postmodern world truth is what works, or makes one feel good! This does not mean that Christians can no longer engage in evangelism and must surrender any concept of truth! It means that Christians have to approach evangelism in a manner that addresses skeptical minds. Christians should begin by establishing a relationship with people by respecting them where they are and gaining their respect by demonstrating a genuine life of concern for others. When the postmodern perceives Christians to be genuine, and that Christians believe in following someone who is genuine, they might be willing to listen to what Christians have to offer!

What Christians have to offer is a lifestyle and teaching about Jesus and his kingdom that is genuine and truly interested in and concerned for others, especially those who are hurting, and the observable advantages of living under the power of a great and genuine savior.

In a postmodern age a rational creedal approach to evangelism, defined in the sense of convincing people regarding doctrine and converting them to that doctrine most often results in a reaction against *doctrine* as the center of faith in favor of simply having a right relationship with God!

In this postmodern age we hear such remarks as "I am not interested in doctrine or church; I am concerned rather about having a right relationship with Christ." But this is what doctrine as Christian *instruction* regarding church life is all about; *bringing us into a right relationship with Christ and instructing us in how to live in a right relationship with Christ.* However, before the postmodern world will listen Christians will have to demonstrate through their faith and in their lives what such a right relationship with Christ really means. Only then will the postmodern be willing to listen.

As mentioned above doctrine understood as a set creedal form of rules and regulations is an imprecise definition of the Greek or biblical term *didaskalía* translated as *doctrine*. *Doctrine* as we have observed in a biblical theological context refers to *instruction*;[27] that instruction which "coaches" one regarding a right relationship with Jesus.

Effective evangelism, therefore, involves biblical instruction regarding the *good news* (*gospel*) relating to a new king who was willing to die for his community. The gospel relates to telling the real meaning of the story of the death and resurrection of this new king, Jesus, who is the center to God's plan for redeeming his hurting world. The gospel includes the teaching of a life lived in a good relationship with Jesus.

Evangelism is not simply Christians teaching a set of rules and regulations which must be rationally accepted and obeyed, but involves telling or demonstrating in their life the meaning of the story of Jesus in such a way that people will fall in love with Jesus, be instructed from Scripture how to believe in him, and how to be united with him in baptism.[28]

Evangelism therefore becomes convincing people, church members and the unchurched, about the advantages of living for Jesus. Yes, this does involve teaching them the good news revealed in Scripture regarding the genuineness of Jesus.

---

[27] Instruction or what is taught is the appropriate definition of the term doctrine. Cf. *didaskalía*; a noun from *didáskō*, to teach. *Doctrine is teaching or instruction*, Zodhiates, *The Complete Word Study Dictionary of the New Testament*.

[28] This is not the place to engage in a full discourse on the process of conversion or atonement other than to say that Scripture does explain that there is an appropriate response to believing the good news regarding Jesus. Certain texts such as Acts 2:17-41, Peter's great Pentecost sermon resulting in the conversion of over 3,000 Jews; Acts 8:26ff, the conversion of the Ethiopian Eunuch; Acts 10: 34-38, the conversion of Cornelius; Acts 16:25-33, the conversion of the Philippian jailor and his household each explain what people were taught after they believed in the story of Jesus. In each case when they heard the story of Jesus and believed this story, they desired to be baptized, thus being united with Jesus in baptism in his death and resurrection to a new life, Rom 6:1-5. Cf. also Gal 3:25-29.

My point is that evangelism is not a bad word that the church should shy away from. It is simply explaining to people that we have a great story and savior to which there is an appropriate response to believing in the great story of Jesus. In a postmodern age the approach of evangelism should not be through a rational recitation of rules and regulations to be believed and obeyed. *One lays the groundwork in evangelism by demonstrating to people that Christians are genuinely interested in them and that as Christians we have a story we would like to share with them about a savior that loves them and who can through a meaningful relationship with him empower them to rise above their present circumstances. The opening of peoples' lives to Jesus in many cases will only come through Christians demonstrating Jesus' love for people through their genuine love and concern for them.*

Before you have a religious faith heart attack and write me and this book off as heresy, you should note that scripture and doctrine correctly understood and interpreted is the foundation on which Christian faith is built. Good works and benevolence, as explained earlier, are the vehicle that opens the door to sound biblical instruction, and not the foundation of faith in Jesus and a good relationship with Jesus. That is the role of Scripture and doctrine.

The story of evangelism is not complete with doing good deeds and benevolent activity without explaining that a real relationship with Jesus results from truly believing (*faith and trusting*) in Jesus as a genuine leader, and deciding to turn one's life over to him (*repentance*) thus being *united* with him in baptism (Rom 6:1-5; Gal 3:25-29). But that is not the end story of evangelism! By the example of our own lives and leading the seeker to a life of discipleship in Jesus through Christian instruction and example, we all grow into a new creation in Jesus (Eph 4:23, 24; Col 3:10; 2 Cor 3:18).

My paraphrase of Matthew 28:19-20 puts this in a proverbial nutshell, "Go therefore and *make disciples of Jesus* among all nations, *baptizing and uniting them to Jesus* in the name of the Father and of the Son and of the Holy Spirit, [20] *teaching and instructing* them *by word and example* to observe all that I have commanded you *about Christian living*; and lo, I am with you always, to the close of the age."[29]

---

[29] For the purist I emphasize again, this is my personal paraphrase of the great commission based on Matthew 28:19-20.

Evangelism and doctrine are not bad news and something we should shy away from. *Evangelism* is *good news* showing by example and telling people the genuineness of Jesus; what God has done for them through Jesus' death and resurrection, and what he wants to do for them in a real relationship with himself. *Doctrine* is instructing one regarding the kind of life that best testifies to the genuineness of faith in Jesus. *Evangelism must first be lived then told!* Doctrine is the telling! Evangelism is incomplete until the full story is told. That is what spiritual formation is all about!

The Church

As mentioned previously, contrary to popular conception, the *English* term *church* actually derives from the German word *Kirche* which in turn derives from the Greek *kuriakós* meaning "belonging to the lord." The word *church* in our English versions of the Bible is a poor "translation" of the Greek world *ekklēsia* which actually means an *assembly,* a *congregation,* or a *community* of people who have *gathered* together for some purpose; civic or religious.

However because of our heritage in the Wycliffe, Tyndale, and King James Bible legacy we are "stuck" with this unfortunate translation! I am nevertheless comfortable with the concept that *church* refers to the *people who attend* some *congregation* or church and *who worship and serve God and Christ* in that *church congregation*! I do like the concept ensconced in the German Kirche from *kuriakós* which implies that the church is a body of people who *belong to the Lord*!

The background behind the New Testament use of *ekklēsia* lies in both a Greek and Jewish usage of *ekklēsia,* both related to the root meaning of the word. In the Greek sense it referred to a *community* or *gathering* of people in an *assembly* to *conduct business of some sort.* The Septuagint Jewish use of the word referred to the *congregation* of Israel who *assembled* or lived in *community* around the Tabernacle or Temple which represented the presence of God in their midst. The Jews were the *congregation* of Israel or the Lord.[30] When Jesus established his *ekklēsia,*

---

[30] Cf. L. Coenen, "Church," *New Testament Theology,* ed. Colin Brown, Vol. 1, pp. 291ff; Hans Kung, *The Church,* pp. 81ff.; Ferguson, *The Church of Christ, A Biblical Ecclesiology for Today,* pp. 129ff.; Arndt and Gingrich, *A Greek-English Lexicon of the New Testament,* Cambridge: University of Chicago Press, *ekklēsia.*

church, or *community of believers,* he took the place of the Temple representing the presence of God in the believer's lives. The *church* became the *community* of "Jesus believers" who *assembled* in *worship and service* of God and *to carry out God's Missio Dei.* This *ekklēsia* of Jesus, which soon after its establishment as a community of "Jesus Believers" spread widely throughout Judea and the Mediterranean region. They gathered or *assembled* in *local congregations* in order to worship God and Jesus, support one another, and bring forward God's *Missio Dei*.

One of the interesting features ensconced in the term *ekklēsia* is that the calling out of the people was primarily forward looking to a meeting with a purpose in mind involving some action or decision.[31] Thus, if we prefer to emphasize the sense of a group *called out,* we should include the sense *of being called out* to a meeting *for a purpose,* not simply a calling out of the world. The focus should be on the purpose, not the source of the group called!

When we speak of the church we do not have in mind a building although the term *ekklēsia* could be used to refer to the place of the assembly. When Jesus said to Peter in Matt 16:18 "on this rock *I will build my church* and the powers of death shall not prevail against it..." (RSV) he did not have in mind a building! He had in mind a *community of believers* who as his disciples would build their new lives on and around his divinity and carry out is mission.

The church is therefore a *community* of *"Jesus people"*! They are followers of Jesus, the Messiah. They are not like Judaism, centered on the Law of Moses and the Temple or Synagogue! They are not like the Gentile world, focused on idolatry. They are different! *They are "Jesus people"*! Their lives are built on and established in the person of Jesus and his mission. They are *a new community* of believers *born again* into the kingdom, John 3:3-5. They are the new family of God; a *community* built on and following Jesus!

The question that challenges many is whether Jesus had in mind a *universal church* or community of believers as opposed to a *local church* or community of believers. It is my opinion that this misses the point! It is misleading to think that one can separate the two churches, the universal and the local. They are one community of believers in contrast to the

---

[31] Cf. Zodhiates, ἐκκλησία, *ekklēsia*.

Jewish and Gentile communities who comprised two "communities." Christians by their faith in Jesus and obedience to his gospel were brought into *a new community of Jesus people*. They found themselves *assembling* in *local communities* or *congregations*[32] of believers! At Matt 16:18 Jesus was merely speaking of a new messianic community of believers in contrast to the nation of Israel.

Some find in Eph 1:22 and Col 1:18 references to a universal church since in these texts the church is identified as the body of Christ which in the mind of some surely should be universal. However, that is not necessarily the case since at 1 Cor 12 Paul is obviously referring to the local congregation when he observes that by the one Spirit they have all been baptized into the one body. The issue in Corinth was that they were dividing the body into several elitist groups, ignoring the poor, instead of preserving the unity of the body, the Corinthian church, 1 Cor 1:10-17.

Some scholars challenge whether there is such a separate entity as the universal church since all Christians in Scripture are found in local congregations! Others focus on the universal or catholic[33] nature of the church recognizing that the local church is but a reflection of the universal church.[34] The question in my mind as I read Scripture is moot in that all Christians are in the new community of believers in Jesus, both Jew and Greek, slave and free, male and female, Gal 3:26-28, but they find themselves living and serving in local communities or congregations.

Others observe in a somewhat negative reaction to church membership, "Is not the kingdom greater than the church or churches! Is it not possible for a Christian to be a member of the kingdom of God and not be a member of a local congregation?" The answer to that should be obvious; of course the kingdom is greater if we mean older or more encompassing than the term or concept of church since the kingdom has

---

[32] We must remember that the terms church, assembly, community, and congregation are all translations according to context of the one Greek word, *ekklēsia*. They are a *community* of believers who *assemble* in different *congregations* to carry out the messianic mission.

[33] By *catholic* I do not have the Roman Catholic Church in mind. The term *catholic* means *general, the whole,* or *universal*. It derives from the Latin *catholicus* or Greek *kathalou*, Shorter Oxford English Dictionary, 1933, 1972.

[34] L. Coenen, "Church," *Dictionary of New Testament Theology*, vol. 1, pp. 298ff; Hans Kung, *The Church*, pp. 169ff; 342ff, *passim*; Ferguson, *The Church of Christ: A Biblical Ecclesiology for Today, passim* but notably pp. 129ff.

existed since creation. The question we must ask is what we mean by greater! Greater in what sense? Perhaps we should rephrase the question and ask "Does the term or concept of kingdom involve more than the church?" The answer to that is also obvious since the kingdom of God predates the church of Christ by several thousand years! Israel as *the former community of God* had been part of God's kingdom but by losing faith Israel had lost that privilege. The church as *the new community of Christ* came into existence as the new community of God and Christ only after his death and resurrection. Yet the church as the new community of God and Christ forms an important and vital part of the overall kingdom of Christ.

It is simply neither biblically nor theologically possible for a person to be a Christian and member of the church which belongs to Christ and not be a member of the kingdom, and likewise it is neither biblically nor theologically possible for a Christian to be a member of the kingdom and not be a member of the church or community of believers that belongs to Jesus!

As we will learn in this study, the terms kingdom and church point to or define two different concepts or characteristics of the people of God. The *kingdom* defines those who have always lived under the *reign* and *sovereignty* of God. This reign and sovereignty of God would have included faithful Abraham and faithful Israel who were the community of Israel under YHWH but were not yet the community of the Messiah, Jesus. The *church* refers to those who through Jesus' death are born again into the kingdom of God and the *community* or church of Jesus and who assemble for worship and service in the *Missio Dei* in local congregations.

The *church* or *community* of Jesus is those who have been united with Jesus' death and resurrection through being baptized into his death and resurrection, Rom 6:1-11, and who now are alive to God *in Christ Jesus*. They assemble in congregations of "Jesus believers" who worship God and carry out his *Missio Dei*. My point is if you are a Christian you have been *united with Christ in his body which is the church*, not simply born into the kingdom! Note Gal 3:26 "for in Christ Jesus you are all sons of God, through faith. [27] For as many of you as were *baptized into Christ have put on Christ.*[28] There is neither Jew nor Greek, there is neither slave nor free, there is neither male nor female; for you are all one in Christ Jesus." Note also 1 Cor 12:13, "For by one Spirit we were all *baptized into one body*—Jews or Greeks, slaves or free—and all were made to drink of one Spirit." We must keep this text in context! When Paul speaks of the body in 1 Corinthians he is speaking to members of the *church* or *congregation* in Corinth.

Unfortunately, there are times when members of the kingdom living as members of a local congregation by their lifestyle individually or corporately demonstrate that they are not living under the reign of Christ in that they live more in the world than in Christ. It would be difficult to define them as members of the kingdom or reign of Christ since they are not living in Christ and do not manifest the characteristics of disciples of Christ!

Likewise, there have been and are times when Christians are not active members of a local community! This is unfortunate! It is a characteristic of true Christians that they are members of the kingdom of Christ and the community of Jesus believers that they identify in community with fellow Jesus believers. Aquila and Priscilla were expelled from Rome and travelled throughout the Christian world as "missionaries" or "teachers" but when they arrived at a place where a Christian community or church existed they immediately attached themselves to the Christian fellowship and community, Acts 18:1ff.

> After this he (Paul) left Athens and went to Corinth. *² And he found a Jew named Aquila, a native of Pontus, lately come from Italy with his wife Priscilla, because Claudius had commanded all the Jews to leave Rome. And he went to see them; ³ and because he was of the same trade he stayed with them, and they worked, for by trade they were tentmakers. ⁴ And he argued in the synagogue every sabbath, and persuaded Jews and Greeks ... After this Paul stayed many days longer, and then took leave of the brethren and sailed for Syria, and with him Priscilla and Aquila. At Cenchre-ae he cut his hair, for he had a vow. ¹⁹ And they came to Ephesus, and he left them there; but he himself went into the synagogue and argued with the Jews. ²⁰ When they asked him to stay for a longer period, he declined; ²¹ but on taking leave of them he said, "I will return to you if God wills," and he set sail from Ephesus. ²² When he had landed at Caesarea, he went up and greeted the church, and then went down to Antioch. ²³ After spending some*

> *time there he departed and went from place to place through the region of Galatia and Phrygia, strengthening all the disciples.*
> *^{24} Now a Jew named Apollos, a native of Alexandria, came to Ephesus. He was an eloquent man, well versed in the scriptures. ^{25} He had been instructed in the way of the Lord; and being fervent in spirit, he spoke and taught accurately the things concerning Jesus, though he knew only the baptism of John. ^{26} He began to speak boldly in the synagogue; but when Priscilla and Aquila heard him, they took him and expounded to him the way of God more accurately.*

Wherever they were and whenever there was a church community meeting Aquila and Priscilla attached themselves to the local congregation and worshipped and worked as members of that congregation.

The New Testament picture of Christians is that they are baptized into the one body of Christ which is the *church or community of Jesus believers*. In that body they became members of the "universal" church but also of a local congregation in which they serve and worship God and Jesus and carry out God's *Missio Dei*.

In the New Testament the congregations were called *churches* implying they formed *communities* established by Jesus' life, death, and resurrection. The concept of a Christian floating free from a local church or congregation yet being a member of the kingdom is completely alien to the New Testament. It may sound sociologically elitist and "postmodernist," but it is profoundly unbiblical and out of sync with Scripture!

Timothy Tennant speaks to the concept of personal salvation and possible membership in the kingdom in a discussion on salvation and church membership:

> Third, the theology of missionaries, especially Protestant missionaries, has tended to be influenced by an overly individualistic and pietistic understanding of salvation … Let me clearly say at the outset of this point that I believe in the necessity of personal conversion and its centrality to the New Testament kerygma. However, let me also clearly state that biblical salvation encompasses much more than individual conversion. Salvation also inherently implies incorporation into a community. We are not

just baptized by faith; we are baptized into a faith that is shared by a community that exists in space around the world and back through time. *Indeed, there are aspects of salvation that can be experienced and known only within the church as the redeemed community and cannot be realized in isolation from that community.* The New Testament celebrates a salvific transformation that has both vertical and horizontal dimensions. Personal salvation in the New Testament is inextricably linked to becoming part of the new humanity of Eph 2:15.[35]

Commenting further to the point that salvation, church membership, and kingdom are an integral part of both soteriology and ecclesiology Tennant quotes Simon Chan;

> ... the church is not merely an instrument to accomplish God's purposes; the church is the "expression of God's ultimate purpose itself ... We need to see ecclesiology as an intrinsic part of the doctrine of the gospel of Jesus Christ, not an administrative arrangement for the sake of securing practical results."[36]

My purpose in introducing Tennant's and Chan's observation at this point is to emphasize that it is neither biblically nor theologically sound to separate personal salvation, membership in the church, and membership in the kingdom.

The separation of the church and the kingdom into two separate and independent entities is unsustainable both theologically and scripturally. Likewise to separate kingdom living from church living cannot be supported either theologically or ecclesiologically.

In the minds of some the term *church* today carries with it a negative connotation. This has been and still is true in some situations or mindsets. There have been times when churches have not lived up to the lofty calling to which Jesus called them but that is no justification to denigrate or discard the concept of or term church. Because of the failure of some churches, some reject the concept of church mainly *because of negative personal issues with the church*. Others do so because they have bought into a postmodern secular negative propaganda regarding religion and

---

[35] Tennent. *Invitation to World Missions: A Trinitarian Missiology for the Twenty-first Century*, kindle locations 572ff.
[36] Tennent, kindle location 580ff.

church. *Unfortunately, such perceptions are mostly based on personal experience and on what has been heard via the various news, or read in the printed media, or on what others have said.* In many cases the perception is based more on what a secular or postmodern culture has imprinted in their minds rather than on fact. This is unfortunate! These comments however are not to imply that some have not had negative experiences with church life. We have to admit and confess that Christians and churches have not always conducted themselves in a manner desired of followers of Jesus.

However, in contrast to such negative perceptions, many people are most positive about their experiences in churches and not in any manner negative about the concept of church or their experience in church life. They have found much to be commended in church membership and church fellowship.

In contrast to such negative propaganda many Millennials and others from similar young generational or gender groups are being drawn to the church all over the world because of the positive environment provided by fellowship in churches while living in a hostile and corrupt world. We need only to notice the growth of non-traditional churches, bible churches, fellowship churches, and community churches in the United States and all over Africa and other parts of the world.

I recognize that in some regions and nations the church is in decline but one should not extrapolate from this or these experiences that this decline is universal. Christianity and churches are growing and flourishing in many nations throughout the world. In Europe and parts of the United States a secular and disinterested mindset has developed, but in Africa, South and Central America, Asia and the East this is not the case and one should not project a negative Western experience or attitude toward church into a universal mindset.

For instance, it has been argued by some in Rwanda that because of the genocide of 1994 in that nation people are negative about church because of the failure of the church to stand against the genocide, and in some cases, to propagate it. We must admit that some churches failed miserably, mostly due to ethnic and political prejudices.[37]

---

[37] Cf. Timothy Longman, *Christianity and Genocide in Rwanda*, Cambridge: Cambridge University Press, 2010.

The issue, however, in Rwanda was not simply a church versus political/cultural phenomenon but rather ethnic Hutu versus Tutsi cleansing and positioning for power. The deplorable failure of some churches and the political community in Rwanda during the genocide years has been well documented. However, in the years succeeding the resolution of the genocide atrocities new churches calling themselves churches are today being planted in Rwanda in an encouraging manner, and they are growing. A simple survey on the internet will reveal positive church growth and expansion in Rwanda. It is my opinion, based on research in the era of 1995-2012 regarding church growth in Rwanda, that those making a case that church has a negative impact on Christianity and evangelism in Rwanda are basing their views more on personal presuppositions and persuasions than on fact.[38] This should not be interpreted to mean that the suffering from the genocide was not real and lasting, or that there remains no negative reaction to the church in Rwanda. Nor should it be interpreted to mean that there are not some difficulties to be dealt with in church planting in Rwanda for government regulation does impose some restrictions. However, the gospel has through centuries of church and Christian persecution thrived because of the positive message proclaimed and lived by sincere Christians in a negative and corrupt world.

We should remember that Christians in the first century were not doing church work, mission, and evangelism in a friendly culture! The Roman Empire did not appreciate their allegiance to Jesus Christ as Lord! Churches and Synagogues ran into continued problems in Rome and Christians and Jews were repeatedly expelled from Rome as in the case of Priscilla and Aquila. Calling on Jesus as Lord could and often did result in a most cruel death. The pivotal center of Christian faith and theology was the crucifixion of Jesus. Crucifixion in the Graeco-Roman culture had a negative connotation and defined one as either a criminal or a traitor but Christians did not deny the term crucifixion or drop it from their vocabulary because it could lead to ridicule and rejection by their pagan

---

[38] Southern Baptist, Missionary Baptist, Lutheran, Seventh Day Adventists, and several other Christian mission efforts have enjoyed considerable success over the last decade in church planning in Rwanda.

neighbors! Paul records[39] that in spite of Corinthian and Jewish rejection of the crucifixion he still made it the central point of his gospel.

The Jews were as guilty as the Romans in their persecution of the Christians and many Christians were reported to the Romans for persecution and martyrdom because of their rejection of Jewish traditional religious practices and culture. The Jews and the Synagogue in Smyrna played a significant role in the martyrdom and death of the aged Christian bishop of Smyrna, Polycarp.[40] Church history reports that it was the Jews that collected the wood for burning Polycarp at the stake. Government and cultural opposition did not discourage or negate Christian preaching of the Lordship of Jesus and establishing communities of Jesus believers.

Whenever missionaries carry the Christian message into new and foreign cultures some resistance can be expected but this should not result in a rejection or denial of fundamental Christian doctrines such as resurrection and church.

Certainly, church planting and evangelism have had to be revisited and re-defined in the face of the failure of Christians to live up to the standards outlined in the Gospels. The challenges of postmodern concerns have fortuitously caused Christians to rethink their approach to evangelism.

However, in spite of the failure of churches in the Western culture and in nations like Rwanda, Christianity and church planting continue to thrive all over the world albeit in different degrees of success. My point is that Christians need not drop or retreat from significant concepts like the church, the crucifixion, resurrection, and Jesus Christ, simply because some do not like the concepts or have had poor experiences with the church and similar Christian faith fundamentals.

Since Jesus introduced the term church and died for it, and since the term and concept of church appears over 100 times in 106 verses of our New Testament,[41] one would assume that church is a significant and central element in the Christian faith and one for which we hope we would be willing to die rather than one from which we would simply walk away!

---

[39] 1 Cor 1:17- 25.
[40] Eusebius *Ecclesiastical History*, Vol. 1, Loeb Classical Library, pp. 335ff, *passim* on early Christian martyrdom for the name Jesus.
[41] The Greek word for church, ἐκκλησία, *ekklēsia* in its various forms likewise occurs over 100 times in regard to the *church, congregation,* or *community* of Jesus.

Dean Flemming in his insightful book on *Patterns for Theology of Mission, Contextualization in the New Testament* observed with keen perception and understanding the conflicting cultural issues missionaries face when working under difficult and sometimes hostile situations. Earlier in his discussion and definition of contextualization Flemming comments regarding the danger of missionaries compromising their gospel message because of local culture "taboos":

> With economic hardship, social ostracism and perhaps some form of local persecution awaiting those who spurned the normal cultural expectations, the temptation to accommodate would have been intense.[42]
>
> ... I take contextualization, then, to refer to the dynamic and comprehensive process by which the gospel is incarnated within a concrete historical or cultural situation. This happens in such a way that the gospel both comes to authentic expression in the local context and at the same time prophetically transforms the context. Contextualization seeks to enable the people of God to live out the gospel in obedience to Christ within their own cultures and circumstances.[43]

My point is that missionaries and evangelists *need not* jettison fundamental doctrines in new cultures but must be able to contextualize their message in order to be relevant in the new situation or context. One way to contextualize church in a negative culture is to demonstrate by Christ-like and Spirit-filled living that church when appropriately understood has much to offer new cultures.

Social Justice and Benevolent Concerns and Interests

The Lausanne Covenant of 1974 brought together Evangelical missiologists from a broad spectrum of traditions. The influences of the post-Death of God and the Secularization of Christianity movement of John A. T. Robinson and Harvey Cox was apparent in the concerns

---

[42] Dean Flemming. *Contextualization in the New Testament: Patterns for Theology and Mission*, kindle locations, 3407f.
[43] Flemming, *Contextualization*, kindle location, 123. I refer readers seeking further information regarding Christianity and culture to Abraham Malherbe's 1983 publication, *Social Aspects of Early Christianity*, Philadelphia: Fortress Press.

expressed, as was the influence of emerging Liberation Theologies following Jürgan Moltmann's "theology of hope" and Gustavo Gutiérrez, and others liberation thinking. Serious concern was expressed over traditional mission theology's neglect of the social injustices of a large population of what would soon be defined as developing nations. The ethnic and social inequities experienced in many advanced nations such highlighted by the Civil Rights movements in the USA, the anti-Apartheid rebellions in South Africa, and the economic disparities of India weighed heavily on the missiologists' thinking and concerns. In many instances the conclusions that were drawn weighed more heavily on the social justice side of the balance than on the spiritual side. The spiritual evangelistic side of the equation of missiology was not ignored but became more of a secondary concern to social injustices.

Integrating two major concerns, the spiritual and the social human conditions challenged many such as Lesslie Newbigin and leaders in the Church Growth Movement of the former Fuller School of World Mission, now the Fuller School of Intercultural Studies. The discussions among followers of the Lausanne Covenant resulted in a meeting of missiologists in Manila in the Philippines in 1989. That conference produced the Manila Manifesto in support of the Lausanne Covenant. In recent years since the Manila Manifesto several evangelical scholars have addressed this integration of the spiritual/evangelization and social justice concerns. I will shortly likewise address this integration under Figure 4 below.

The Kingdom of God and Jesus, Church, Mission, and the *Missio Dei*

Theologically we must understand that the concepts of the *Missio Dei*, the kingdom of God, the church, and mission are integrally and inseparably related. Failure to understand the *Missio Dei* as the mission of God in which he has been engaged since the call of Abraham truncates the full understanding of kingdom theology. Failure to see the mission of Jesus and the church in the context and theology of the *Missio Dei* of bringing the whole world under God's sovereign reign and kingdom mission will result in a shrunken view of kingdom theology. Failure to understand that God has called the church into his *Missio Dei* will naturally result in our not fully understanding the real meaning of the kingdom of God. A failure to understand that the kingdom of God is all about the *Missio Dei* and is therefore fundamentally *missional* and involves the church engaging actively in the *Missio Dei* will result in a truncated view of the kingdom. We should note that the *Missio Dei* and kingdom theology are intricately not internally *centripetally* focused but are outreaching and *centrifugally* driven. The sad point is that today many churches are more concerned and driven by internal concerns than for God's and their mission in the world.

Four Figures Relating to Kingdom Theology, the *Missio Dei*, Church, Mission, and Missions

In the following **Four Figures** I have schematically diagrammed my understanding of the relationships between kingdom theology, the *Missio Dei*, mission, the local church, church ministries, and a lost and alienated world. I encourage you to examine these figures carefully in order to grasp the integration and interrelationships of these kingdom and *Missio Dei* concepts.

Figure 1 will set the four figures in the context of God's *Missio Dei* by citing Eph 1:3-12 and setting the kingdom of God within God's eternal purpose.

Figure 2 will demonstrate that Mission, Benevolence, Spiritual Formation, Social Justice, and Kingdom Living are all ministries within the *Missio Dei*.

Figure 3 explains that in the *Missio Dei* God works through churches which function within the kingdom of God.

Figure 4 demonstrates that kingdom churches function through a variety of ministries.

FIGURE 1

THE KINGDOM OF GOD
AND
THE MISSIO DEI
What is God Doing in the World?

God is putting the world right again!
He is doing this through His covenant with Abraham
to bless all nations.
He achieves this through Jesus Christ
and
the many ministries of the Church.

Christians bring glory to God and the *Missio Dei*
through Christ and the church!
Eph 1:3-12

"Blessed be the God and Father of our Lord Jesus Christ, who has blessed us in Christ with every spiritual blessing in the heavenly places, [4] even as he chose us in him before the foundation of the world, that we should be holy and blameless before him. [5] He destined us in love to be his sons through Jesus Christ, according to the purpose of his will, [6] to the praise of his glorious grace which he freely bestowed on us in the Beloved. [7] In him we have redemption through his blood, the forgiveness of our trespasses, according to the riches of his grace [8] which he lavished upon us. [9] _For he has made known to us in all wisdom and insight the mystery of his will, according to his purpose which he set forth in Christ_ [10] _as a plan for the fulness of time, to unite all things in him, things in heaven and things on earth._ [11] In him, according to the purpose of him who accomplishes all things according to the counsel of his will, [12] we who first hoped in Christ have been _destined and appointed to live for the praise of his glory._"

Figure 1

The Kingdom and the *Missio Dei*

As I will explain more fully in later chapters one must always keep kingdom thinking and the *Missio Dei* within God's covenant promise to Abraham and Israel. In his covenant with Abraham God has been working to set the world right again after the fall of man. For many the quick fix is to begin with the various formulations of the Great Commission contextually repeated in the four Gospels. However, mission and the *Missio Dei* must be seen and interpreted within the greater story of God's redemption which began with God's call and covenant with Abraham unfolding through the history of Israel in the Old Testament and culminating in Jesus' kingdom ministry as outlined in the Gospels, and carried forward by the church.

The danger of losing sight of the inextricable relationship between the *Missio Dei* and God's covenant with Abraham and kingdom theology is that the dynamic and power of the church's missiological and ministry efforts is either diminished or possibly even abdicated. Kingdom living, kingdom ministry, and kingdom mission have meaning and purpose only when set within or driven by the *Missio Dei* and consequently by kingdom missional theology. Mission, ministry, and kingdom living thus become misguided and lacking a suitable compass point when removed from or not driven by kingdom theology and the *Missio Dei*.

Kingdom theology and the *Missio Dei* serve to remind us of what God is doing in our world, and what the real purpose of the church is.

Eph 1:3-12 reminds us that we have been called by God to be his children according to a purpose God inaugurated even before creation. His purpose in Christ was to unite all creation and restore it back to its created order. The church was destined by God in Christ to so live that it would bring glory to God through Christ as Christians play their preordained role in God's purpose or *Missio Dei*.

FIGURE 2

THE MISSIO DEI
What is God Doing in the World?

He is putting the world right again!
He is doing this through His covenant with Abraham
to bless all nations.
He achieves this through Jesus Christ
and
the many ministries of the Church.

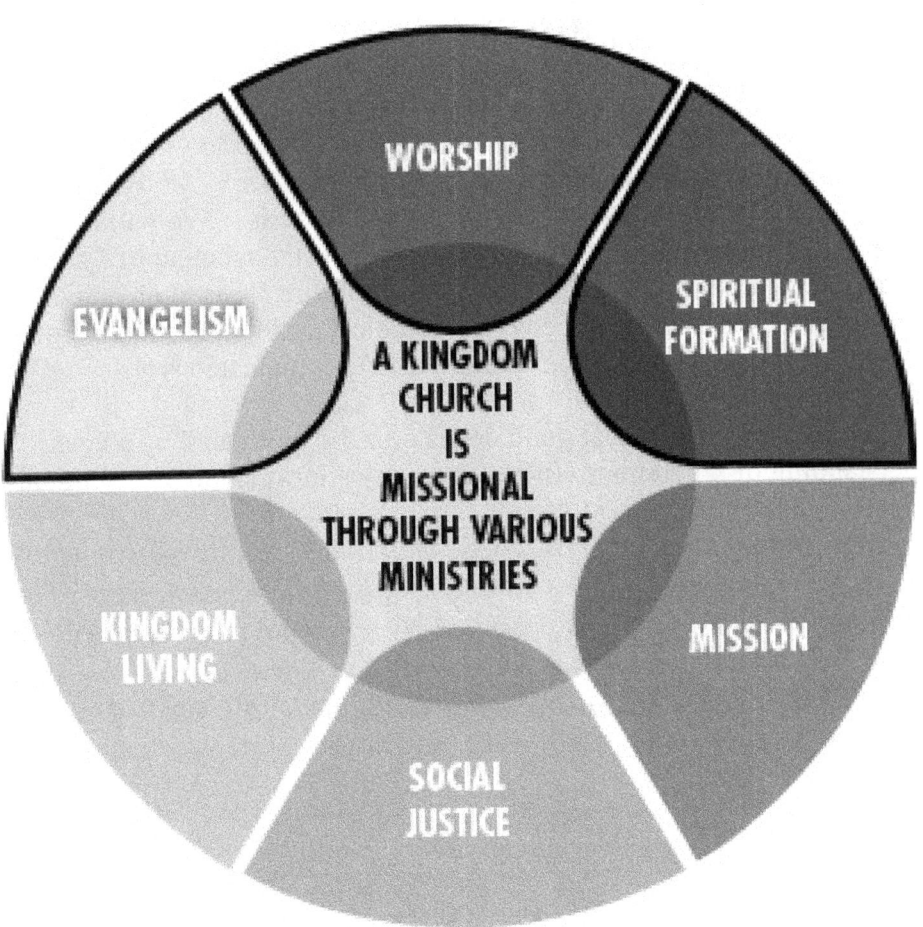

Figure 2

The *Missio Dei* and the Kingdom:

We will learn that Jesus' ministry and mission was all about restoring the kingdom of God on earth. Through Jesus God was fulfilling his promise to Abraham and putting the world right again. This is the fundamental nature of the kingdom; God reigning in the lives of people and through those people reaching out into the world, extending his kingdom. That is the heart of mission! That is the heart of the kingdom! The kingdom is essentially missional in nature. The church or God's people reach out to the world through many ministries such as Worship, Evangelism, Missions, Benevolence, Spiritual Formation (Christian education and maturation), Benevolence, Social Justice and other service efforts. When these are not motivated by an evangelistic awareness of the *Missio Dei* and kingdom theology they are reduced to good deeds more of a social concern than of a redemptive nature. Christians are good people and want to do good deeds but when this loses its *Missio Dei* dynamic the good deeds become simply a benevolent social function. We will note in figure 4 that the goal of kingdom mission is the establishment of communities of believers, churches, whose lives are focused on and driven by Jesus as they nurture the needy and homeless and witness to the power of Jesus' death and resurrection through the communicated word, evangelism and good deeds.

Figure 2 reminds us that good deeds must be motivated by a keen understanding of kingdom missional theology and what God is doing in this world, hence, the *Missio Dei*.

The kingdom reign of God must always maintain its missional dynamic for this is what God intended in his covenant with Abraham and this is what he is doing in his world! He is preeminently missional in his concern for his world. When the church is not missional and engaged in mission then the church is not engaged in the kingdom of God and the Missio Dei!

FIGURE 3

THE MISSIO DEI
What is God Doing in the World?

He works through local churches which function within the Kingdom of God

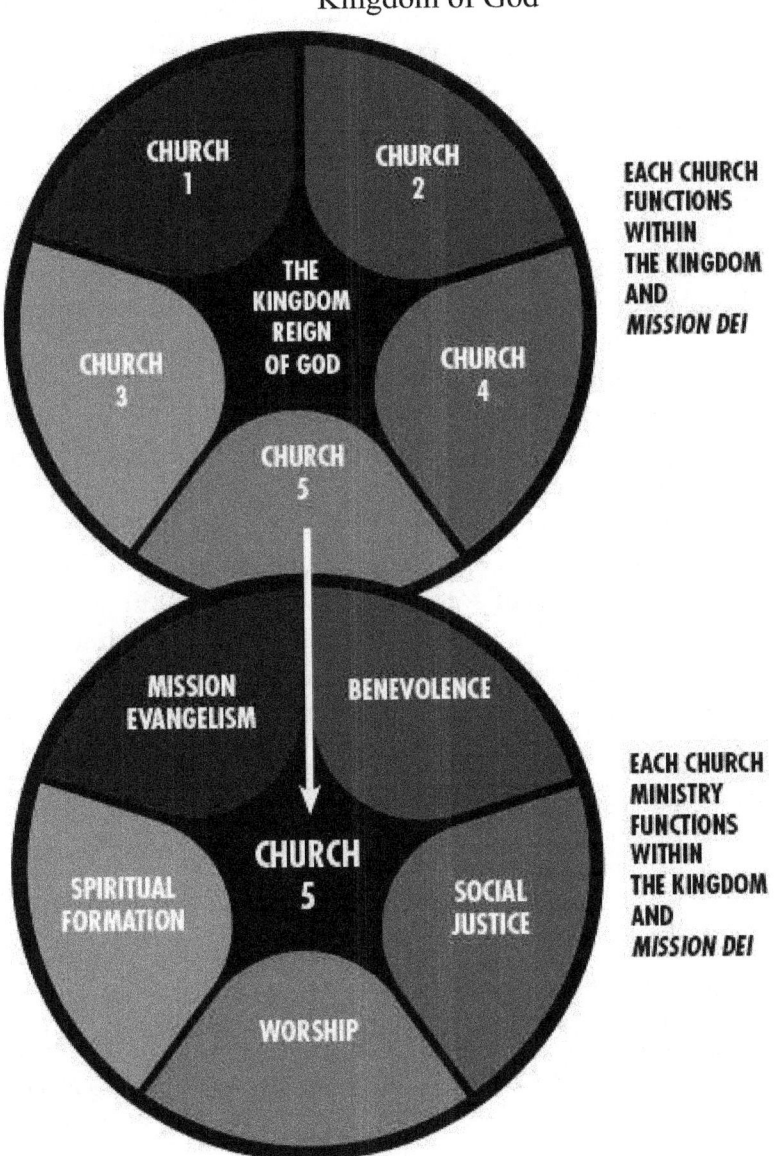

Figure 3

The Kingdom and the Church:

Understanding the relationship of the church to the kingdom has been a challenge to Christian theology for centuries, giving rise to much millennial confusion. At times more emphasis has been given to the church[44] than to the kingdom and at other times more to the kingdom[45] than to the church! Scholars are correct in pointing out that one should not equate the kingdom and the church, but at the same time one should not place one above the other! Both are essential ingredients in the *Missio Dei*.

In our postmodern culture many are raising questions as to the importance and necessity of the local church or the role that a local church should play in the *Missio Dei*. On the mission field a younger generation of "missionaries"[46] finds no need to be in the church business in the sense of planting churches or getting involved in evangelism and the conversion of the people they might be working with. I hear the remark that mission work is working or living alongside the "natives"[47] helping them deal with the sociological issues and injustices of their culture. I will argue on solid biblical and theological grounds that this is not kingdom mission but is kingdom benevolence!

There is a trend on the part of a postmodern generation to denigrate or discard the notion of church since churches have in many cases become a negative concept in the minds of some. This is not the first time that an alien and hostile world has turned against Christians and the church. Ever since the first century the church as an organized body has been criticized, demeaned, and persecuted. The same phenomenon can be traced in

---

[44] This was a major fault in the Restoration Movement of Churches of Christ in the USA especially in the divisive era following the civil war, and later following the conflict-ridden debates over premillennialism, 1940-1960.

[45] This is seen particularly in the kingdom millennial issues of postmillennialism, premillennialism, and dispensational theology.

[46] I use the term missionary lightly as it is common to use the term broadly to cover any kind of involvement on a distant field whether it is more benevolent, social justice, or some other form of ministering to the needs of people. I hold to the classical use of the term as in David Bosch, *Transforming Mission: Paradigm Shifts in Theology of Missions*, Eckhard Schnabel, *Paul the Missionary: Realities, Strategies and Methods, passim*.

[47] I use the term native in a non-derogatory manner to refer to the peoples of the mission field who are *native* to that field.

different situations through the centuries of church history with the church itself at times persecuting the church!

The church can be seen in at least two ways; *one*, as a community of people who driven by their human fallibility have failed to be the living body of Christ. In this regard church history reveals that the church has a poor record of being the kingdom. Or, *two*, the church can be seen as a community of people for whom Christ died and who have been brought into a new relationship with God through the body of Christ, the church, and who through that body or church seek to serve God and their fellow man to the best of their ability in the spirit of Christ.

I recognize that Jesus had more to say about the kingdom than he said about the church, but then again the Apostle Paul had more to say about the church than the kingdom! The reality is a matter of context, that is, the context of their ministries. Jesus' ministry was to inaugurate the kingdom of God and a community of people, the church *(ekklēsia)*, who would play a profound part and ministry in Jesus' kingdom. Paul came to explain how in the context of his mission to the Gentiles the *Missio Dei* would become a real living entity in the context of communities or congregations of Christians which we call the churches *(ekklēsiai)* but who function under the kingdom or reign of God.

The kingdom expresses the reign of God in people's lives as they are brought into the kingdom of God through a new birth (John 3:3-5). They become a new creation in the image of God (Col 3:17; Eph 4:23, 24; 2 Cor 5:17). The term church, *ekklēsia*, describes how these "new creation" Christians live together in community and carry out the missiological nature of the *Missio Dei*. They witness to the power of Jesus' death and resurrection, reshaping and renewing their own lives. They take care of their members and demonstrate the love and concern of God for their neighbors through their personal lives and loving service to others. All of this they do in the name of Jesus and through their churches. It is no wonder that Paul could bring praise to God in his magnificent letter to the churches in Asia as seen in his letter to the Ephesians.

Note particularly Eph 3:10-21. Paul in a hostile Jewish and Gentile world did not flee from the word church but featured it prominently in his mission preaching:

> *"Of this gospel I was made a minister according to the gift of God's grace which was given me by the working of his power.* [8] *To*

me, though I am the very least of all the saints, this grace was given, to preach to the Gentiles the unsearchable riches of Christ, ⁹ and to make all men see what is the plan of the mystery hidden for ages in God who created all things; ¹⁰ <u>that through the church the manifold wisdom of God might now be made known to the principalities and powers in the heavenly places.</u> ¹¹ This was according to the eternal purpose which he has realized in Christ Jesus our Lord, ¹² in whom we have boldness and confidence of access through our faith in him. ¹³ So I ask you not to lose heart over what I am suffering for you, which is your glory.

¹⁴ For this reason I bow my knees before the Father, ¹⁵ from whom every family in heaven and on earth is named, ¹⁶ that according to the riches of his glory he may grant you to be strengthened with might through his Spirit in the inner man, ¹⁷ and that Christ may dwell in your hearts through faith; that you, being rooted and grounded in love, ¹⁸ may have power to comprehend with all the saints what is the breadth and length and height and depth, ¹⁹ and to know the love of Christ which surpasses knowledge, that you may be filled with all the fulness of God.

²⁰ Now to him who by the power at work within us is able to do far more abundantly than all that we ask or think, ²¹ to him be glory in the church and in Christ Jesus to all generations, for ever and ever. Amen."

Certainly the kingdom is greater than the church in that it predates the church and reaches out beyond the church into all creation. But the church is an essential part of the kingdom and loses its true nature when not defined within and by the kingdom. *To play down the existence of the church in contrast to the kingdom is to severely denigrate the church and misunderstand the kingdom.* It is a common fallacy to compare the failures of Christians with the sovereignty of the kingdom and to define the church by those failures. However, the "institutional" church is an essential component of the kingdom and kingdom theology.

To put it mildly, one cannot be a member of the kingdom of God that was inaugurated by Jesus and not be a member of the body of Christ, the church or community that was established by Jesus and found in local congregations!

The kingdom reign of God is carried out in the world through the lives of congregations of Christians who have experienced the new birth and new creation into the kingdom.

It has become a catch phrase of some to say that they want to be Christians or kingdom people but not a part of an organized church. This sounds appealing to some but it runs contrary to Scripture. Christians today as in the past must decide whether to be defined by Scripture or the current mood of a secular society.

According to Jesus he established his community or church as a part of his kingdom ministry. At Matt 16:18 Jesus himself said "I will build my church ... and I will give you the keys of the kingdom of heaven." According to Paul, Jesus in his messianic ministry loved the church and gave himself for the church, Eph 5:25. *If Jesus so loved the church one would think that his disciples would also love Jesus' church!* If the church is the body of Christ then the body is made up of individual members of that body. Christians are those members, cf. Eph 1:22, 23; Col 1:18; 1 Cor 12:13ff; Rom 12:4ff. Again, it is contrary to biblical theology and Scripture to hold that one can be a member of the kingdom and not of the church!

Figure 3 emphasizes that it is through the church, that is, through local congregations that the *Missio Dei* and kingdom ministry is carried out into the world. *Paul is clear that it is through the church which is the body of Christ and the fulness of God who fills all things that Christians bring glory to God and carry out his ministry in the world in and through the church.* Note the following collage of scriptures from Paul's letter to the Ephesians whose theology is that Christians should bring glory to God through Jesus and His church. Again I turn to Paul's letter to the Ephesians to stress this profound point.

> Eph 1:11-23. *"In him, according to the purpose of him who accomplishes all things according to the counsel of his will, [12] <u>we who first hoped in Christ have been destined and appointed to live for the praise of his glory</u> ... [17] that the God of our Lord Jesus Christ, the Father of glory, may give you a spirit of wisdom and of revelation in the knowledge of him, [18] having the eyes of your hearts enlightened, that you may know what is the hope to which*

he has called you, what are the riches of his glorious inheritance in the saints, ^{19} and what is the immeasurable greatness of his power in us who believe, according to the working of his great might ^{20} which he accomplished in Christ when he raised him from the dead and made him sit at his right hand in the heavenly places, ^{21} far above all rule and authority and power and dominion, and above every name that is named, not only in this age but also in that which is to come; ^{22} and he has put all things under his feet and <u>has made him the head over all things for the church, ^{23} which is his body, the fulness of him who fills all in all</u>."

Eph 3:7-21. *"Of this gospel I was made a minister according to the gift of God's grace which was given me by the working of his power. ^{8} To me, though I am the very least of all the saints, this grace was given, to preach to the Gentiles the unsearchable riches of Christ, ^{9} <u>and to make all men see what is the plan of the mystery hidden for ages in God who created all things; ^{10} that through the church the manifold wisdom of God might now be made known to the principalities and powers in the heavenly places</u> ... ^{20} <u>Now to him who by the power at work within us is able to do far more abundantly than all that we ask or think, ^{21} to him be glory in the church and in Christ Jesus to all generations</u>, for ever and ever. Amen."*

In summary then of figure 3 we conclude that it is through the ministries of the local congregation, the local church that the *Missio Dei* is carried out in the world. The church's involvement in the *Missio Dei* is to extend God's reign or kingdom through the entire world. It is through the church as a ministry of the *Missio Dei* and the kingdom that Christians bring glory to God. This does not imply that individual Christians in their daily lives cannot and do not bring glory to God. However, it is the divine office or commission of the church as a corporate body of believers to so practice its faith and ministry through the church that it serves the *Missio Dei* and brings glory to God.

FIGURE 4

THE MISSIO DEI
What is God Doing in the World?

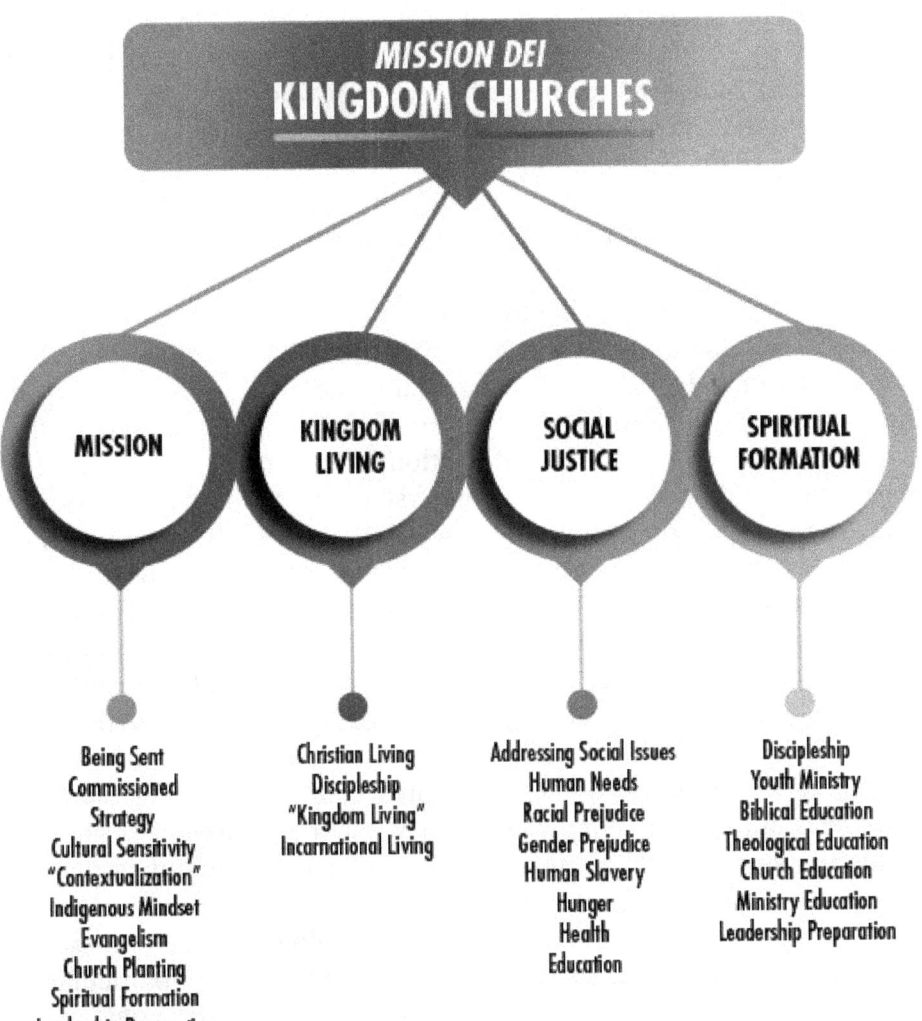

153

Figure 4

The *Missio Dei* and the Kingdom Church:

This figure diagrams some of the various works or ministries available to the church as it seeks to carry out its kingdom mission throughout the world. Most missiologists agree that mission is the function of the church, or of the members of the church who carry out the kingdom mission into the entire world according to Jesus' various commissions to the disciples in the Gospels and Acts.

Questions arise however regarding how one should define the word mission. Some prefer to identify the singular term *mission* with the church's mission to carry out the *Missio Dei* in the world in the more traditional manner of referring to the *mission work of the church and missionaries*. Others see the plural *missions* as referring to the overall concept of God's *Missio Dei*, understanding the plural term *missions* to refer to the *various missions or ministries* by which the church does this. I have no serious issue with this bifurcation of the terms but feel that it is unnecessary in the sense that most understand the plural term *missions* to be the *functions* of the church as it carries out the *mission* of the *Missio Dei* in the world. To clarify my understanding I see *mission* as the mandate of the church to carry out the *Missio Dei* in the world and *missions* to refer to the different ministries by which the church does this. I understand *mission* to refer to the process of evangelism that results in planting churches in new regions, far and near and not necessarily defined by geography. I see *mission* as one of the *ministries* or *missions* of the church along with benevolence, social justice, kingdom living, etc. However, I am in agreement with the view that the church does not simply do mission work; it is by definition missional and an integral part of God's *Missio Dei. The church is the Missio Dei!*

I am indebted to several outstanding missiologists and biblical scholars for clarifying the difference in these two terms. In particular I have found David Bosch, Lesslie Newbigin, Christopher Wright, and Eckhard Schnabel[48] to be most helpful in refining and clarifying this. Eckhard Schnabel's definition of missions highlights this view:

---

[48] Cf. the bibliography for the relevant references.

> The term "mission" or "missions" refers to the activity of a community of faith that distinguishes itself from its environment in terms of both religious belief (theology) and social behavior (ethics), that is convinced of the truth claims of its faith, and that actively works to win other people to the content of faith and the way of life of whose truth and necessity the members of that community are convinced...[49]

Missionaries integrate the new believers into a new community. The new converts become disciples. Being a follower of Jesus Christ is not a private philosophy or an individual ethic. It is a transforming reality that connects all believers as "children of God" in a community where they worship God and Jesus Christ. They learn from God and Jesus Christ by studying the Scriptures of Israel and the words of Jesus. And they learn to care for one another. Thus, missionaries establish contact with non-Christians, they proclaim the news of Jesus the Messiah and Savior (proclamation, preaching, teaching, instruction), they lead people to faith in Jesus Christ (conversion, baptism), and they integrate the new believers into the local community of the followers of Jesus (Lord's Supper, transformation of social and moral behavior, charity).[50]

The issue that is "troubling" the church in the 21st century arises from the secular forces or impulses that are being read increasingly into the precise definition of missions. Since the Evangelical thrust of the Lausanne Congress on Missions dating from 1974 there has been concern to see the *Missio Dei* in a broader definition than traditional missions which focused more on the spiritual evangelical dimension of mission than on the human condition in our world. The downside of this movement has

---

[49] Schnabel, *Paul the Missionary: Realities, Strategies and Methods*, kindle locations 340-343.

[50] Schnabel, *Paul the Missionary: Realities, Strategies and Methods*, kindle locations 450-456. Schnabel's strength is that he brings several elements to his scholarship in missiology. He holds a Ph.D. in biblical theology from the University of Aberdeen. He is the Rockefeller Distinguished Professor of New Testament Studies at Gordon-Conwell Theological. He has taught previously at Trinity Evangelical Divinity School, the Freie Theologische Akademie, at Giessen, Germany, the Wiedenest Bible College at Bergneustadt, Germany, and at the Asian Theological Seminary, Manila, Philippines. His academic and missionary experience in Germany and the Philippines enrich his outstanding biblical foundation to missions.

been a decline in appreciation for the evangelistic church planting emphasis of mission in the mind of postmodern persuasion Christians.

In this regard, you may recall the story mentioned earlier in this book of the two men I encountered in the beautiful village of Teyateyaneng, Lesotho. I, and a missionary colleague, had been working with a recently planted church in the Blue Mountain area of Lesotho. I had asked the two men which church they had been working with as missionaries expecting them to identify some denominational church in the area. To my surprise they were not supported by or working with any church! They were involved with a community education development program in the area and were supported and worked under the leadership of UNESCO. We had engaged in a discussion as to the nature of doing mission work! It was obvious that they were working under a definition of mission different from mine in the tradition of Lausanne and I was working with the traditional model of church planting and spiritual evangelism. We were literally continents apart in our understanding of mission!

Connecting the apparent disparity of emphases between the traditional evangelistic mission mindset and the Lausanne social concerns Christopher Wright,[51] Lesslie Newbigin,[52] Richard Bauckham,[53] Eckhard Schnabel and others have drawn attention to the fact that "spiritual/evangelism mission" and "social justice mission" are both necessary ingredients of the broader *Missio Dei* which involves Christians and the church understanding that in God's scheme of kingdom restoration both the spiritual/evangelistic and social justice dimensions are essential elements. Christians should be concerned about the spiritual wellbeing of the world, but they should also recognize the humanitarian needs of those living in a world alienated from God. The question is whether these concepts are equal in order or whether one should be prior or the foundation of the other. Wright, Newbigin, Bauckham, and Schnabel agree that spiritual evangelism should be the foundation of social justice and not vice versa! The point is that mission without spiritual evangelism conversion and the creation of a community of believers, the church, is not mission and that social justice without spirit evangelism conversion and

---

[51] Christopher J. H. Wright, *The Mission of God's People, passim.*
[52] Lesslie Newbigin, *The Open Secret: An Introduction to the Theology of Mission, passim.*
[53] Bauckham, *passim*, pp. 20, 25, 88.

the establishment of a community of believers, the church, although a noble enterprise, is likewise not mission but merely social involvement.

However in a postmodern age it is conceivable that without a sound foundation in social concern and benevolent interest evangelism may not be the entrance to addressing the real needs of a new community or ethnic group. To express this in other words, social justice in the absence of planting a new community of believers which involves evangelism, conversion to Christ, maturation, and nurturing in which the new converts are loved, cared for and taught how to live in harmony with God's kingdom which obviously engages social issues is simply not a mature kingdom mission in the *Missio Dei*!

Perhaps it might help if I described my view of Christian mission. My views have been profoundly shaped by my theological education at Abilene Christian University and the University of KwaZulu Natal in South Africa, by membership in the Southern Africa Missiological Society, over 15 years of active mission work in South Africa, over 40 years of mission engagement, and over 40 years in the seminary and university context preparing students for ministry and mission work.

First, I am comfortable with the singular and plural words, *mission* and *missions*. I understand the singular *mission* to refer to the church being involved in kingdom mission and the *Missio Dei* through spiritual evangelism. This is normally done through the church sending out missionaries to evangelize and plant and mature churches or communities of believers in Christ. The church is engaged in mission to extend God's kingdom in all the earth to all nations and peoples. I understand that this might be a church mission or an individual Christian's mission. I understand the plural *missions* to refer to the many mission outreach ministries available to churches and Christians in the kingdom through benevolence, social justice, etc. Obviously missionaries will not be oblivious to the social needs and injustices of their mission communities and congregations and will work in whatever fashion is available to address these.

Second, I hold that the goal of mission is evangelistic church planting in which truly indigenous and contextualized churches are planted. This involves evangelism, faith, repentance, baptism (all eschatological kingdom issues which will be discussed in later chapters in this book), spiritual conversion, being born anew by God's Holy Spirit, being united with Christ in his body, being taught, mentored, loved, and nurtured. I have no interest and have never engaged in what some refer to as the colonization[54] of missions in which the mission church is an extension of the sending church and is "governed" be a sending entity. Mission churches should be truly self-governing, self-propagating, self-supporting, and self theologically contextualizing. I recognize that initially the new mission church will be led and nurtured by the missionary but transition to indigenous leadership should be high on the agenda in the mission strategy. David Bosch has appropriately added a fourth self-category, self-theologizing referring to the contextualizing of theology on the mission field.[55]

Third, I understand this mission endeavor to agree with Matt 28:19-20 where Jesus commissioned his disciples to go and make disciples of all nations. Most serious missiologists in the heritage of the Lausanne Covenant agree that this text is fundamental to all mission efforts![56]

It does not take an advanced biblical scholar to understand this commission, but a little help is in order! Jesus' words were, "*Go* therefore and *make disciples* of *all nations, baptizing* them in the name of the Father and of the Son and of the Holy Spirit, [20] *teaching* them to observe all that I have commanded you; and lo, I am with you always, to the close of the age."

In this text the controlling verb is *make disciples, mathēteusate* from *mathēteúō*.[57] The verb is a present active imperative which means *you*

---

[54] While I recognize the broader aspects of this term I understand colonization to refer to bringing the new mission church under the umbrella of some overseas home mission society or sending church in which the new church is answerable or under the oversight and control of the mission board or sending church.

[55] The three-self indigenous concept is not new and has been around since Henry Venn and Rufus Anderson in the mid eighteen hundreds. It has persisted in various formulations through the last 200 years as a workable philosophy of mission. Melvin Hodges published a work based on his mission experience in Nicaragua in 1950, *On the Mission Field: The Indigenous Church*. David Bosch has renewed interest in the concept in his *Transforming Mission*, originally published in 1994 but republished in 2012.

[56] Cf. Bruce Ashford, Richard Bauckham, David Bosch, Alan Hirsch, Leslie Newbigin. Craig Ott, George Peters, Eckhard Schnabel, Christopher Wright, et al. See the references in the bibliography.

[57] μαθητεύω *mathēteúō*; to be a disciple or follower of another's doctrine ... to make a disciple (Matt. 28:19; Acts 14:21); to instruct (Matt. 13:52) with the purpose of making a disciple, Zodhiates, *The Complete Word study Dictionary: New Testament*.

must continue to make disciples, or *be making disciples*. The other three verbal forms in the text are all active modal participles explaining how the disciples are to make disciples. They are to do this first by *going*, then by *baptizing*, and then by *instructing*. The *destination* of the commission is *all nations* not merely Israel!

This commission was intended by Jesus to instruct the disciples what to do when they carried out his messianic mission. They were to *go and make disciples*. They were not to stay put in Jerusalem or Judea in order to make disciples; they were to go to all nations, into all the world (Mk 16:15), beginning in Jerusalem, then to Judea, Samaria, and ultimately to the end of the earth (Acts 1:8). They were being commissioned as missionaries[58] to go and *make disciples* of Jesus and the kingdom. Jesus did not leave any questions as to how disciples were to be made; "*baptizing* them in the name of the Father, and of the son, and of the Holy Spirit and *teaching* them to observe his teachings." The *missionary* sense was added by the participle "*going.*" Missionaries make disciples by *going*, *baptizing*, and *teaching*! Notice that the full godhead is involved in this action of commissioning, adding both urgency and seriousness to the commission.

There are enough teachings on baptism in the New Testament to inform one as to the purpose of the action and purpose of baptism. Rom 6:3-11 highlights the meaning and purpose of baptism!

> "*Do you not know that all of us who have been <u>baptized into Christ Jesus were baptized into his death</u>? ⁴ We were buried therefore with him by baptism into death, so that as Christ was raised from the dead by the glory of the Father, we too might walk in newness of life. ⁵ For if <u>we have been united with him in a death like his, we shall certainly be united with him in a resurrection like his.</u> ⁶ <u>We know that our old self was crucified with him so that the sinful body might be destroyed, and we might no longer be enslaved to sin.</u> ⁷ For he who has died is freed from sin. ⁸ But if we*

---

[58] There are some that make the argument that the word missionary is not found in the Bible. This is not a well-informed observation since the English word missionary is built off the Latin words *missio or mittere*. The Greek words behind the Latin *missio* and *mittere* are *apóstolos,* to be an *apostle* or *apostéllō to go*. An apostle is *one sent with a purpose or commission*, hence a missionary! The word can be used in the *general* sense as *anyone* sent on a mission or in the *specified* sense as an *apostle of* Christ.

have died with Christ, we believe that we shall also live with him. [9] *For we know that Christ being raised from the dead will never die again; death no longer has dominion over him.* [10] *The death he died he died to sin, once for all, but the life he lives he lives to God.* [11] <u>*So you also must consider yourselves dead to sin and alive to God in Christ Jesus. Let not sin therefore reign in your mortal bodies, to make you obey their passions.*</u> [13] <u>*Do not yield your members to sin as instruments of wickedness, but yield yourselves to God as men who have been brought from death to life, and your members to God as instruments of righteousness.*</u>"

    In this one magnificent pericope Paul encapsuled the process of spiritual conversion. The text of Rom 6:13 continues by engaging in a principle of *sanctification* which carries the sense of dedication, commitment, and purpose. Sanctification includes living faithfully in the kingdom by kingdom principles and working against the social injustices of this world.

    In baptism the new convert and new Christian goes through a dying to this world, being born again, being united with Christ and being raised to live a new life of righteousness in a right relationship with Christ and God. A new birth is experience through the power of the Holy Spirit, John 3:3-5, Titus 3:4-7. As explained by John at John 3:3-5, one is born again and becomes a member of the kingdom of God. Without a new birth in Christ social injustice is of little significance, but after a new birth and being united with Christ in his kingdom social injustice becomes a serious concern.

    The final imperatival participle "*teaching* them to observe all that I have commanded you" is vital yet unfortunately given little emphasis in the process of conversion. New disciples need to be taught, mentored, set an example, and instructed in the new life they have just begun to enjoy. This involves a principle which Jesus himself indicated in his kingdom parables of Matt 13, the leaven and the mustard seed; kingdom growth may be slow but it is incremental. Growth in the kingdom takes time, love, care, and nurturing. It is at this stage that the new disciples are taught about sin and social injustice and to take a stand against the prevailing ways of the world.

Notice that this impressive and profound Matthean commission pericope covers several necessary and urgent stages of the mission process. Mission involves *going* and *making disciples*. The remaining modal participles in this pericope explain how those disciples are to be made, *baptizing* and *teaching*! The teaching covers instruction as outlined in Jesus' great Sermon on the Mount and elsewhere which encompasses caring for the socially disenfranchised, the poor, and the homeless.

Fourth, once the disciples are converted and in process of being instructed and nurtured they are brought into a community of believers which the New Testament identifies as the loving and caring body of Christ, the church.[59] *The church is not simply a formal institution. It is a loving caring group of believers in Christ who have chosen to proclaim and live the love of Christ in the world.* Paul identified the church as the body of Christ which Christ loved and for which Christ had died, Eph 1:23, 24; Eph 5:25ff. Paul further explained that it is in baptism that disciples are baptized into the one body of Christ, 1 Cor 12:12, 13. He later explained that it is through or in that one body that the disciples function in Christ-like service, 1 Cor 12:27ff. *It is in the church that disciples are loved, nurtured, mentored, and taught the meaning of the kingdom of God and the responsibility of mission and evangelism.* Missionaries are in the business of maturing new converts into a loving maturing body of caring serving believers.

Fifth, the process of missionaries planting churches on a "foreign" or in a culturally diverse community must involve *contextualizing* the gospel message to address the needs of the recipients. Here David Bosch has coined the term *self-theologizing*. This involves planting indigenous churches that fit into and are relevant to the culture of the community while staying true to the gospel message. A church that looks like the "home" church of the missionary and that worships like the "home" church will not survive long in a culturally diverse environment. This is not the place to discuss the complicated process of theologically

---

[59] I have little time for Christians who denigrate the church! I recognize that the church has failed on many occasions and those outside the church or body of Christ like to point to this. However, Jesus loved the church and died for the church. Christians demonstrate the love of Christ when they love the church which means not simply an institution but involves loving and caring for people. Christians, the body of Christ, or the church, live in such a way that they demonstrate the love of Christ for others.

contextualizing the gospel while remaining true to its core but I simply wish to draw attention to this vital need as a necessary requirement of planting indigenous churches.

Sixth, a fundamental principle that I espouse in the process of indigenizing a local church involves never establishing a model of church that the native culture cannot support and physically sustain. Primarily this involves financial considerations but goes far beyond mere finances. The scale of the mission program should be tailored to the economy and development of the target community.

Seventh, leadership development must be a key concern for the mission church planting team. New congregational leaders, both men and women, need to be taught and mentored. The process can be slow and frustrating but it is an essential ministry in congregational maturation. What the mission team initially did when planting the new Christian community the new church must assume as their own responsibility. They must become leaders in their own congregations and communities, make disciples, perhaps even go, baptizing disciples and teaching them kingdom living and mission, training leaders, and maturing congregations.

Eighth, at the root of mission philosophy and possibly even theology, the missionary or mission sending church should have a firm strategy of withdrawing from engagement with the local church as soon as possible. Cultural differences prohibit setting a timetable for this withdrawal, but such should be fundamental to mission strategy. This does not preclude return visits for enrichment and encouragement for this was a fundamental principle in the Apostle Pauls' mission church planting effort.

In Figure 4 I have attempted to diagram the process of kingdom churches.[60] Each church or Christian community, however one chooses to describe them, is to be a missional kingdom church involved in the *Missio Dei*. There should be no question that churches are the primary vehicle for carrying out the *Missio Dei*. This does not imply that individual Christians

---

[60] I will speak often in this study of *the kingdom church* implying churches that are defined by the concept of the kingdom of God as expressed in this study. I have in mind churches that respect the unity of the body of Christ, who are opposed to division of the body, and who surrender to the will of God in Jesus in God's *missio*nal kingdom mindset. This may refer in context to a universal church but more preferably to local churches under the kingship of Christ. By implication it may be seen that some churches do not fall under this umbrella and who are extremely cultic and divisive.

may not be involved in some fashion in the *Missio Dei* but it should be obvious that they will be restricted in the scope of their mission. Each church in the kingdom has a variety of opportunities for carrying out the *Missio Dei*. These include *mission* which involves evangelism and church planting, doing good deeds such as *benevolence* and *addressing social injustice* in the mission community.[61] Benevolence should not be limited only to financial giving but should include all acts of kindness extended to others both within and outside the church community. The new community or church should become involved in some fashion in addressing social injustice, but primarily by example.[62] The new church should be seen by its community as a servant church serving the hurts of its community, whether spiritual, physical, or social injustice. Spiritual formation in some form of religious education in Scripture and nurturing should feature prominently in the mission strategy of the congregation. In Figure 4 I have not listed all the ministries available to churches and Christians seeking to carry out kingdom ministry, only those that are more commonly identified.

    My *final*, yet in my opinion *profound point* is that churches and Christians should not confuse these ministries. Each ministry has a unique nature and function. *Mission* is church planting, evangelism, nurturing, and spiritual formation within the church community planted by the mission effort. *Benevolence* such as taking care of orphans and feeding the hungry may be part of the church planting effort but independent of church planting is not mission. *Addressing social injustice* may be a demonstration of the kingdom of God but apart from church planting it is

---

[61] Benevolence, a disposition to do good deeds, acts of kindness, generous giving to others. From Latin *bene* and *volens*, choosing to do good deeds. I consider addressing the needs of the poor, the hungry, and the homeless as such benevolent good deeds. They demonstrate the love of God and kingdom concerns for the hurting world.

[62] I caution that one should not interpret this as liberation theology for contrary to the views of some the New Testament neither supports nor encourages such. The theology of revelation does not call for political reaction, and engagement against Rome and Jesus may not be biblically defined as a zealot as some have attempted. That Christians may oppose civil injustice certainly is a personal decision but such is never mandated of the church in the New Testament. Christians should teach against social injustice and become involved in charitable deeds that seek to correct social injustice.

not *mission* in the technical sense of evangelism and planting churches, but remains social concern.

The kingdom of God is broader than the local church but the local church is part of the missional kingdom of God and the *Missio Dei*! The *Missio Dei* is broader than *mission* but kingdom *mission* in the technical sense of evangelism/church planting is a fundamental and primary ingredient of the *Missio Dei*. *Benevolence*, feeding the hungry, and taking care of the homeless is part of the *Missio Dei* but is not necessarily mission in the sense of evangelism/church planting. We should call each ministry by its unique ministry identifier! *Mission is mission, benevolence is benevolence, social justice is social justice, and spiritual formation is spiritual formation*!

A Fallen World View

Paul at Rom 1:18-32 describes in explicit terms how man's original relationship with God degenerated into a base one in which man lost respect for God and created order and lowered himself to the pits of depravity.

> "*For the wrath of God is revealed from heaven against all ungodliness and wickedness of men who by their wickedness suppress the truth. [19] For what can be known about God is plain to them, because God has shown it to them. [20] Ever since the creation of the world his invisible nature, namely, his eternal power and deity, has been clearly perceived in the things that have been made. So they are without excuse; [21] for although they knew God they did not honor him as God or give thanks to him, but they became futile in their thinking and their senseless minds were darkened. [22] Claiming to be wise, they became fools, [23] and exchanged the glory of the immortal God for images resembling mortal man or birds or animals or reptiles.*
>
> *[24] Therefore God gave them up in the lusts of their hearts to impurity, to the dishonoring of their bodies among themselves, [25] because they exchanged the truth about God for a lie and worshiped and served the creature rather than the Creator, who is blessed for ever! Amen.*

^{26} For this reason God gave them up to dishonorable passions. Their women exchanged natural relations for unnatural, ^{27} and the men likewise gave up natural relations with women and were consumed with passion for one another, men committing shameless acts with men and receiving in their own persons the due penalty for their error.

^{28} And since they did not see fit to acknowledge God, God gave them up to a base mind and to improper conduct. ^{29} They were filled with all manner of wickedness, evil, covetousness, malice. Full of envy, murder, strife, deceit, malignity, they are gossips, ^{30} slanderers, haters of God, insolent, haughty, boastful, inventors of evil, disobedient to parents, ^{31} foolish, faithless, heartless, ruthless. ^{32} Though they know God's decree that those who do such things deserve to die, they not only do them but approve those who practice them."

The fall of man described in Gen 3 resulted in a broken relationship with God and a broken relationship with creation. What had been intended to be a blessing, the earth, the vegetation, and the animals now became a burden, and a curse. Man was expelled from his idyllic garden home which God had created for him; man became a servant of Satan and the degeneration described by Paul set in.

As man's relationship with God degenerated, man replaced God with the creaturely world and worshipped that world in place of the eternal God. In the process man devised other gods that he could control to take the place of the One God, YHWH, and turned the plan of God on its head with man subservient to and worshipping creation and its powers. Man created his own gods which he could control. In many situations this is where man has arrived in the 21st century! Many questioning whether there is an ultimate God or reality have replaced the ultimate God with an ultimate universe. Consequently man decries any need for a higher creating God who is over all. Creation with a purpose has been replaced by a creation in chaos.

Paul's description of the fallen world in his day at Rom 1:28-31 describes precisely where many find themselves in our age today.

"^{28} And since they did not see fit to acknowledge God, God gave them up to a base mind and to improper conduct. ^{29} They were

> *filled with all manner of wickedness, evil, covetousness, malice. Full of envy, murder, strife, deceit, malignity, they are gossips, [30] slanderers, haters of God, insolent, haughty, boastful, inventors of evil, disobedient to parents, [31] foolish, faithless, heartless, ruthless."*

> Unfortunately, many find themselves in this world *"at sea without a rudder and wind."*

Chaos surrounds man and frustration and hopelessness rises to the surface. At Eph 2:12 Paul describes the situation in clear terms: *"having no hope and without God in the world."* This is precisely why Jesus taught his disciples to pray that God's will and kingdom would be experienced on earth just as it is in heaven, Matt 6:10, and gave his life for that will and kingdom to become a reality.

But God had foreseen this and in love had a rescue plan ready to redeem fallen man. Notice how Paul describes this in magnificent praise of God at Eph 1:3-14,

> *Blessed be the God and Father of our Lord Jesus Christ, who has blessed us in Christ with every spiritual blessing in the heavenly places, [4] even as he chose us in him before the foundation of the world, that we should be holy and blameless before him. [5] He destined us in love to be his sons through Jesus Christ, according to the purpose of his will, [6] to the praise of his glorious grace which he freely bestowed on us in the Beloved. [7] In him we have redemption through his blood, the forgiveness of our trespasses, according to the riches of his grace [8] which he lavished upon us. [9] For he has made known to us in all wisdom and insight the mystery of his will, according to his purpose which he set forth in Christ [10] as a plan for the fulness of time, to unite all things in him, things in heaven and things on earth.*
>
> *[11] In him, according to the purpose of him who accomplishes all things according to the counsel of his will, [12] we who first hoped in Christ have been <u>destined and appointed to live for the praise of his glory</u>. [13] In him you also, who have heard the word of truth, the gospel of your salvation, and have believed in him, were sealed with the promised Holy Spirit, [14] which is the guarantee of our inheritance until we acquire possession of it, to the praise of his glory."*

The image of the creator in man at the creation, lost in the fall, can be restored in Christ and the redemption according to God's predetermined plan. This plan was set in motion with God's missional call and covenant with Abraham. It is demonstrated in the rescue of Israel from Egypt, the return from the exile of Israel to Babylon for disobedience and loss of faith in God's plan, in the restoration of Israel under Ezra and Nehemiah, and eventually in the ministry and death of Jesus, the suffering servant of God.

God's kingdom plan, the *Missio Dei*, the rescue of his fallen creation, the restoration and inauguration of the kingdom in Jesus, *is now the ministry of the church*. The church living within the kingdom reign of God and Jesus carries out the *Missio Dei* through its various ministries. *It is vital however for the church to understand that the kingdom has from the beginning and especially in the ministry of Jesus, been centrifugal, been missional, reaching out beyond any kind of "Jerusalem"*[63] *to the ends of the earth and the nations. This is kingdom theology!*

As Paul pointed out in his description of fallen man in Rom 1:18-32 man turned away from God and substituted false gods in the place of the one sovereign God. The paganism of the world, both ancient and modern demonstrate how humans have substituted false gods in the place of this one sovereign God; gods of their own desire and making and in doing so have rejected any notion of the kingdom of God.

Unfortunately, the church too often like the fallen world has also too often turned away from kingdom of God theology, a missional concept of the kingdom of God, and focused attention on preserving its own turf and identity! Christians call this world that has turned away from God and substituted false gods a fallen world. The purpose of the kingdom theology and the *Missio Dei* is to restore this fallen world to its original state of a real and full relationship with God. W*e refer to the restored world as the kingdom of God and the process of the restoration of this kingdom of God we call the missional nature of the kingdom, kingdom theology, and the mission of the church.*

---

[63] Unfortunately the comfort zone of our own local congregation has become a new false Jerusalem beyond which we seldom travel in God's *Missio Dei*!

Summary

It is the purpose of the *Missio Dei* and kingdom theology to correct the fallen condition of God's world and to create the dynamic for God to put the world right again. He has done this through Jesus' ministry and death and resurrection, and has drawn the church into this redemptive plan. It is the ministry of Christians and the church now to assume God's original gift of a nurturing stewardship that he had given to Adam and to witness to God's redeeming work in Christ.

The *Missio Dei*, kingdom theology, and the ministry of the church cannot be broken down into separate units or entities such as mission, benevolence, spiritual formation, and social justice but must be held in tight unity. The remaining chapters of this book will trace the story of kingdom theology and the *Missio Dei* through "Bible history" down to our present time in the eschatological[64] church age.

What we learned in this Chapter

In order to understand the proper relationship between the local church, the *Missio Dei*, and kingdom theology it is essential to remember that the concept of the kingdom reaches back to the creation event in which God in his sovereign power created everything—the earth itself, the vegetation, the animals, birds, and man.

The creation was not only a demonstration of God's power but also of his great love for his creation and desire for man's benefit to have a lasting relationship with man. God's sovereign power and authority were defined by his love for his creation and desire to nurture that relationship.

God demonstrated his love for man in the following three remarkable ways:

1. He established an intimate relationship with man in which he communed with man.
2. He created a female partner for man so man could enjoy a deeper relationship with her than he could with the creaturely world in which he had been placed by God.

---

[64] Eschatology is the theological term that speaks of the end time or final days. It is the Christian understanding that the restored kingdom of God in Christ and the church age are the final days in which this missional propose will be fulfilled.

3. He gave man a ministry of nurturing oversight and care for the creaturely world in which man would be his servant steward over creation.

The special relationship God had with man was broken by man's sin, disobedience, and banishment from his Eden home.

In his sovereign relationship with man and his creation God established a kingdom over which he was the absolute sovereign. This sovereignty he shared with man, placing him over creation with the charge to nurture, shepherd, and care for creation.

We call this special relationship with creation God's kingdom on earth.

After the fall of man God set in motion a method of restoring man and creation to their rightful relationship with himself. We call this process the *Missio Dei*, the mission of God to bring everything back to its original status with himself.

The establishment of the church represents a final step in God's mission to continue what he had promised to Abraham in his global covenant which was brought to fulfillment through the death and resurrection of Jesus, God's suffering servant. The death of Jesus was a demonstration of his faithfulness to God as his suffering servant messiah.

We noted that the kingdom and church represent different aspects of the *Missio Dei* with the kingdom being larger than the church but with the church being an essential ministry related entity within the kingdom of God.

The kingdom of God carries out its ministry through the life and mission of the church. The various ministries of the church are thus the missional ministries of the kingdom in the mission of the *Missio Dei*.

Chapter 8
The Great Commission and the Kingdom

Most concerned Christians recognize Jesus' teachings, instructions, and imperatival commands to go into all the world preaching the Gospel. It is possible that this is seen mostly as a command of Jesus, and a Christian mission, which it certainly is. However, if it is not set firmly within the *Missio Dei* with deep roots in God's covenant with Abraham and the story of Israel's settlement in Canaan, its theological impact is diminished. In fact, if Jesus' great commission is not set firmly in the context of what God began when he created everything and charged Adam and Eve to multiply and populate the world we miss its kingdom impact!

Either way, to separate the kingdom from God's *Missio Dei missional* dynamic, or to separate Jesus' great commission from the creation understanding of the kingdom is likewise to impoverish God's missional *Missio Dei*.

Likewise, to see kingdom *living, concern for social justice, and benevolence toward the underprivileged*, as important as they are to the life of the kingdom, as fulfilling Jesus' great commission is to have missed the *Missio Dei* teaching and commissions of Jesus to his disciples.

It is apparent that the early disciples and the Jerusalem church did not fully grasp the full impact of the *Missio Dei* and kingdom theology. I will shortly comment on this more fully, but from our study of the New Testament we learn that it took the intrusion of the Holy Spirit into Peter's ministry to get him to come to a mature understanding of kingdom theology (Acts 10, 11).

Paul encountered Jewish opposition to his evangelistic mission at almost every stop in his missional journeys which resulted in his magnificent grasp of God's covenant with Abraham expressed so graphically in his epistle to the Galatians.[1]

Paul recognized that the mission of Christ, as a fulfillment of God's *kingdom Missio Dei* was also a fulfillment of God's covenant promises to Abraham. *The inclusion of the blessings to the Gentile nations obviously involved and included a centrifugal evangelistic missional kingdom*

---

[1] Cf. N. T. Wright who has expressed this so cogently in his three fine works, *Justification*, *Paul*, and *Paul and the Faithfulness of God*.

mission to the nations which Ananias clearly articulated to Paul at his conversion. Cf. Acts 9:15-18 and Acts 22:12:

> *Acts 9:15* But the Lord said to him, "Go, <u>for he is a chosen instrument of mine to carry my name before the Gentiles and kings and the sons of Israel</u>; ¹⁶ for I will show him how much he must suffer for the sake of my name." ¹⁷ So Ananias departed and entered the house. And laying his hands on him he said, "Brother Saul, the Lord Jesus who appeared to you on the road by which you came, has sent me that you may regain your sight and be filled with the Holy Spirit." ¹⁸ And immediately something like scales fell from his eyes and he regained his sight. Then he rose and was baptized, ¹⁹ and took food and was strengthened.
>
> *Acts 22:12.* "And one Ananias, a devout man according to the law, well-spoken of by all the Jews who lived there, ¹³ came to me, and standing by me said to me, 'Brother Saul, receive your sight.' And in that very hour I received my sight and saw him. ¹⁴ And he said, <u>'The God of our fathers appointed you to know his will, to see the Just One and to hear a voice from his mouth; ¹⁵ for you will be a witness for him to all men of what you have seen and heard.</u> ¹⁶ And now why do you wait? Rise and be baptized, and wash away your sins, calling on his name.'

At Acts 22:21 Paul acknowledged that God had chosen him to go to the Gentiles, "*And he said to me, 'Depart; for I will send you far away to the Gentiles.'*"

From where we sit today, having become familiar with Paul's epistles, the flow of thought reflected in these few citations from Acts falls into a natural sequence of events, but from Paul's context, they presented life shaping, kingdom changing theological challenges! Having encountered the risen Jesus, Paul, the strict Pharisaic Jewish devotee, became a transformed kingdom *Missio Dei missionary* with a passion for the lost, Jew and Gentile. He reread his Mosaic inclinations and traditions through the lens of the *Missio Dei* Abrahamic promises. Perhaps we need in our own lives to refocus our understanding of the *kingdom* and the *Missio Dei* along with Paul through the lens of God's Abrahamic covenant!

For the seriously biased Pharisaic Jew, Paul, to have written his epistle to the Galatians with the following theological depth of thought,

God's covenant with Abraham became a new polar star. True, Moses and the Law remained for Paul a firm foundation to his life, but understanding the *missional* nature of the *Missio Dei* implications wrapped up in the Abrahamic Covenant, with Christ becoming the seed of the promise, this new grasp of the Abrahamic covenant opened new horizons to Paul's understanding of the real nature of the *Missio Dei*.

Notice the transformation in Paul's theological thinking reflected in Gal 3:21ff:

> *Is the law then against the promises of God? Certainly not; for if a law had been given which could make alive, then righteousness would indeed be by the law.* [22] *But the scripture consigned all things to sin, that what was promised to faith in Jesus Christ might be given to those who believe.*
>
> [23] *Now before faith came, we were confined under the law, kept under restraint until faith should be revealed.* [24] *So that the law was our custodian until Christ came, that we might be justified by faith.* [25] <u>*But now that faith has come, we are no longer under a custodian;*</u> [26] *for in Christ Jesus you are all sons of God, through faith.* [27] *For as many of you as were baptized into Christ have put on Christ.* [28] *There is neither Jew nor Greek, there is neither slave nor free, there is neither male nor female; for you are all one in Christ Jesus.* [29] <u>*And if you are Christ's, then you are Abraham's offspring, heirs according to promise.*</u>

As disciples of Jesus we appropriately speak of Jesus' great commission to his disciples, cf. Matt 28:18ff, and it certainly was great. However, perhaps we might speak more appropriately of a great commission if we reset our *Missio Dei* focus on God's calling of Abraham in Gen 12:1ff where God called Abraham out of the Ur of Chaldea and sent him toward Canaan and a land of great theological promises. At first these may not have been seen by Abraham as great theological promises, but in God's commission this calling and these promises became the foundation of God's future with Israel and his *Missio Dei*!

We understand that the great commission ensconced in Jesus' instruction at Matt 28:18ff was based in and driven by his death and resurrection. However, we need to recognize that the foundation of Jesus' death and resurrection lies within God's *Mission Dei* plan of redemption which was enabled by his calling of Abraham and the faithfulness of Abraham to that calling.

Now that we have theologically reset the foundation of Jesus' great commission in the *Missio Dei* and Abrahamic covenant, we turn to Jesus' commission as recorded for us in Matt 28:18ff:

> *And Jesus came and said to them, "All authority in heaven and on earth has been given to me. [19] <u>Go</u> therefore and <u>make disciples</u> of all nations, <u>baptizing</u> them in the name of the Father and of the Son and of the Holy Spirit, [20] <u>teaching them</u> to observe all that I have commanded you; and lo, I am with you always, to the close of the age."*

We begin by observing the obvious! Jesus was speaking by the full divine authority of the trinitarian godhead: Father, Son, and Holy Spirit. Obviously, this command carries with it all the planning and imperatives of God's *Missio Dei*.

As we examine the text carefully we note that the only verb involved is the *plural aorist active imperative, μαθητεύσατε, you must make disciples*. Accompanying this imperatival verb are several *modal* participles which draw the imperatival form from the main verb. Modal participles explain *how* the disciples were to make disciples! The modal participles are *go, πορευθέντες*; *baptizing, βαπτίζοντες*; *teaching, διδάσκοντες*. Jesus' command to his disciples, therefore, was *you must make disciples*! You do this by *going, baptizing*, and *teaching*.

Note the missional sending evangelistic kingdom intention of this command! You do not do this by staying at home! You *go* and find people who are willing to hear the message of Jesus whom you can *teach*. You *baptize* them into Christ and teach them the *principles* of Christ (kingdom living). Kingdom living is the outgrowth of *Missio Dei* (note the full trinitarian emphasis on this command)! Missional evangelistic teaching is the purpose and mission of the *Missio Dei*!

This great commission is causally related to *kingdom theology* and *the kingdom of God*! At the beginning of Matthew's account of the gospel story he drew attention to the fact that *Jesus <u>came</u> preaching the gospel of the kingdom*. Now at the close of his gospel Matthew explains how Jesus' mission was to be extended by the disciples <u>going out</u> to make disciples by preaching the kingdom Gospel of Christ!

Luke sharpens the edge of this narrative by setting this story in a slightly different context. Luke 24:44ff fits into Matthew's account in a dramatic way:

> Then he said to them, "These are my words which I spoke to you, while I was still with you, that everything written about me in the law of Moses and the prophets and the psalms must be fulfilled." [45] Then he opened their minds to understand the scriptures, [46] and said to them, "Thus it is written, that the Christ should suffer and on the third day rise from the dead, [47] and that repentance and forgiveness of sins should be preached in his name to all nations, beginning from Jerusalem. [48] You are witnesses of these things. [49] And behold, I send the promise of my Father upon you; but stay in the city, until you are clothed with power from on high."

Luke continues his narrative in Part 2 of his accounting the Gospel story, the book of Acts. The following citation Acts 1:1-8 is long but is critical to the great commission story we are examining:

> In the first book (Luke), O The-ophilus, I have dealt with all that Jesus began to do and teach, [2] until the day when he was taken up, after he had given commandment through the Holy Spirit to the apostles whom he had chosen. [3] To them he presented himself alive after his passion by many proofs, appearing to them during forty days, and speaking of the kingdom of God. [4] And while staying with them he charged them not to depart from Jerusalem, but to wait for the promise of the Father, which, he said, "you heard from me, [5] for John baptized with water, but before many days you shall be baptized with the Holy Spirit."
>
> [6] So when they had come together, they asked him, "Lord, will you at this time restore the kingdom to Israel?" [7] He said to them, "It is not for you to know times or seasons which the Father has fixed by his own authority. [8] But you shall receive power when the Holy Spirit has come upon you; and you shall be my witnesses in Jerusalem and in all Judea and Samaria and to the end of the earth."

At least three major points stand out in this remarkable account of Jesus' commission recorded by Luke. First, this gospel to which the disciples were to be *witnesses* was a *kingdom gospel*. Jesus had spent 40 days teaching them about the kingdom. *Second*, they were to *go out beginning from Jerusalem through Judea, Samaria, and to the end of the earth! Third*, it was in every sense a *kingdom missional gospel* and commission! *Fourth*, it was obviously to be evangelistic since the disciples were to witness to Jesus' death and resurrection. *Fifth*, and alarmingly, the disciples were still focused on *restoring the kingdom to Israel*!

Where had their brains been? However, we must cut them some slack, for the kingdom message is a transforming message which took them time and the power of the Holy Spirit to grasp. We learn from Acts 10, 11, that even Peter needed the intervention of the Holy Spirit to set this kingdom story in the context of the *Missio Dei* at the conversion of Cornelius, the Roman centurion! Likewise, even after 2000 years many of us have still not yet grasped the real full impact of the *global, missional impact* of the *Missio Dei* and the kingdom message! We still struggle to learn the difference between kingdom living and kingdom theology!

It took all of the theological skill and courage of the apostle Paul to traverse all of the facets of the theological diamond God had created in the beginning, and to convince even the leaders of the Jerusalem church, cf. Acts 15 and his Galatian epistle, that the kingdom of God was greater than just one of its obviously essential growth parts, Judaism and the Law of Moses. The beauty of God's creative genius and kingdom reality can only be appreciated when set in his kingdom missional *Missio Dei* plan!

To conclude and emphasize this great commission kingdom point I refer once again to Eph 1:3-14 which reflects Paul at his theological best!

> *Blessed be the God and Father of our Lord Jesus Christ, who has blessed us in Christ with every spiritual blessing in the heavenly places, ⁴ <u>even as he chose us in him before the foundation of the world, that we should be holy and blameless before him.</u>*
> *⁵ He destined us in love to be his sons through Jesus Christ, according to the purpose of his will, ⁶ to the praise of his glorious grace which he freely bestowed on us in the Beloved. ⁷ In him we have redemption through his blood, the forgiveness of our trespasses, according to the riches of his grace ⁸ which he lavished upon us. ⁹ <u>For he has made known to us in all wisdom and insight the mystery of his will, according to his purpose which he set forth</u>*

in Christ [10] as a plan for the fulness of time, to unite all things in him, things in heaven and things on earth.

[11] In him, according to the purpose of him who accomplishes all things according to the counsel of his will, [12] we who first hoped in Christ have been destined and appointed to live for the praise of his glory. [13] *In him you also, who have heard the word of truth, the gospel of your salvation, and have believed in him, were sealed with the promised Holy Spirit,* [14] which is the guarantee of our inheritance until we acquire possession of it, to the praise of his glory.

Chapter 9
The Apostolic Practice and the Mission and Expansion of the New Testament Church and Kingdom *Missio Dei*

This chapter presents a historical explanation of the disciples carrying out Jesus' great commission at Matt 28:18ff and Luke 24:44ff which we discussed in the previous chapter. My plan is to see how the 12 apostles and early church carried out this commission as reflected primarily in Luke's account in Acts. The comment and word we will focus on to begin this survey is Acts 1:8, *"you shall be my <u>witnesses</u> in Jerusalem and in all Judea and Samaria and to the end of the earth…"* The word witness, μάρτυρες, *martures*, is interesting in that, as Zodhiates points out, it is peculiar to the New Testament, implying that it had become somewhat of a technical term. The root noun for this term is *μάρτυς mártus*, which Zodhiates points out primarily means:

> One who has information or knowledge of something, and hence, one who can give information, bring to light, or confirm something (Matt. 18:16; 26:65; Mark 14:63; Luke 24:48; Acts 1:22; 5:32; 7:58; 2 Cor. 13:1; 1 Tim. 5:19; Heb. 10:28). It denotes that the witness confirms something, though in many cases that witness may have been bribed or otherwise persuaded to make a false statement (Acts 6:13). In the sense of a simple confirmation (2 Cor. 1:23); of the Apostle's faithfulness and spiritual integrity (Rom. 1:9; Phil. 1:8; 1 Thess. 2:5, 10; 1 Tim. 6:12; 2 Tim. 2:2). Heb. 12:1 refers to the "cloud of witnesses" is mentioned. This may refer to them as spectators at a race, but seems to imply that they also testify, whether by word or deed, regarding the race they themselves have run.[1]

In an explanation of the use of the term *μάρτυρες, martures*, Zodhiates adds:

> Peculiar to the NT is the designation as mártures (pl., witnesses) of *those who announce the facts of the gospel and tell its tidings* (Acts 2:32; 3:15; 10:39, 41; 13:31; Rev. 11:3). Also mártus is used as a

---

[1] Zodhiates, *μάρτυς mártus*.

designation of those who have suffered death in consequence of confessing Christ (of Stephen, Acts 22:20; of Antipas, Rev. 2:13; see Rev. 17:6. These verses, however, should not be understood as if their witness consisted in their suffering death, *but rather that their witnessing of Jesus became the cause of their death*). The Lord Jesus in Rev. 1:5 is called "the faithful witness," the faithful one (see Rev. 3:14).

Several extended studies of the term μάρτυρες, *martures* develop the thoughts emphasized above by Zodhiates, drawing attention to the fact that the concept of witnessing had deep roots in both the Hebrew and Greek traditions. These traditions included not only faithful personal witness to the facts being born, but also the *missional apostolic responsibility of proclaiming the meaning and of the facts*.

Darrell Brock observes that Jesus' concern was not an eschatological one of dating the establishment of the kingdom, but of testifying to the truth and significance of his death and resurrection. In an extended comment he writes:

> The disciples' calling, concern, and mission are not to focus on the timing of the end. Rather they are to receive the enablement that God will give in the Spirit. They will be Jesus's witnesses from Jerusalem to the end of the earth. The Spirit is tied to power (δύναμιν, dynamin), which refers here to *being empowered to speak boldly by testifying to the message of God's work through Jesus* ... So they are to be "witnesses" (μάρτυρες, martyres) for Jesus ... A witness in this sense is someone who helps establish facts objectively through verifiable observation. As such, a witness is more than someone with merely subjective and personal impressions. This objectivity and fact-based quality of the witness are why the direct experience of Jesus's ministry and resurrection are required of Judas's replacement in Acts 1: 21– 22, a passage that shows what stands behind Luke's use of this term. *Thus "witness" is a key term in Acts for those who experienced Jesus and saw him in a resurrection appearance (1: 22).* <u>This experience means that they can testify directly to what God did through Jesus</u> *(Luke 24: 48)*. The disciples' direct and real experience of Jesus

and his resurrection qualifies them as witnesses, but the Spirit will give them the *capability to articulate their experience with boldness.*[2]

Strathmann in Kittel, *Theological Dictionary of the New Testament* ties this discussion together well:

> The addition ὑμεῖς μάρτυρες τούτων shows why the disciples are fitted for this task, and *how they will discharge it*. They are fitted because from experience they can bear witness to the factuality of the suffering and resurrection of Jesus, and also because they have grasped in faith the significance of Jesus, and can thus attest it. *They discharge the task by proclaiming both the facts and their significance V 4, p 493 as they have grasped this in faith*. Only thus does the kerygma become the kerygma. As special equipment they have the prospect of the Spirit whom the Father has promised and whom Jesus will send (v. 49).
>
> What is intimated in Lk. is developed in Ac. *The missionary charge to the apostolic band is repeated with the phrase ἔσεσθέ μου μάρτυρες (1:8). The primary thought is that they can and will proclaim from first-hand knowledge the story of Jesus (1:22; 10:39) and especially the fact of His resurrection (2:32; 3:15; 5:31 f.; 10:41)*. But in so doing they will always emphasise its saving significance (cf. esp. 10:42). It is at once apparent that this condition can be met only by a select circle whose members had the honour of personal encounter with the risen Lord (10:41; 1:22). These are μάρτυρες αὐτοῦ πρὸς τὸν λαόν (13:31).[3]

We can safely conclude from these observations that Jesus' instruction to the soon to be twelve disciples was a commission to *go and proclaim the truth of his death and resurrection* to the ends of the earth, and to do this faithfully to the facts. In the context of Acts, this was a *Missio Dei, kingdom, missional, evangelistic*, teaching and proclaiming commission! Witnessing did not mean that they were simply to go out and

---

[2] Bock, *Acts*, kindle locations 2024-2044; cf. also Polhill, Acts: 26: The New American Commentary, p. 85.
[3] Strathmann, G. Kittel, *Theological Dictionary of the New Testament*, vol. 4, pp. 492–493

do good social justice and benevolent deeds, which obviously were part of their Messianic mission, but they were *primarily commissioned to go out and evangelistically preach the truest facts of the gospel, Jesus' death and resurrection, and convert people to the faith of Christ*, and mentor them in that faith. This is the heart of the *Missio Dei*, the missional kingdom message.

For a while the apostles remained in Jerusalem preaching the death and resurrection of Jesus, for this was in keeping with Jesus' instruction, "beginning in Jerusalem." They waited for the power of the outpouring of the Holy Spirit and when this occurred, Acts 2, Peter did precisely what Jesus had commanded, he witnessed to the death and resurrection of Jesus in his great Pentecostal sermon, and 3,000 men were baptized! Acts 2:14-36:

> *But Peter, standing with the eleven, lifted up his voice and addressed them, "Men of Judea and all who dwell in Jerusalem, let this be known to you, and give ear to my words. [15] For these men are not drunk, as you suppose, since it is only the third hour of the day; [16] but this is what was spoken by the prophet Joel:*
> *[17] 'And in the last days it shall be, God declares, that I will pour out my Spirit upon all flesh,   and your sons and your daughters shall prophesy,   and your young men shall see visions, and your old men shall dream dreams; [18] yea, and on my menservants and my maidservants in those days I will pour out my Spirit; and they shall prophesy ...*
> *[22] "Men of Israel, hear these words: Jesus of Nazareth, a man attested to you by God with mighty works and wonders and signs which God did through him in your midst, as you yourselves know— [23] <u>this Jesus, delivered up according to the definite plan and foreknowledge of God, you crucified and killed by the hands of lawless men. [24] But God raised him up, having loosed the pangs of death, because it was not possible for him to be held by it</u> ... <u>This Jesus God raised up, and of that we all are witnesses.</u>*
> *[33] Being therefore exalted at the right hand of God, and having received from the Father the promise of the Holy Spirit, he has poured out this which you see and hear ...*

> *36 Let all the house of Israel therefore know assuredly that God has made him both Lord and Christ, this Jesus whom you crucified."*

Acts 2 was not a kingdom living, social justice, benevolent time! It was a *kingdom missional theology* time!

Shortly after this great kingdom theology time an occasion arose for a kingdom living, social justice, benevolent time! Acts 6:1-7:

> *1 Now in these days when the disciples were increasing in number, the <u>Hellenists murmured against the Hebrews because their widows were neglected in the daily distribution</u>* (a social justice benevolent time). *2 And the twelve summoned the body of the disciples and said, "It is not right that we should give up preaching the word of God* (a kingdom theology evangelistic time) *to serve tables. 3 Therefore, brethren, pick out from among you seven men of good repute, full of the Spirit and of wisdom, whom we may appoint to this duty. 4 But we will devote ourselves to prayer and to the ministry of the word." 5 And what they said pleased the whole multitude, and they chose Stephen, a man full of faith and of the Holy Spirit, and Philip, and Prochorus, and Nicanor, and Timon, and Parmenas, and Nicolaus, a proselyte of Antioch. 6 These they set before the apostles, and they prayed and laid their hands upon them.*
>
> *7 And the word of God increased; and the number of the disciples multiplied greatly in Jerusalem, and a great many of the priests were obedient to the faith.*

Early in the life of the church in Jerusalem Jewish persecution and opposition arose, Stephen was martyred, and Saul of Tarsus arose on the scene, persecuting Christians in the name of the Jewish leaders in the Sanhedrin. Acts 8:1-6:

> *And on that day a great persecution arose against the church in Jerusalem; and they were all scattered throughout the region of Judea and Samaria, except the apostles. 2 Devout men buried Stephen, and made great lamentation over him. 3 But Saul was ravaging the church, and entering house after house, he dragged off men and women and committed them to prison.*
>
> *4 Now those who were scattered went about preaching the word. 5 Philip went down to a city of Samaria, and proclaimed to*

them the Christ. ⁶ And the multitudes with one accord gave heed to what was said by Philip, when they heard him and saw the signs which he did.

The young disciples in Jerusalem had not forgotten Jesus' commission and the apostles teaching. Kingdom theology was still alive in the church. They went everywhere preaching the good news of Jesus, witnessing to Jesus' death and resurrection!

The gospel good news of Jesus' death and resurrection was witnessed and proclaimed in Judea and even Samaria just as Jesus had commanded!

Although Paul had done some preaching and teaching in Damascus after his baptism, this was primarily in the synagogue. Luke records in Acts 9:19f:

For several days he was with the disciples at Damascus. [20] And in the synagogues immediately he proclaimed Jesus, saying, "He is the Son of God." ²¹ And all who heard him were amazed, and said, "Is not this the man who made havoc in Jerusalem of those who called on this name? And he has come here for this purpose, to bring them bound before the chief priests." ²² But Saul increased all the more in strength, and confounded the Jews who lived in Damascus by proving that Jesus was the Christ.

In keeping with the divine plan, it took the Holy Spirit to motivate Peter to begin preaching the gospel to the Gentiles. This narrative and the events that took place are pivotal in understanding the full nature of the *Missio Dei* kingdom theology that is so deeply imbedded in the Abrahamic promises of Genesis 12, *et al*.

We read this interesting initiative in Acts 10 and 11. Peter was living in Lydda when he was told to go to Joppa where one Cornelius, a Roman centurion, lived and to teach him the good news about Jesus' death and resurrection. We learn from the narrative that Cornelius, although a Gentile was a devout person and apparently an attendee at the synagogue. He lived in the Roman administrative city of that region, Caesarea on the coast of Israel. The initial reaction for Peter, a Christian but still a devout Jew, was that this was not *"kosher"* permissible!

John Polhill discusses the profound significance of this saga of events:

Chapter 10 marks a high point in the church's expanding mission. God led Peter to witness to the Gentile Cornelius.

Through that experience Peter became fully convinced of God's purposes to reach all peoples and hence became one of the greatest advocates of the mission to the Gentiles. The Hellenists had been the leaders in this outreach, Philip having evangelized Samaria and having baptized the Ethiopian eunuch. The latter incident in many ways parallels that of Peter and Cornelius. Like Cornelius, the eunuch seems to have been both a "God-fearer" and a Gentile. The significant new development in chap. 10 is that Peter became committed to the Gentile mission. His testimony would be instrumental in leading the mother church in Jerusalem to endorse the Gentile mission and thus lend it legitimacy and continuity with the ministry of the apostles (11:1-18; 15:7-11).

The place of his residence is of some importance, since Caesarea was from A.D. 6 the provincial capital and place of residence of the Roman governor. Unlike Lydda and Joppa, which were mainly inhabited by Jews, Caesarea was a Hellenistic-style city with a dominant population of Gentiles. Originally a small town named Strato's Tower, it was rebuilt on a grand style by Herod the Great, complete with a man-made harbor, a theater, an amphitheater, a hippodrome, and a temple dedicated to Caesar. There was a substantial Jewish minority there and considerable friction between the Jews and the larger Gentile community. It was fitting that it should be the place where Peter came to terms with his own prejudices and realized that human barriers have no place with the God who "does not show favoritism."[4]

Since the Cornelius event held significant theological import in the globalization of the gospel message, and Jesus' command to witness to the end of the earth, I am including Luke's account of a portion of this interesting narrative. The narrative of the conversion of a Gentile held a pivotal role in Luke's theological argument to Theophilus, a prominent Gentile. Luke devoted two chapters in his account in Acts to cover this event. For the sake of brevity I will cite only Luke's closing comments,

---

[4] Polhill, *Acts*, pp. 249-252.

but encourage the reader to read the full narrative in Acts 10 and 11. Acts 11:5ff:

> ⁵ "I was in the city of Joppa praying; and in a trance I saw a vision, something descending, like a great sheet, let down from heaven by four corners; and it came down to me. ⁶ Looking at it closely I observed animals and beasts of prey and reptiles and birds of the air. ⁷ And I heard a voice saying to me, 'Rise, Peter; kill and eat.' ⁸ But I said, <u>'No, Lord; for nothing common or unclean has ever entered my mouth.'</u> ⁹ But the voice answered a second time from heaven, <u>'What God has cleansed you must not call common.'</u> ¹⁰ This happened three times, and all was drawn up again into heaven. ¹¹ At that very moment three men arrived at the house in which we were, sent to me from Caesarea. ¹² And the Spirit told me to go with them, making no distinction. These six brethren also accompanied me, and we entered the man's house. ¹³ And he told us how he had seen the angel standing in his house and saying, 'Send to Joppa and bring Simon called Peter; ¹⁴ he will declare to you a message by which you will be saved, you and all your household.' ¹⁵ <u>As I began to speak, the Holy Spirit fell on them just as on us at the beginning.</u> ¹⁶ <u>And I remembered the word of the Lord,</u> how he said, 'John baptized with water, but you shall be baptized with the Holy Spirit.' ¹⁷ <u>If then God gave the same gift to them as he gave to us when we believed in the Lord Jesus Christ, who was I that I could withstand God?"</u> ¹⁸ When they heard this they were silenced. <u>And they glorified God, saying, "Then to the Gentiles also God has granted repentance unto life."</u>

To carry this saga of the historical globalization of the gospel forward from Jerusalem through Judea, Samaria, and the end of the earth in the life, we follow the disciples of the early church as they manifest their understanding of witnessing to the death and resurrection of Jesus. We turn to Paul as he began his lifelong mission to the Gentiles as recorded by Luke in Acts. We know the story well! From Antioch on the coast of Syria, Paul with companions Barnabas and Silas embarked on three great mission journeys.

Follow Luke as he begins his discussion of Paul and Barnabas' first mission effort, Acts 13:1ff. But before you do, note also the interesting empowering of the Holy Spirit in this narrative, and recall Jesus' commission at Acts 1:6:

> So when they had come together, they asked him, "Lord, will you at this time restore the kingdom to Israel?" ⁷ He said to them, "It is not for you to know times or seasons which the Father has fixed by his own authority. ⁸ But <u>you shall receive power when the Holy Spirit has come upon you; and you shall be my witnesses in Jerusalem and in all Judea and Samaria and to the end of the earth</u>."

Acts 13:1ff:

> Now in the church at Antioch there were prophets and teachers, Barnabas, Simeon who was called Niger, Lucius of Cyrene, Mana-en a member of the court of Herod the tetrarch, and Saul. ² <u>While they were worshiping the Lord and fasting, the Holy Spirit said, "Set apart for me Barnabas and Saul for the work to which I have called them."</u> ³ Then after fasting and praying they laid their hands on them and sent them off.
>
> ⁴ So, <u>being sent out by the Holy Spirit</u>, they went down to Seleucia; and from there they sailed to Cyprus. ⁵ When they arrived at Salamis, <u>they proclaimed the word of God in the synagogues of the Jews</u>. And they had John to assist them. ⁶ When they had gone through the whole island as far as Paphos, they came upon a certain magician, a Jewish false prophet, named Bar-Jesus. ⁷ He was with the proconsul, Sergius Paulus, a man of intelligence, who summoned Barnabas and Saul and sought to hear the word of God. ⁸ But Elymas the magician (for that is the meaning of his name) withstood them, seeking to turn away the proconsul from the faith. ⁹ But Saul, who is also called Paul, filled with the Holy Spirit, looked intently at him ¹⁰ and said, "You son of the devil, you enemy of all righteousness, full of all deceit and villainy, will you not stop making crooked the straight paths of the Lord? ¹¹ And now, behold, the hand of the Lord is upon you, and you shall be blind and unable to see the sun for a time." Immediately mist and darkness fell upon him and he went about seeking people to lead him by the hand. ¹² <u>Then the proconsul believed, when he saw what had occurred, for he was astonished at the teaching of the Lord</u>.

Paul's and Barnabas' mission was not to spread *kingdom living, engage in social justice, and engage in benevolent works!* Their kingdom mission was to preach the gospel, plant churches, and establish them in the faith. This is kingdom theology, missional theology, the Missio Dei in action!

As we have walked with the disciples as they followed Jesus' witnessing commission we note that the activity involved was *witnessing* to the death and resurrection of Jesus, *teaching,* and *preaching* the message of Jesus' death and resurrection.

A good closing point to this discussion would be Paul's own statement to the Corinthians at 1 Cor 1:17ff:

> [17] *For Christ did not send me to baptize but to preach the gospel, and not with eloquent wisdom, lest the cross of Christ be emptied of its power.*
> [18] *For the word of <u>the cross</u> is folly to those who are perishing, but <u>to us who are being saved it is the power of God</u> ...,* [23] *but we preach <u>Christ crucified</u>, a stumbling block to Jews and folly to Gentiles,* [24] *<u>but to those who are called, both Jews and Greeks, Christ the power of God and the wisdom of God</u>.* [25] *For the foolishness of God is wiser than men, and the weakness of God is stronger than men.*
> [2:1,] *When I came to you, brethren, I did not come proclaiming to you the testimony of God in lofty words or wisdom.* [2] *For <u>I decided to know nothing among you except Jesus Christ and him crucified</u>.* [3] *And I was with you in weakness and in much fear and trembling;* [4] *and my speech and my message were not in plausible words of wisdom, but <u>in demonstration of the Spirit and of power</u>,* [5] *that your faith might not rest in the wisdom of men but in the power of God.*

Now that is *kingdom theology*, the missional *Missio Dei* in action. *Kingdom living* is surely part of the function of the church and disciples as they *live the life of Jesus* in their daily living and *witness* to the *lifestyle* of Christ.

Kingdom living is certainly a witness to the quality of life lived and taught by Jesus, but it is not *kingdom theology* as implied by Jesus in his great commissions of Matt 28:18ff, Luke 24:44ff, and Acts 1:6-8!

Chapter 10
What does a Missional Kingdom Church Look Like?

We have in the previous nine chapters explored the biblical theological dynamic, or "genetic" makeup, of a *kingdom missional church*. What remains is to close this discussion by examining what a few real-life kingdom missional churches may look like. That is, what does a church look like that has "inherited" this "kingdom missional gene" and transcribed this into a real-life situation!

I am sure that there are many churches and para-church organizations that I could refer to in this real-life scenario, and I beg the forgiveness of those whom I have apparently ignorantly or unknowingly overlooked. Typical para-church organizations such as the *Continent of Great Cities Ministries* (now *Great Cities Missions*), *World Bible School, and the Sunset School of Preaching* in its earliest configuration, have successfully incorporated the kingdom missional mindset into their global mission programs. Although these ministries are to be praised, they originated in the disappointment in congregations of Churches of Christ not engaging in concentrated world missions. In these parachurch programs individual mission-minded Christians chose to step out and engage world evangelism. We thank our God for such Christians and programs who have caught and handed on the mission bug! Any discussion of global kingdom missional outreach would be lacking without mention of such great global mission programs. But I have two next generation church stories to tell, so hang in there with me!

I am sure that there are several fine churches in our USA Church of Christ fellowship that I will overlook in this survey of great missional kingdom churches. This failure is due mostly to my own limited knowledge of our wide-spread brotherhood interests. Some careful research could solve that issue! However, such an extensive survey is limited due to the space constraints of this book!

One American church of my personal experience in kingdom mission stands out: the Sunset Church of Christ in Lubbock, Texas. For over 60 years this congregation in one of its forms of *Sunset School of Preaching* (now *Sunset International Bible Institute*) has engaged in world evangelism church planting in almost every nation imaginable. Originally, the program, in the mind of Cline Paden its founder, functioned as a parachurch movement until it came under the leadership of the Sunset congregation. As I have traveled extensively internationally engaging in academic, mission, and church related business, the presence of an international Sunset missional program has stirred my missionary heart. Certainly, any story of kingdom missional effort without mention of this great mission program would be incomplete!

So now, for what I have called a *next generation* kingdom missional narrative we move primarily to Africa! Because of my own national heritage, being a South African by birth, and by my "new birth" into Christ as a result of a kingdom mission effort, I will explore three African kingdom missional church stories. The same story could be repeated in Brazil, and several other nations, but such other great stories I leave to those more informed than I!

I begin with the Church of Christ in Caluza, Edendale, KwaZulu Natal, South Africa, 1968! Following this challenging narrative we will explore the missional growth of this congregation in Lusikisiki, Transkei, South Africa. We will then move north to central Africa and the Nsawam Road Church of Christ in Accra, Ghana, all three movements have mission roots dating back to 1956 and 1968.

In 1964, an American missionary, Robert Harold (Tex) Williams, working in South Africa became disappointed and concerned over the fact that due to several reasons, mostly the Apartheid program of the white governed Nationalist party, no *active* concerted mission outreach had been engaged by the South African white and American backed churches in South Africa.[1] Some black conversions had taken place, and a limited program of outreach was present. No serious effort, either South African or American, was made to reach the vast majority of black and colored *mulatto* peoples in South Africa.

---

[1] This comment is based on research reflected in a speech I delivered at a *Restoration Quarterly* Annual Meeting at Abilene Christian University in 2003 on the occasion of a *Festschrift* in honor of my work as the Dean of the College of Biblical Studies at Abilene Christian University in 2003. Research in the annual volumes of the Southern African *Christian Advocate* dating from 1950 revealed no evidence of any effort to establish churches among the black citizens of South Africa. Most of the articles in the early volumes were intended as reports to "supporting churches" in the USA of mission progress and church planting.

Because I was reasonably trilingual, speaking English, Afrikaans, and Zulu, Williams invited me to join him with a Zulu Christian, Samson Peters, in an effort to engage in such a program.

Due to the fact that neither Williams nor I had any serious theological or missiological training, a requirement of the Nationalist South African Government for a license to work among the native black populations in South Africa, in 1965 we decided to enroll in Abilene Christian College in Texas to pursue such degrees. During the three years at Abilene Christian college we researched and planned a mission program for our return to South Africa in 1968.

Backed by two churches in Texas, assisted by numerous interested Christians and other congregations, we returned to South Africa in August 1968, accompanied by another Texan and his family, Delbert and Betty McLoud, to join Samson Peters in establishing a Zulu congregation in Edendale, a black suburb in Pietermaritzburg, in the province of Natal. Williams joined the program in 1970. At the time there was a white congregation in Pietermaritzburg, but due to the Apartheid restrictions, black membership in the white congregation was forbidden. There were two Zulu congregations in the Zulu townships adjacent to the city of Pietermaritzburg, one in Sobantu Village, the other in Edendale.

This story of kingdom missional outreach is actually the story of this congregation in Edendale which in time became known as the Caluza Church of Christ. An original charter ministry purpose in the establishment of this congregation was to engage in an evangelistic church planting program, and the training of Zulu ministers and church leaders who would continue the mission whenever white missionaries and ministers would be banned from such leadership under the extremely progressive Apartheid laws.

Beginning in 1968, and then continuing in 1974 under the leadership of Zulu leaders, teachers, and ministers, this program under the ministry of the Zulu led Natal School of preaching has been responsible for planting over 300 churches in the region. The driving force of this new mission program was to evangelize the surrounding regions, plant new congregations, and mentor the new converts and congregations. The *modus operandi* was to conduct classroom instruction in the rented house of the newly established Natal School of Preaching Monday through Thursday, and to leave for the surrounding rural regions for practical evangelistic teaching wherever contact points could be established. In a short period of time we had more contact points than we could service!

Our original goal was for Fair, McLoud, and Peters to conduct and lead the program for 10 years, and then to hand the leadership over to Peters and the Zulu church leaders to conduct. The goal included establishing 100 new congregations, training 100 full time students in ministry, and 100 part time church leaders. The goal for 100 new congregations was exceeded in 2 years, and 100 full time ministers in five years!

In 1969 the Natal school of Preaching hosted the first Zulu/Xhosa Lectureship to be held, hosted by the Edendale/Caluza congregation. This lectureship for the black Christians in KwaZulu-Natal and the Transkei/Eastern Cape was to parallel the lectureship offered by the white school of preaching in Benoni whose annual lectureship, due to Apartheid laws, excluded attendance by black native Christians. Approximately 500 attended the new Natal School of Preaching held at the Edendale/Caluza church of Christ. In 2019 the Caluza congregation celebrated the 50th anniversary of the original Natal School of Preaching Lectureship. Over 2000 were in attendance.

The Caluza congregation still considers its primary purpose as evangelism, planting new congregations, and ministering to its own members. Recently when the COVID Pandemic in South Africa seriously restricted travel and outreach, the Caluza congregation did not mourn over its gathering restrictions, working out of house churches. They mourned their restrictions on travel and engaging in missional evangelism. An e-mail message to me from their leadership asked for our prayers that such restrictions would soon be lifted. The prayers were answered, for on September 27, 2020 life was back to normal! *This is what a kingdom missional church looks like!* They take care of their local members, but see their calling as an evangelist, church planting, kingdom missional outreach! We praise God for this congregation, its native Zulu leaders such as Samson Peters and his family, and a congregation that is infested with the kingdom missional gene!

But the missional viral "contamination" did not stop here in Caluza! In 1972 a Xhosa leader living 250 miles away from the Caluza congregation heard of the Caluza Church of Christ. He wanted to hear about this work. His name was Alfred Thezi. He was not a Zulu, but of the

Xhosa tribe, cousins of the Zulus. He was the elderly leader of a small clan of people living near Lusikisiki in the Transkei region of South Africa. He visited with the school of Preaching in Edendale, spent about 6 weeks with the congregation at Edendale, then returned home for the "crop plowing and planting season," having gained a promise that Samson and I would visit him in his home "kraal" (a collection of houses in a family community), near Lusikisiki. We made the journey about six months later after the crop harvest, supposedly to preach to and convert his large family. To our surprise, this elderly illiterate Christian had converted and baptized his large family of over 87 members, and built a nice church building able to seat about 100 people. Our visit was not what we expected and had planned for! We preached to and taught, encouraging Alfred and his family to continue in their great ministry. Alfred pleaded for us to return for another visit.

As we prepared to leave for our home in Edendale, I stood outside the church building Alfred had built, and pointed out to the surrounding hills, each hill with a community of houses. Partially joking, I encouraged Alfred to see that when we did return there would be a congregation on each hill. Approximately two years later when we did return Alfred informed us that they had planted 12 congregations in the region of his home! Years later, after Alfred had passed on to his Lord, Samson Peters, now himself over 80 years old, told me that on his last contact with the church leaders at Lusikisiki there were now over 25 congregations in the region. Now, that is a kingdom missional story and what a kingdom church looks like!

The Edendale/Caluza congregation and Natal School of Preaching Christians clearly understood their *Missio Dei*,[2] *missional evangelistic* gene and dynamic, but they also clearly understood that ensconced in them lay also an extensive *kingdom living* serving ministry. They diligently take care of their people and serve their local community but have higher visions of their kingdom horizons!

---

[2] They may not have known the full meaning of the *Missio Dei* concept, but they clearly understood their *missional evangelistic* gene and dynamic. This had been ingrained in them by their own conversion, teaching, and early mission outreach programs. *They had been taught that this was their fundamental theological ministry and purpose.* The *Missio Dei* and kingdom theology principles are inculcated in the primary purpose of Scripture.

May I challenge you without making you my enemy? How does your church look alongside the Caluza and Lusikisiki churches? Your church may be doing a number of good things, but does it look like a *kingdom missional* church? How does it measure its impact on the *Missio Dei missional kingdom* scale? It may score well on the kingdom *living* social justice, benevolence, and church and Christian mentoring[3] scale, and that is fine, but in this study we are more focused on the larger *Missio Dei missional evangelistic* element of *kingdom theology* and the church.

You have to travel several thousand miles from Caluza and Lusikisiki, South Africa, to our next "port of call"! We plan to visit Accra, Ghana, and the Nsawam Road Church of Christ in that city. Accra is the large capital city of Ghana with a population of more than 2.5 million people, many of them of the Akan tribe speaking the English and Twi dialects.

Before I explain the story of the Nsawam Road Church of Christ in Accra, I need to acknowledge the presence of another fine Ghanaian church, the Church of Christ in Kumasi, a major city in Ghana in the northern region of Ghana. This congregation, through its leadership and school of preaching played a major role in the early life and development of the Nsawam Road Church in Accra. The church and school of preaching in Kumasi continues to be a major influence among churches, notably in the Northern regions of Ghana and surrounding districts.

The process of doing evangelism and establishing new congregations of churches in Ghana, and specifically in Accra, as in the case of the Edendale church and the Natal School of Preaching, became the *modus operandi* of church growth in Ghana, driven by the *missional evangelistic* principle of *teaching, conversion,* and *the establishment of new congregations.*

The *Missio Dei, missional kingdom theology*, was taking place simultaneously in Edendale and Accra, a world distant from any "home churches" in the USA! Jesus' commission to go into all the world preaching the Gospel, converting people, and planting new communities was the driving force behind these events.

---

[3] I use the term church and Christian *mentoring* in regard to the need for new Christians and new congregations to be *mentored* and taught by those parenting and planting individuals and churches in the vein of the Apostles Paul and Peter, and Barnabas, Timothy, *et al.*

Somehow, on the mission field, the *missional* understanding of *evangelism* and *planting new churches* defined the new mission programs. They inherited, out of need and practice, a *missional evangelistic* lifestyle. The missional practice of growth by evangelism and conversion was the normal rather than growth by membership transfer as was the practice in many USA home churches. The difference in mindset is one of understanding the difference between kingdom theology and *kingdom living*; both necessary ingredients in the *Missio Dei*, with either the one gaining the ascendency or the other.

The churches in Accra, namely the Nsawam Road Church of Christ, have roots dating back to 1968. However, the beginning of Churches of Christ in Ghana was associated with the conversion of Ghanaian denominational preacher John Gaidoo.

John Gaidoo had learned of a free Bible correspondence course offered by a Church of Christ in Athens, Alabama. This church had placed an advertisement in a Moody Monthly Newspaper offering a free Bible correspondence course. Little did they know where this would lead!

Gaidoo enrolled in the study. Eventually, Gaidoo completed the study and requested that someone come to Accra and teach him and his congregation the Scriptural view of the church. The church contacted Wendell Broom, an American missionary serving as a missionary in Nigeria, asking him to go to Ghana and find Gaidoo. Broom and four Nigerian Christians did so, and found Gaidoo in June 1958. During a second trip to Ghana, Broom and his team stayed from October 22 through November 20, 1958 and they met with and studied with Gaidoo and his congregation. Gaidoo was impressed as were some of the members of his local church who were baptized, but most of his previous congregation rejected the teaching.

Gaidoo's conversion began a *missional kingdom* movement of Churches of Christ in Ghana in 1958. At this point we are introduced to a Ghanaian, Daniel Asiamah, who was baptized in 1967, in the Eastern region of Ghana, the result of an evangelistic outreach conducted by the church of Christ in Kumasi. Asiamah enrolled in the Ghana School of Preaching where he met another Ghanaian, S. B. Obeng of the Kumasi Church of Christ and School of Preaching. Asiamah was encouraged by an American Missionary in Kumasi, Gerald Fruzier, and S. B. Obeng who were teachers at the Ghana School of Preaching, to move to Accra and establish a church in Accra. Fruzier was supported by a church near Lubbock, Texas.

Records reveal that the church in Accra was established on Sunday, May 19, 1968 by Asiamah, with 14 people in attendance, mostly Bible Correspondence enrollees. They originally met on the veranda/porch of a house belonging to a friend of Gerald Fruzier. It is interesting that this date is almost the same as the date that the Natal School of preaching was established in Edendale with the Edendale church! The *kingdom evangelistic missional* bug was sweeping across Africa!

In 1970 Asiamah was joined by an American missionary, George Boersman, his wife, and two children who came from a congregation near Lubbock, Texas. They rented a garage, the local term for an automobile workshop, in 1970 to house the new Accra School of Preaching. This building was remodeled into a church meeting place with some space provided for student study. This meeting place was initially leased for 25 years as the home of the new Accra congregation. Since the building was located on Nsawam Road, the church was called the Nsawam Road Church of Christ, with a School of Preaching.

Asiamah was joined by several American missionaries in the Accra School of Preaching and evangelistic program. The primary purpose of the school was clearly understood to be evangelistic, to train Christian men to become evangelists, to plant new congregations, and to minister to any new congregations.

The first group of students graduated in 1972 and settled in different parts of Ghana but the school had to close down in 1976 due to leadership struggle among the missionaries.

In January 1982, Daniel Asiamah, who was also the preacher for the Nsawam Road congregation, started the National Bible Institute (NBI) with five full-time students using the facilities of the previous Accra School of Preaching. The curriculum included a Saturday program for training men in the Nsawam Road Church by instruction and in practical evangelism.

Some of the men in the church who received training included Samuel Twumasi-Ankrah and Douglas Boateng, both of whom became leaders in that congregation. Boateng became a leader in church planting in Ghana and surrounding nations. Asiamah, the original teacher of NBI would travel with the students in a truck to the outlying villages preaching, teaching and converting people to Christ. Twumasi later became a leader in the school of preaching and evangelistic program of the church, and eventually President of the Heritage Christian University College in Accra.

At this point, 1981, an American missionary, Daniel McVey moved to Accra and associated with the Nsawam Road Church, placing himself and his family under the leadership of the Nsawam Road Church. In 1984, following Daniel Asiamah's departure to Lome, Togo to expand an evangelistic program in that nation, McVey assumed the leadership of the school of preaching known as the National Bible Institute.

The National Bible Institute, apart from the teaching of Daniel McVey, was an entirely Ghanaian program under the supervision and support of the Nsawam Road church incorporating the *missional evangelistic* program of church planting and leadership development.

The Nsawam Road Church of Christ clearly understood its *Missio Dei missional kingdom theology* roots and dynamic, but likewise, clearly understood that as a kingdom church they needed to reach out to their neighbors with *kingdom living* social justice, benevolence, and educational mentoring services. Their *kingdom living* ministry has never dimmed their *kingdom theological evangelistic missional* purpose.

Several outstanding *kingdom living* programs have grown out of the Nsawam Road Church as a result of ministering to the needs and interests of their members. Early in the life of the congregation one of the members noticed that there were several deaf people visiting their services. This resulted in the establishment of a deaf ministry and congregation meeting in the same building as the main congregation, and an outgrowth of this ministry to other congregations in Ghana.

Some church leaders noticed that in some community villages the quality and supply of water was lacking. Working with the community leaders they established a water drilling program in 1989 which in turn led to a government recognized and operated mechanized drilling machine. Several communities in the Northeastern region of Ghana, a Muslim religious area of Ghana, heard of this program and invited the drilling program to work in their communities. This led to a friendly relationship with the church members and some congregations being established in these regions.

Like most developing nations, Ghana has struggled with the problem of young street people not being able to find employment. The Nsawam Road Church initiated localized training programs in mechanical, woodworking, leather working, and similar experiences. This involved both young men and women gaining experience in life skills. The ever-present problem of orphans, with the aid of interested Christians, led to the establishment of an orphan home, a school system, and a high school program. Each of these programs has received local and national recognition, opening more doors to congregational outreach programs.

Such was the dynamic and genetic nature of the National Bible Institute that its graduates had initiated an ever-expanding evangelistic ministry with literally hundreds of congregations being established in Ghana and neighboring nations. For years it was a requirement that a student graduating from the Bible Institute would need to establish a working congregation before he received his graduation diploma. For people in the USA this might not be seen as a serious negative, but for South Africans and most Africans raised under a British educational system, the formal graduation ceremony was a high point in personal enrichment and social setting. The net result of this policy was two-fold; one, that many congregations were established, and two, the concept of Biblical and theological maturity for individuals and congregations was that the mission of churches and individuals was missional, planting and mentoring new congregations through evangelism. Certainly the second point was more effective in the life of the missional dynamic of churches in Ghana.

This brief survey of three churches in South Africa and Ghana is not intended in any way to be critical of any other churches in Africa or the USA. Its only purpose has been to demonstrate what a *kingdom church* working in the *Missio Dei*, and with a *kingdom theological* mindset, might look like.

One significant point is that these churches who have each been in existence for more than 50 years have not lost their identity as *kingdom churches* working in the *Missio Dei* and under a *kingdom theology*, have not lost their genetic structure and purpose as evangelistic churches working as agents of God's Abrahamic kingdom purpose.

We thank God for all churches that seek to work under the will and purpose of God as kingdom churches and witness to Jesus in a world that sorely needs to see a brighter hope.

AUTHOR

Ian A. Fair (PhD)
Professor Emeritus of New Testament
and New Testament Theology
Graduate School of Theology
College of Biblical Studies
Abilene Christian University

TEACHING & SPECIALIZATION	SEMINARS AND WORKSHOPS
Revelation	Revelation
Romans	Romans
Prison Epistles	Matthew
Synoptic Gospels: Matthew	Strategic Planning
1 & 2 Thessalonians	Leadership
Leadership	Unity in Diversity

Education

Ph.D. in Systematic Theology, University of Natal, South Africa
Dissertation: *The Theology of Wolfhart Pannenberg as a Reaction to Dialectical Theology*
MA in New Testament Theology, University of Natal, South Africa
Thesis: *The Resurrection of Jesus in Three Contemporary Theologians*
BA Honors in Bible and Theology, University of Natal, South Africa
BA in Bible, Abilene Christian University, Abilene, Texas, USA.

Books by Dr. Ian Fair published by HCU Media
(available in paperback & Kindle Formats)

Conquering in Christ: Commentary on the Book of Revelation

Ephesians: Studies in the theology of Paul's Letter to the Ephesians

Paul's Epistle to the Galatians

Philippians: A Remedy for the Spiritual Blahs

A Biblical Theology of Worship

A Biblical Kingdom Theology

WHO WE ARE
HCU Media LLC

Publishing in support of

Heritage Christian University – Ghana (HCU Ghana)

www.hcuc.edu.gh

HCU media has been established to support the publication of materials, both paper and electronic, created by faculty and friends of HCU Ghana. These materials will be offered initially in the USA & Ghana but may become available globally via other outlets.

www.ingramcontent.com/pod-product-compliance
Lightning Source LLC
Chambersburg PA
CBHW070842160426
43192CB00012B/2280